The (New)
Manual For Life

The (New)
Manual For Life

Bennet Wong, M.D.
and
Jock McKeen, M.D.

PD Publishing
Haven By-the-Sea
RR1, Site 9, 240 Davis Road,
Gabriola Island, B.C. Canada V0R 1X0
Email: jockben@island.net
Website: www.island.net/~jockben

Canadian Cataloguing in Publication Data

Wong, Bennet, 1930-
    The new manual for life

        Includes bibliographical references and index.
        ISBN 0-9696755-4-2

        1. Self actualization (Psychology). 2. Interpersonal relations.
        3. Self-help, health. I. McKeen, Jock, 1946- II. PD Seminars.
        III. Title. IV. Title: Manual for life.
        BD431.W79 1998   158'.1   C98-910771-X

Printed and bound in Canada by Hignell Printing Limited

This book is printed on acid-free paper.

Cover illustration "Bamboo" by courtesy of Sarah Lam

Contents

Dedication

For Reps
and
Virginia Satir.

Your undaunted and wise spirits
continue to inspire us.

Foreword

When I first became convinced that my survival depended upon my willingness and ability to make things right for others, I had no words or concepts that might account for this experience of infancy. Even now, I have only the faintest understanding of how these pre-verbal images were transformed into personal choices that drew me away from my thespian fantasies and carved out an uneasy career as a professional helper.

As a young student of psychology I was rebuked by my teachers for polluting their pristine rivers of knowledge with reflections of the "irrelevant" and seemingly chaotic experience of my own life. By the time I entered the hallowed halls of Graduate School, however, I had learned to rise above these undisciplined urges and join my fellow students in their relentless search for the truth about the nature of the organism. I entered practice wondering if these organisms would, in fact, conform to my newly acquired body of knowledge, while fearing the possibility that they might not respond to my carefully rehearsed interventions.

Fitting my clients with their "diagnostic" strait-jackets was relatively easy although it was painfully obvious that, once contained, I had no key with which to set them free. For the first year or so, I was quite prepared to accept that their apparent resistance to change was something to do with me and I applied myself diligently to mastering the tools of my trade. In later years I urged myself to believe that it was their own pathological obstinance that thwarted my efforts, but the strain of trying to fix other lives was becoming increasingly unbearable. By the time the humanistic movement was in full swing in the late sixties, I was ready to look at some alternative ways of meeting my needs and bolstering my struggling ego. Here was a new orientation with some new techniques. Again, I prepared myself to become the expert in my chosen field. I tried to fill my emptiness with more concepts and more words, and continued to maintain the illusion.

By the time I met Bennet Wong and Jock McKeen in 1985, I was barely hanging on. My role as a professional offered only the flimsiest veil of assurance and the "irrelevant and seemingly chaotic experience of my own life" was speaking back to me in a foreign tongue. Encouraged by my partner Judith, I participated in one of the programs offered by *PD Seminars* and, fighting my own resistant pathology, I slowly—very slowly—began the painful task of unravelling the chronicles of an unreflected life by coaxing myself into the experience of the moment. In this strange, and sometimes empty, place, an emerging sense of Self began to challenge the textbook beliefs of my Psychology.

Somewhere along the way, I had failed to grasp the simple empirical principle that the nature of phenomena changes in accordance with the stance of the observer. Slowly it began to dawn on me that other lives could only be understood in relation to my own life and that I was using my quest for objectivity to obscure the totality of one side of the equation. It was obvious to me that Ben and Jock were not only exploring this other side but had thrown the doors of learning wide open by revealing one side to the other, first in their own relationship and then in their work with program participants. I had never witnessed or experienced anything like it before and my excitement, tempered by fears about what I might discover, challenged my courage to leap across the chasm. But Englishmen prefer to build bridges.

When Ben and Jock graciously agreed that I should write a book about them and their relationship, I had in mind that I could use their trestles to pick my way across and begin the search for my own wisdom. It was clear from the outset that this would be no true biographical or pure scientific enterprise and I marvelled at their willingness to have their lives projected through such a crude and contaminated filter. Despite their assurances that "truth" is an experiential reality, I harboured serious doubts about the integrity of my "investigation." Then it occurred to me that my fascination with the relationship of Bennet Wong and Jock McKeen could become a legitimate scientific enquiry, but only as long as I was prepared to examine my own experience in the process. Whatever the beliefs of my old academic mentors, I was obliged to explore the world of my own subjective experience.

I am now convinced that a true psychology must reach down into the core of the lived experience—from the unheralded moment of spiritual enlightenment to the habituated minutiae of daily life. From here, our most cherished and time-tested concepts must remain open and responsive to the raw experience of being. It is from this foundation that Wong and McKeen have carved out their own beliefs, using philosophy and theory only when these abstractions fit the data—"until further notice." It is for this reason that *A Manual For Life* represents a radical and unique contribution to the literature.

Philosophers of the phenomenological tradition certainly have stressed the primacy of subjective reality and many psychologists have attempted to speculate about the nature of the experiential world. But philosophy has generally remained cold and distant while humanistic psychology has failed to produce the necessary analytic methodologies. In both cases the issues have been reduced to untestable polemics designed to challenge the so-called "scientific tradition." Meanwhile, those who have constructed their "knowledge" from Newtonian physics and Cartesian dualism have continued to abstract the life from the very lives they purport to study. *A Manual For Life* neither negates nor embraces these positions.

In the work of their own lives, Wong and McKeen have simply moved beyond the tedious debates that have separated the various schools of thought. Through their courage to confront the "isness" of their own experience they have detached themselves from the closed world views of philosophical prescriptions and, in their commitment to the integrity of their own truth, they have avoided the "rightness" and "wrongness" of academic psychologizing. Above all, within their own relationship, they have created a living experimental laboratory with standards of discipline and rigour capable of intimidating even the most zealous scientist-practitioner.

For many years now, Bennet Wong and Jock McKeen have been sharing their work and their world with those who come to participate in their programs on Gabriola Island. Their respect for each individual experience, combined with the elegance of their methods, serves to create a place of learning in which the shared truth of individual lives generates a constant flow of living data. Over these years they have meticulously sifted through the grist of personal and collective experiences in the development of their own ideas about our place in the universal order. Up to this point, the intensity of their engagement in this process has left little time for writing but their decision to publish *A Manual For Life* represents an important step toward sharing some of these ideas with other students of life. Hopefully, it is only a beginning.

As Editor of *The Journal of Child and Youth Care* I was delighted to have had the opportunity to participate in this project. Having published a number of fine articles contributed by these authors, I jumped at the prospect of assisting in the publication of this volume and, like many Wong and McKeen watchers around the world, I have no hesitation in asking for more.

—Gerry Fewster, Ph.D.

Introduction

Introduction to *A Manual For Life* (1992)

In response to many requests, this manual was first prepared as a compilation of many of the papers we had written for different journals, newsletters, and other publications, along with some new articles. They afforded a glimpse of some of the basic concepts that we use in our work with *PD Seminars* at *Haven By-the-Sea* and in workshops we have given in North America, Europe and Asia.

The manual was not intended to be a comprehensive body of information. Rather, it summarized the ideas that are presented in the "Come Alive" workshops and the "Phase Programs." Those of you who have taken these will find the ideas familiar, and perhaps helpful for review. We hope you will also discover some new meanings to the experiences you had in the workshops, strengthening any transformational process that you may have begun. Those of you who have not attended any workshops may find the information useful in your everyday life and relationships, helping you to arrive at some insights into your life choices and patterns. The articles have been written with all of you in mind.

This version of *A Manual For Life* is an updated extension of the original collection. Friends and clients have commented on the density of the *Manual's* contents; we ourselves have recognized this. We had fully intended to expand it into a more readable, more anecdotal, more easily digestible book, with examples gleaned from our readers, and possibly some graphics. More and more, however, we heard from people who loved wrestling with our ideas, and the ideas of others, that we had included in our writing. They reported that they could digest only a few pages at a time, and certainly could never relax into a state of easy reading. Nevertheless, they appreciated that in a book, much as we ourselves have done.

People increasingly wrote from all parts of the world requesting permission to use parts of the *Manual* for their teaching: the condensed writing suited their purposes very well. Many people said that they were using the *Manual* in their personal lives as a stimulus for discussion (or argument, depending on the state of their relationship). Such people liked the opportunity to fill in the blanks of our ideas with their own, using ours only as a catalyst for their own thought. Those who took our seminars were able to see the ideas in practice, in their interactions with fellow participants. Finally, we were told that the *Manual* would be used as a reference book for some courses in child care and human development if it were published in a more finished form.

As a consequence, instead of rewriting the *Manual* to make it more readable and less dense, we set about editing what we had already written to give it more consistency and integrity. Then we proceeded to write more, as densely as before, but filling in gaps in the continuity of thought. Thus, the volume of the original manuscript was increased by half as much again. Consequently, we regret that we cannot offer relief to those of you who have loyally and patiently waited in hopes of simplification; we seem to have replaced density with more density. We hope that stimulation will more than make up for the disappointment.

Out of the great morass of philosophical and psychological theories in which we all swim, we believe that we have been able to select and refine some very interesting and useful concepts. They have been tested by many of you during your very willing participation in our experiential workshops. By acting as evaluators you have contributed to the rapid growth of *PD Seminars* and *Haven By-the-Sea*. To you we dedicate this writing, and we hope that these words will be personally meaningful to you.

We extend our appreciation to our *Haven* colleagues and support staff, who have helped to create the loving environment that provides such an effective context for learning; our friends (particularly Gerry and Judith Fewster), who encouraged and supported our writing; our sons, Kevin, Randy, and Justin, who have become so engaged with their own individual goals in life in such a responsible and shared fashion; and finally, we appreciate each other for our unwavering dedication to our own relationship, which has elucidated so many of the concepts that we have attempted to explicate in our own personal way.

Introduction to The (New) Manual For Life (1998)

Since *A Manual For Life* was published in 1992, we have continued to work on these ideas, and develop others. We found a different expression in *As It Is In Heaven* (1993), and *In And Out Of Our Own Way* (1995). Much of our work on relationships has found its place in print in *The Relationship Garden* which was published in 1996. We will refer to these works from time to time in this book, to cross-reference material rather than repeat it. Now we return to the original book, for a re-vamping of the presentation.

With the experience of writing *The Relationship Garden*, we found a form to express our ideas that we think is more readable and accessible than the original *A Manual For Life*, which had grown organically from a collection of a hodge-podge of papers, lectures and musings. Thus, we set out to put the next edition of *A Manual For Life* into the more readable format and presentation.

At the beginning, we intended to make this book a second edition to *A Manual For Life*, anticipating cosmetic upgrading, and modest additions. As we delved into the body of the material, we were somewhat shocked to find how much the ideas contained in the original volume have now ripened and matured in our ongoing experiences with ourselves and our clients and friends. We have patiently worked on the original volume, word by word, and done some considerable modifying of the original text. Indeed, there are places where the material was either discarded altogether, or almost completely re-written.

In reviewing the first version of the book, we have concluded that the material was quite "choppy" and not well coordinated, making it sometimes difficult to read. In this new book, we have endeavoured to place the material into specific sections, and to cross-relate the material, as well as refer to the appropriate sections in our other books.

We have added some material to this book that was not in the original edition of *A Manual For Life* too. In recent years, we have been speaking and writing about memory, and its place in psychology and human experience. Hence, we have added chapters to this edition that reflect our thinking on this subject. Specifically, "The Walking Wounded" chapter and the "Memories of Abuse" chapter reflect our current thinking on this subject.

So, we have discovered that this is a new book. We have decided to retire the original volume, and not reprint it or make a second edition. Instead, welcome to the first edition of *The (New) Manual For Life*. We have incorporated suggestions from many people into the rewriting of these ideas. We hope you find them a step forward.

—Bennet Wong and Jock McKeen
Gabriola Island, February 1998

Part One:
PROCESSES

Yesterday I met a whole man. It is a rare experience but always an illuminating and ennobling one. It costs so much to be a full human being that there are very few who have the enlightenment, or the courage, to pay the price—one has to abandon altogether the search for security, and reach out to the risk of living with both arms. One has to embrace the world like a lover, and yet demand no easy return of love. One has to accept the pain as a condition of existence.

—Morris West [1]

1. Morris West, *Shoes of the Fisherman* (London: William Heinemann 1963), p. 204.

A Fable

Once upon a time, the entire Universe was filled with unrestricted, free-flowing energy that danced joyously and chaotically in all directions in the Garden of Energy. For eons, the Universe enjoyed this existence, this freedom. However, since everything was so perfect and predictable, the Universe gradually began to feel a disquieting sense of boredom. Then, one day while at play, just for fun, it decided to create some beings. Separating out pieces of its own energy, it shaped and embodied one pattern of a being into a triangle, and another into a circle. These were coloured with the pigments of the rainbow and were named "Triangulus" and "Circula" so that they could be easily identified. Although both of their energy flows remained connected to the source and thus to one another, the Universe allowed them unrestricted freedom to move, travel and play in order for them all to enjoy life to its maximum. And so they did!

Triangulus and Circula enjoyed their existence together with one another and with the Universe, exploring all the nooks and crannies of the Garden of Energy that was bathed in a warm, glowing light. The sky, the earth and all beings in them which were connected to one another and to them were theirs to discover. What delight! Since the energy that flowed through Triangulus and Circula was the same energy that flowed through the Universe and all the other Beings therein, they felt no fear. Curiosity was their gift.

Just as had occurred to their creator previously, after eons of play all things became known to them. Circula and Triangulus began to feel a sense of sameness that gradually grew into a disquieting sense of boredom. Wanting some unpredictability to provide spice, they developed a game of hide-and-go-seek which they played not only with one another but also with the Universe and all of the other Beings therein. What fun!

Over more eons of time, the playing of hide-and-go-seek became other than fun—it became compelling! As it became more competitive, they

the hiding became more effective when their connection
~r and with All Beings was disrupted and hidden. Soon,
riencing more disconnection than connection, and each
)lated and alone. Since they no longer knew what each
other was thinking or doing, the game of hide-and-go-seek began to take
on aspects of anxiety and desperation. The fun turned into fear and the
business of life became serious!

Now that they could no longer depend upon the basic connection of the
flow of energy between themselves and other Beings, Circula and
Triangulus desperately developed means of controlling one another and
the Universe. They were unable to tolerate the dreadful sense of isolation
that they felt *even in the company of one another*! So each began to develop
ways of manipulating, seducing and bargaining with the other; together
they began to bend the Universe to their *will*, overcoming and destroying
much of the rest of the Universe so that they could feel more secure. The
more that they did this, the more they lost the connection of their energy
with all else and the more suspicious they became of one another and the
entire Universe. The light turned harsh and piercing.

As they looked across to one another and to the Universe, they now
experienced a frightening abyss between them. Instead of returning to
their roots where their energy was already connected (although
forgotten), they focused upon building bridges across that chasm in order
to contact one another. Such bridges included social skills, fantasy
diversions, religions, scientific discoveries, new and better ways of
communication and transportation, and groupings into common
languages, families and couples. All of these were jealously protected, for
fear of losing advantage and control over one another. Out of this fear
grew experiences of jealousy, hurt feelings and ultimately, vengeance and
violence. The Universe felt sad!

In spite of all of this, they retained a concern for one another—since at
root, *they were one another*! Unable to feel the flow of energy connecting
them, they instead began to make connections at a more superficial level.
Instead of feeling *at one* with one another, when they were not competing
they began to feel a sense of *sympathy* and *empathy* for others. They

developed a desire to *take care of* one another. In such a way, they managed to maintain control of their relationships, and began to feel secure again. Institutions and religions were developed around moral systems, and smugness and pride in righteousness were natural outcomes.

Now, across the great abyss, Triangulus and Circula expressed to one another their great need for one another, and each swore to take care of the other. Of course, what they had forgotten was the fact that each of them was already whole and already connected to one another. So the belief in needing one another was a Big Lie. However, since they were able to dress up the Big Lie with hearts and flowers, they made it very appealing indeed, calling it their "Romance!" Now, they wanted each other to swear allegiance for life, even though by doing so they were committing themselves to a death of their own individual selves. The price that they had to pay was the sacrifice of their own personal potential of being! However, that did not matter to them, because to submit to the control of the other was exciting and full of the promise of security. Now, they did not have to stare across the big abyss. Rather, they spent their time in the movie house and fun palaces that made them forget about Reality! They could spend their time *taking care of one another instead of having to care about one another.* Although they no longer could feel their connection with one another, they worked hard to get to know one another so that they could please one another.

In fact, what Circula and Triangulus now felt for one another was the certainty of *possessiveness* and *control*. For a long time, that did not matter—at least not until the control stopped working! Eventually, the stark realism of being alone tended to leak out, sometimes because of natural aging, or loss of roles, or the falling out of Romance by one of the people involved. When that happened to either Circula or Triangulus, each would feel the pain of loneliness. Finding that pain too difficult to bear, they converted it into hurt feelings and anger and each began to blame the other. This maneuver was a desperate attempt to prevent the self from falling into the abyss. So long as the other was to blame, this angry energy provided a temporary sense of meaning to an otherwise horrifying experience of nothingness and depression. Out of this tendency to blame arose a whole new approach to life—becoming a victim in which the other became responsible! Now life became not only serious, it became irresponsible!

Gradually, the institutions took over the responsibility for everybody, leaving each person only the right to do what was *politically correct*. To make life more predictable, Triangulus and Circula were forbidden to look triangular and circular; each was made to look like a grey box. Spontaneity, individuality and personal freedom became a thing of the past! The light of the Universe dimmed in the Garden of Energy as all movement, sound and colour became legislated.

However, Circula and Triangulus, trapped in their politically correct grey box, yearned to return to their original shapes and colours—to be themselves! When they saw each other's personal pain, they felt sorry for one another and wanted to *help* one another. Realizing the original trap of wanting to take care of one another, they refused to do that any longer; they knew that they could not take away the other's pain. Instead, they learned how to be *responsible* for their own pain, to be *present* to witness the pain of the other, to *share* rather than blame. While so doing, they began to feel the connection of their energy at their roots, discovering that their hurt was the pain of their separation. When they felt their connection, they knew that each of their pain was one another's pain—that it was not just similar, it was the same! Now, they were able to *resonate* with one another's feelings, and no longer felt alone.

With that resonance, colour and aliveness returned to the lives of all Beings. The Garden of Energy began to flower and energy flowed freely again. For Triangulus and Circula, life again became liberated, full of light and movement. They danced and sang, played and worked with full hearts. And the Universe smiled!

THE BEGINNING . . . .

Waiting at the Station

Most people seem to believe that destiny has some particular goal for them, that they were meant to become something special. To such persons, the task in life is to discover exactly what that goal is, to figure out the destination before being prepared to commit time and effort to getting there. This is a common life-stance among adolescents, who believe that education is a waste of time until they decide on an occupational goal. Many people live much of their lives in this immature pattern, whiling their time away until they know their exact destination.

In effect, such people believe that there is a specific train that will carry them to a particular locus of success; so they wait in the train station watching all the trains (opportunities) go by, entertaining themselves at the computer games with all the other waiting people. They might closely examine each passing train to see if it is the right one; but, because the destinations are never clearly marked, each train passes without being boarded.

In the station, these waiting people become restless and discontent, wondering when they will be given specific instructions about which train to catch. Even when they are advised to board a specific train, they find fault and raise doubts rather than taking the risk of embarking. They are afraid of wasting time by getting on the wrong train—they fear that they might arrive at a wrong destination and then have to return to this station to catch the right train. So trains keep passing them by. Yet they do nothing but waste time in the train station.

What such people do not realize is that *all* of the trains have the same destination—death. They may have different itineraries, with different stop-offs en route (e.g., a different career); but ultimately, the terminus is the same. That being the case, these people would do well to board the very next train, take the first opportunity to become involved with the activities on the train, and be present for the trip. If they were to do so, they would notice their fellow travelers, the ever-changing passing scenery, and the pleasure of the motion of the train. While on the train, their challenge would be to discover creative uses of time and talents, especially in relationship to the other passengers.

An important element in selecting a train to board would be the character of the passengers already on board. Are they serious minded or revelers, musicians or poets, relaxed or tense, morally righteous or libertarians? These qualities will give some clue to the atmosphere that might be expected on a prolonged journey.

Giving up the investment in a future goal allows a person to enjoy the journey in the present. At any of the stops, it is possible to get off a particular train and board another. The danger in disembarking is that one might once again get stuck in the waiting room of another train station—to become uninvolved—instead of throwing oneself onto another passing train, to have yet another new experience!

A Model for Communication

Context (Background)

Each time you enter a new situation, you carry with you a context that is based upon your past experience (both recent and more distant). So you do not enter new situations fresh; you colour them in terms of other experiences you have had. For example, if you have been having a bad day and feel irritable, when you meet a new person you will begin your interaction in an irritable frame of mind. On the other hand, if you have been feeling buoyant and happy and then enter a difficult situation, you will begin in a positive frame of mind.

The context is the *background* or *substrate* against which immediate situations are viewed. Thus, one can benefit from a periodic checking with one's internal world to see what the context is. One should not take the context for granted, as it can shift and change. A moment of closing your eyes to investigate thoughts and feelings will give you an impression of the background you bring in. As you observe your thoughts and note your feelings, you will find what might be seen as trivial experiences—repetitive thoughts, or a vague mood that doesn't seem to have any origin. Note these—they will be colouring the situations you enter. Indeed, the context will even help select, out of the infinite variety of possible perceptions, those that you will notice.

Perception (Five Senses)

As you open your eyes to observe another person, you will begin to absorb information about that person. If you do not attempt to communicate, but instead permit the impressions of the other to wash over you, you will develop a "soft eyes" impression of the other. You can appreciate the other as you would relish a fine sculpture in a museum. In a matter of seconds you will take in hundreds of items of information through your senses—seeing, hearing, smelling, tasting, and touch. Although most of this is done subconsciously, you *do* quickly take in this vast array of data. What is interesting is that none of these hundreds of pieces of information means anything—they are simply the result of stimulation of your nervous system. They are experienced by your brain as raw sensory information—shape, colour, texture, smells, and sounds.

Note that these are *impressions*—a hint of a fragrance, a subtle sound, a shading of expression on the face of the other. The perceptions do not mean anything in themselves; in order to make our world understandable, we go to work subconsciously on each of these hundreds of pieces of information to *make them mean something*—we perform the mental operation of interpreting. The perceptions are sensory; the interpretations are the mental operations that provide the meaning.

Interpretation (Meaning Attribution)

As you observe your partner, you will have impressions of the way he or she is sitting; the colour of skin; the position of hands; the colour and type of clothing, jewelry, skin tone, hair style; and countless other features. From these impressions, you will assemble an overall picture, which you interpret. Now, it is important to realize that your interpretations are not correct—they are a *best guess* at the meaning of what you are witnessing. These interpretations assist you in making intelligible the huge amount of information that you have received from your senses. Although the interpretations are not correct, they are also never wrong. They are simply your way of understanding the information you have.

One should always check with the other person, seeking agreement or disagreement relating to each interpretation. It is impossible to be either correct or wrong; nevertheless, I can check to see if my version of you matches your version of yourself. Note that if you agree with me, I am not right; we simply *agree*. If your opinion differs, I am not wrong; we simply *disagree*. When there is a difference in an interpretation, we do not have to agree; instead, we can become *curious* about the different viewpoints we have, and learn more about ourselves and each other. This attitude of curiosity with no right or wrong permits an openness to ongoing learning; to become fixated on who is right or wrong brings learning to a halt.

Common phrases to express your interpretations are:

- I *interpret* that you are a kind person.
- I *believe* that you are being honest.
- I *think* that you are shy.
- I *assume* that this is difficult for you.
- I *imagine* that you are uncomfortable.
- I *judge* that you are trying very hard to communicate.
- I *speculate* that you are thinking of something else.
- I *fantasize* that you are feeling very young.

Interpreting is a mental operation that involves thinking. A common mistake is to confuse interpretations with feelings. Thus the phrase "I feel that you are ...." *never* describes a feeling; instead, it is a misrepresentation of "I think that you are ...."

Many people are afraid to express their interpretations because the idea of judging someone else has taken on negative overtones. Yet judging (interpreting) is merely your way of making sense of information in order for you to more profoundly know another person. Judgment does not necessarily imply a rejection; indeed, pure judgment simply involves drawing distinctions in order to make sense of random data. It is from these interpretations that all your feelings come: how you interpret the data of your senses will determine whether you wish to move toward or away from another person.

Feeling

Based on the interpretations you make, you will develop your feelings. Feelings are experiences in the body involving changes in blood flow and energy shifts. There are basically two kinds of feelings—positive and negative.

Positive feelings involve an opening up of the blood vessels in the body, and are associated with a sensation of warmth and well-being. When you sense this positive feeling, you will feel like moving toward the person for whom you have the feeling. You would express a positive feeling in these ways: "I like you," "I am drawn to you," "I am attracted to you," "I feel comfortable with you," "I feel close to you," "I feel warm with you," or "I love you." The overall experience is one of feeling close and comfortable, with a desire to move toward the other person.

Negative feelings involve a contraction of the blood vessels in the body, with an accompanying feeling of tightness, discomfort, coolness and a desire to move back. You might express a negative feeling in any of these ways: "I am uncomfortable with you," "I dislike you," "I feel distant from you," "I am repulsed by you," "I don't like you," "I am afraid of you," "I hate you," or "I feel like moving away from you." The overall experience is one of feeling distant, cool, and repelled.

Note that a negative feeling does not imply that the other person is bad or wrong; it simply reflects a judgment within the person who has the negative feeling, who for some reason experiences a desire to move away. For example, when you chose your outfit this morning, you were negative to all the other clothes in your closet; when you choose chocolate ice cream, you are negative to all the other flavors that you could have chosen. So, negative and positive feelings involve *choice* and *valuing*; they do not say anything about the worth of the other person, but rather speak of the valuing process within the person having the feelings.

Also, be aware that the feelings you have are entirely based upon your context and interpretations. The same perceptions can be coloured differently given different contexts and interpretations, and it is possible to feel either positively or negatively about any perception. For example, the sight of a big man with a knife could be interpreted in various ways. If one were to interpret the man as a threatening killer, one would likely have a negative feeling and draw away; if instead one were to interpret him as a chef who is about to carve a roast of beef, one might draw close to get the first piece! The feelings are determined by the interpretations of the perceptions.

Context
(Background)

Perceptions: (Five senses)
I see, hear, taste, smell, touch

Interpretations: (Meanings)
*I believe, think, assume, interpret,
imagine, fantasize, judge, speculate*

> NOTE: Nobody is ever right or wrong
> You can only agree or disagree
> **CHECK** IT OUT!

Feelings: POSITIVE—*like, love, open, warm,
attracted, comfortable, move toward*
NEGATIVE—*dislike, hate,closed,cool,
repulsed, uncomfortable, move away*

Intention: *What I feel like doing, intend to do,
want to do, will do*

Action: *What I do*

Intention

Intention involves the conscious use of the will in translating feelings into action. For each perception/interpretation/feeling complex, it is possible to develop an intention about what you would like to do in response. You do not ever have to follow a feeling; human beings have free will, and can decide to act in opposition to their feelings. For example, you might feel attracted to someone, and decide not to pursue this attraction because of commitment to an established relationship. In a similar manner, you might be afraid of someone and decide to approach that person to talk about your fear, instead of withdrawing and following the feeling. You can always learn about yourself from a situation, whether you follow your feeling or not.

Also, you should always be ready in a dialogue to ask of the other, "What is your intention in telling me this?" This question elevates an encounter from a mundane interchange of ideas to the level of the deeper meanings involved in the communication. For example, if someone's intention were to express anger in order to clear the air and become closer to you, you might be interested in staying to face the anger; on the other hand, if that person's intention was simply to try to intimidate or get control of you, you might not want to stay engaged with the other. Clarifying your intentions can allow the communication to proceed to ever deeper levels.

Action

Once you become clear about your perceptions, interpretations, feelings, and intentions, any decisions to act will be uncomplicated, easily understood by others, and more effectively executed. With this kind of mastery, you can develop increasing amounts of self-responsibility, and your inner strength will grow. More and more, you will recognize how you are constantly creating your own reality. Then the possibilities for personal growth, expansion and transformation are limitless!

The Soup

Although we have described these phenomena of communication as if they occur in a linear, sequential fashion, they usually occur simultaneously. Hence, in communication, it is not necessary to proceed in the order of the above chart. One can start anywhere, and relate the other elements as they come up. For example, some people can readily relate their interpretations, and have to search to find their feelings; other people will easily know their feelings, and will not know the interpretations that are associated. The elements of the communication process are mixed together, just as different foods are mixed in a soup. There is no right way or order to relate all this. Just begin, and describe to your partner the elements that you find!

I've had the joy of others experiencing my pain
Been held, told by strangers that I am loved.
I've searched my soul, experienced my anger and sorrow.
I feel whole and yet there remains a void that needs to be filled
The fullness that only comes from experiencing the special love
And intimacy of one human being caring for another.
It is now easy to write and speak of love.
Even if it be in the abstract and uncommitted to a single soul.

I reached out my arms and cradled people who, hitherto I would
   have felt unwarranted of my time.
I've heard the screams of hurt; sobbed and felt their pain and my own.
I've come alive with the realization that life has its origins
   in the interconnectings of the human spirit
And when we become alone and unwilling to reach out and share that spirit,
We have allowed ourselves to die.
My fortune is that I am me. My salvation is that there was you.
                                                    —Larry Gold [1]

Notes

1.   Larry Gold, Unpublished poem.

Constructivism

The Oxford Dictionary defines epistemology as "a theory of the method or grounds of knowledge."[1] Constructivism is an epistemology that proposes that all of our ideas about reality (our knowledge and belief systems) are *interpretations* of immediate experience. As such, we must continually refer our ideas back to experience-as-a-whole for verification and refinement. Most of this interpretation of reality is done through the use of symbols. The roots of such an approach can be found as far back as the writings of Kant, but more recently in the phenomenology (the study of phenomena) of Husserl, and the pragmatism of William James and John Dewey. Rollo May and Abraham Maslow did much to integrate phenomenology into humanistic psychology through the synthesis of existential philosophy and psychiatry. Fritz Perls incorporated phenomenology into gestalt psychology. For all these theorists, a main point was that *experience* is the most important source of data for psychology, at least equal (if not greater) in importance than data collected through observation (the objective approach of the scientific method).

The Constructivist Approach

Over recent years, the constructivist approach has been explored and applied to achieve insights into the individual, the family, and groups. A critical insight is that symbols are used to interpret and understand natural, social, and psychological worlds. In exploring this view, it is important to recognize the following:

- these symbols themselves are the psychological world
- these symbols create or constellate the social world
- these symbols *systematically influence* and *destabilize* the *natural* world

The existentialists challenged the essentialists' concept that "essence precedes existence," replacing it with Sartre's epigram that "existence precedes essence."[2] The constructivists now propose that "epistemology precedes ontology" (one's theories precede and engender the nature of being or reality). This opens the door to the possibility of innumerable "multiple realities" and "realms of being"—there is then no absolute, correct reality. Each person, organization, or group can construct a unique version of reality by building on some basic underlying common themes; Jung's theory of archetypes describes common patterns that configure particular world views.

Multiple Intelligences

Howard Gardner suggested that humans attempt to organize their understanding of reality through the use of their *multiple intelligences,* of which there are at least six:

- *Logical-mathematical*: the use of symbols and their relationships to one another
- *Linguistic*: the use of language
- *Musical*: the use of sounds in relationship with one another (as in melody)
- *Spatial*: the experience of locating the self in relation to space
- *Bodily-kinesthetic*: the locations of inner experience
- *Personal*: the feelings and experiences unique to the person[3]

Experience and Objectivity

For the past four centuries, scientific philosophy has dominated our exploration of reality, reaching the zenith of its influence on society in the last century. Great strides in knowledge have been accomplished through the use of the logical-mathematical intelligence, with its emphasis on pure *observation* and *objectivity*. Although the study of human behaviour did not readily lend itself to such a scientific approach, behavioral scientists struggled to force a fit in their desire to gain acceptability and credibility with their scientific colleagues. Rebelling against such an unnatural fit, the existentialists had a strong influence in establishing the view that *experience* is as important as *observation* in our understanding of human nature. Such a revolutionary idea struck home in the hearts of psychologists who were searching for the human element in their understanding of the person. The rising influence of humanistic psychology reflects such an awareness.

Early concepts that gained influence in the field recognized the importance of language in shaping reality. With its scientific inheritance, neurolinguistic programming (NLP) developed as one of many systems that attempted to break out of a narrow view of human behaviour, returning to the individual the possibility of constructing a personal experience and reality.

A Variety of Approaches

In the past two decades there has been an upsurge of a great variety of approaches to understanding human experience; since many of these are unscientific and nonlogical, they have been met with resistance from traditional bodies of psychology. The increasing influence of constructivism has been seen to be a threat against the social order. In the area of religion, creation-centred spirituality has been seen to threaten the tenets of the traditional Christian church by maintaining that there is no objective God experience separate from the subject (see below, "Creation-Centred Spirituality"); in the field of healing, holistic health concepts that maintain that the patient is responsible for illness have threatened the traditional medical model (see below, "Individual Responsibility in Illness and Health").

The humanistic viewpoints took considerable interest in bodily approaches to understanding human behaviour. Reichian concepts and their many offshoots (such as bioenergetics, Feldenkrais and Alexander techniques, and rolfing) expanded awareness of the bodily-kinesthetic and spatial elements involved in understanding and appreciating the world as it is created by human experience. Much work still needs to be done to understand more fully the language of the body. From a holistic health perspective, we postulate that physical symptoms represent a message, a form of expression of underlying themes: *the body speaks what the voice cannot.*

The significance of music in constructivist theory has yet to be fully studied. Music obviously has considerable influence on human emotions, and is in turn affected by them. Musical styles and structures vary from one society to another. From the viewpoint of the body approaches, life stances and cultural differences are held in the deep tissue tensions. The patterns of these holdings are expressed in the unique music of that culture. In turn, these musical expressions recreate the deep patterns of that culture. The human body is the medium in which music and culture interface.

Structuralism

Accompanying and closely identified with the constructivist influence were the ideas of *structuralism*, which proposed that human experience was *structured* by deep, underlying patterns of behaviour that are always pressuring for expression.[4] Such an idea is not new, being readily seen in the ancient philosophy underlying acupuncture and traditional Chinese medicine.[5] A resurgence of interest in Jung's ideas about myths and archetypes reflects these same ideas, none of which are very scientific.[6] Despite the opposition of traditionalists, these approaches are becoming increasingly popular.

An Integrative Viewpoint

Ultimately, it is the personal and unique use of all of these intelligences that matters.[7] Each person moves in a social structure that imposes its mark upon the individual. The commonly accepted version of reality that is held today in the western world is still very scientific. When a person's experience of reality differs from the conventional view, that individual has to decide either to abandon this personal perspective (the most usual solution) or to develop ways of surviving while remaining out of step with the rest of society. The more accepting the society is, the easier it is for the individual to acknowledge and share differing or multiple realities. Because such acceptance is not usual, people often find difficulty in maintaining a unique version of reality. Furthermore, they are often reluctant to share unusual experiences and perspectives.[8] Yet, sharing with others can help to further self-discovery and self-acceptance.[9]

Listen

Rest in the sombre shadows
The quiet inner voice
has been talking to you
all your life
Now you begin to listen
and the world opens
Flooding with images
from behind the dam
of social propriety
Accompanied by strange
and haunting melodies
—Jock McKeen [10]

Notes

1. *The Concise Oxford Dictionary* (Oxford: Oxford University Press, 5th ed. 1967), p. 325.

2. J.P. Sartre, quoted in John Macquarrie, *Existentialism*, (Baltimore, Maryland: Penguin Books, 1973), p. 15.

3. H. Gardner, *Frames of Mind, The Theory of Multiple Intelligence* (New York: Basic Books, 1985).

4. Edgar Levenson, *The Fallacy of Understanding* (New York: Basic Books, Inc., 1972).

5. Joseph Needham, *Science and Civilisation in China, vol. II* (Cambridge: Cambridge University Press, 1956).

6. Edward Edinger, *Ego and Archetype* (Baltimore, Maryland: Penguin Books, Inc., 1973).

7. J. McKeen and B.R. Wong, *The Relationship Garden* (Gabriola Island, B.C.: PD Publishing, 1996), p. 29.

8. Ibid., p. 79.

9. Ibid., p.194.

10. J. McKeen and B.R. Wong, *As It Is In Heaven* (Gabriola Island, B.C.: PD Publishing, 1993), p. 181.

The Ideal Self:
Striving for Perfection

Self-Criticism

It is remarkable how often people are self-critical and self-deprecatory. Stuck with a low sense of self-esteem, they are unhappy with their accomplishments, no matter how good they may be in the eyes of others. By society's yardstick, such people are very successful, occupying positions of power and authority. In their personal lives they may appear to have loving families and many important and good friends. However, within themselves they are unhappy, often depressed, with feelings of guilt, seeing their lives as empty and meaningless. They work hard, achieve much, and are good at what they do, but *it is never enough.*

Frequently, the history of these people includes what society would describe as an ideal family; many times, these families that seemed exemplary were actually *dysfunctional.* Parents of such people are often authoritarian or perfectionistic, placing great demands for achievement on the children. Sometimes, the parents seem quite the opposite in terms of *outward* expectations; they may be quite liberal and accepting of their children. But when they themselves have achieved much in lives filled with success, their unspoken requisition often is to "be perfect!" Even if that injunction is absent, the obvious signs of parental success commonly set a base level against which the children compare themselves and find themselves wanting. Sometimes, the background history is one of poverty or family neglect; children may react by vowing to rise above their family's state of helplessness through striving for achievement and power.

The Authentic Self

We assume that each individual is born as an "Authentic Self." This is the basic nature and characteristic personality of the infant. As many mothers will attest, even from the earliest days of life each child has a unique and individual quality, a particular essence of the individual's being (some refer to this as the "soul"). This includes all the potential of that person's being that could come to fruition with time and future experience. Just as no two snowflakes are alike, each human being is unique from the beginning. Even though each individual is so particular, the Authentic Self is at the same time connected to the entire universe; this is our spiritual nature.

Parental Attitudes

It is easy to imagine how the newborn child must feel when being held, cared for, fed, and played with. The parents' attitudes toward the child are being transmitted during all of these interactive activities. Their feelings have considerable effect upon the youngster, and help determine the degree to which the child will experience the world as a safe and accepting place. Parental feelings can range from being ecstatic over having the child to resenting the added burden; most often, they are a combination of both extremes, shifting from time to time, depending on the circumstances.

Expectations

At some level, no matter how much they intend to do otherwise, parents have expectations of their infants; the children have to contend with all of those expectations. Many times, these expectations are a burden, even when they are positive—we have known people who have suffered from a life-long parental expectation that they be happy! Somewhere in the depths of the developing personality, each individual becomes aware that behaviour must be modified to please the parents. This is the normal course of events as a child matures. Through daily experience, children form an image of how they must be in order to please those upon whom they are entirely dependent for survival. That developing image of the self that will be acceptable and will gain approval (and thus ensure survival) is referred to as the "Ideal Self." The expectations, demands, and injunctions become codified, memorized, and incorporated into a *self-regulating system of behaviour* in the maturing person. Thus, children are caught in an early bind. What they want to do, to express the impulses of the Authentic Self, is most often in opposition to what is expected by the parents (and later by all authorities, institutions, and society in general). As those expectations become incorporated within the personality as a self-governing Ideal Self, the struggle becomes an inner one, within the individual. Once this process has been internalized, it occurs even in the absence of the parents or any external authority. This self-controlling mechanism is well established in the first few years of life.

In most cases, the *desires* of the Authentic Self must be surrendered to the Ideal Self's *demands* for acceptance. The result is usually some form of *compromise* that establishes the expressed behaviour of a developing "Actual Self." These "selves" are constellations of a processes; they are not separate or distinct entities (for convenience, we refer to them as nouns). Through such a process, the growing child becomes a relatively well-behaved, disciplined, civilized person prepared to be educated for responsibilities as a future adult. Each person lives as these three selves (Authentic Self, Ideal Self, Actual Self), trying to satisfy all of them in order to maintain some emotional balance and ease ("sanity").

This model corresponds to the ideas about resonance that we wrote in *The Relationship Garden*. The notion of the Ideal Self corresponds to the box of authority in the resonance model; the Authentic Self corresponds to the circle and triangle that individuate in the flow of universal energy. The demands to "become appropriate" in the energy model (represented by boxing the triangle and circle) correspond to the expectations that are depicted in the model of the Ideal Self. The Actual Self would be represented by a circle or a triangle, encased in a box.[1]

From the outside, the emerging struggle between the parts of the self appears relatively peaceful. The youngster is seen to be merely "growing up" and "maturing" into a "good" child, a "cooperative" student, and a "responsible" citizen. The compromises being made are not unreasonable; they are for the child's "good." Unfortunately, every time that the Authentic Self is betrayed in an effort to behave more like the Ideal Self, the person recognizes that abandonment (often unconsciously), and reacts with *self-hatred*.[2] Thus, even though people achieve a great deal through this process, much of their nature is denied, and tension grows.

The "Path of Glory"—and Back!

Self-Hatred Cycle:
1. The child tries to please the parent by striving to become the Ideal Self.
2. Abandonment of the Authentic Self produces self-hatred.
3. The Actual Self establishes *control* in the real world.
4. Recognizing that it has fallen short of expectations, the Actual Self strives toward greater perfection, abandoning the Authentic Self even more, thus generating even more self-hatred and establishing a *self-hating cycle*.

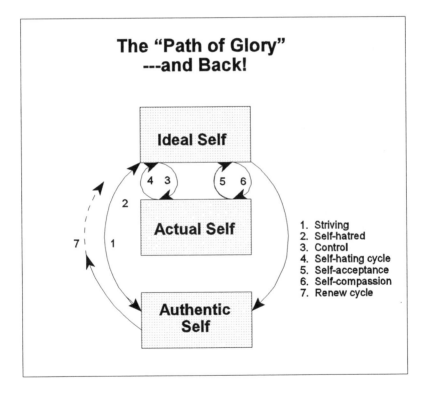

Self-Compassion Cycle:
5. By becoming *aware* of the Ideal Self, the Actual Self can begin to *accept* the totality of the self, with warmth and understanding for

having had to compromise so much in the past.

6. This *self-compassion* leads to an acceptance of all parts of the self, including the part that has found it necessary to abandon its Authentic Self in the face of reality. This leads to a greater awareness of the whole person, including the Authentic Self.

Repetition of the Process:

7. Generally, people repeat the process over and over. The cycle begins once again.

Symptoms of Self-Hatred

To develop the Ideal Self, people learn to adopt and play socially acceptable *roles*; these roles are a social vehicle that help to maintain the image of the Ideal Self, at the expense of the Authentic Self. In order to carry on working against their deep nature, achieving people who are playing their roles become numb or frozen. Their breathing pattern is constrained, and thus they do not fill themselves with the pleasure of being. They lose touch with their feelings, and their bodies eventually manifest symptoms, which can occur physically, psychologically or spiritually.

The growing accumulation of self-hatred can be experienced as feelings of anxiety and depression, or witnessed in compulsively self-destructive behaviour. When patterns of self-defeating behaviour with resulting low self-esteem are established, the person is driven to greater heights of achievement, with ever-increasing amounts of self-hatred. Evidence of being trapped in this cycle will be seen at all levels of the being. As mentioned, emotionally these people might experience anxiety or depression. More often, in order *not* to feel the emotional discomforts related to self-hatred, they develop any number of obsessive or compulsive behaviours or other signs of neurotic maladaptation. Physically, a wide variety of symptoms of illness can develop; such a process often underlies allergies and other boundary illnesses. Phobias often have such a process at their root too. Spiritually, an emptiness (anomie) might be experienced, or a lack of direction in life, or deep sense of guilt. In their desire to numb themselves to the process of self-hatred, such high achieving people will often become addicted to some agent or activity; hence, at the core of alcoholism, addictions and dependencies often lurks a profound process of self-hatred.

In our society, it is these very driven and achieving people that ultimately arrive at the "top" to become our political and economic leaders, many of them filled with self-hatred and anger. Their choices are simple: they can go for more power and achievement (and hate themselves even more), they can somatize their anger and become physically ill, they can manifest self-destructive behaviour (such as failure, addictions of all sorts, or family disorders), or they can direct their anger outward in the form of blame or aggression. Because of the power that society generally affords such leaders, how these people handle this self-hatred has many larger social consequences—wars, social unrest, antisocial behaviour, addictive disorders, and family dysfunctions are a few of the possible symptoms.

A Universal Dilemma

Every person always has these three inner aspects, caught in the dilemma of striving for perfection and generating self-hatred. Through self-awareness, people notice the patterns of achievement and desires for perfection, which mask their underlying self-concept of helplessness, inadequacy, and inferiority. With some warmth and humour ("Here I go again!"), they can recognize the persistence of the pattern. At this point, they have a wide variety of possible reactions:

- They can deny the patterns, or forget about them, and continue with the cycle with all of its accompanying emotional, physical, and spiritual consequences. This is the *Path Of Glory*.[3]
- They can fall into despair or self-pity for having to contend with the inevitability and hopelessness of the situation, developing feelings of depression and anxiety. This is the *Path Of Helplessness*.
- They can focus on blaming others (like parents and other authorities) for their having contributed to the creation of this dilemma, becoming obsessed with revenge and retribution. This will lead the person to become stuck with such patterns of behaviour, with an accompanying accumulation of inner rage and all of its dire

consequences to the body and mind. This is the *Path Of Blame*.
• They can accept themselves for the kinds of persons they are and realize that they have a choice to act or not act on the impulse toward perfection. They may choose to love themselves, to ease up for a change, and pay some attention to their needs for relaxation or pleasure. This is the *Path Of Self-Compassion*.

The Way Back: The Self-Compassion Cycle

To neutralize this cycle of striving for perfection, where much is achieved, but where a load of self-hatred is generated and accumulates, each person must learn about self-compassion. The first step is to become *aware* of these patterns of striving. The next step is to *acknowledge* the patterns, to others as well as to oneself; this acknowledgment overcomes the rigid pattern of denial, and frees up the fixation. In this revealing of the self, *acceptance* is demonstrated and furthered. This can be carried forward in *action*, further sustaining the self-compassion process. We call these the *four A's of self-compassion*: *awareness, acknowledgment, acceptance, action*. People are challenged to accept even the struggle toward perfection itself. Through this acceptance, individuals can develop a growing pattern of self-compassion, thus altering and transforming the repetitive patterns of self-denial and self-hatred. This occurs slowly at first; with time and repetition, people become established in the self-compassion process, which grows increasingly familiar and acceptable to them.

Striving For the Authentic Self

Sometimes, when high achievers grasp this process, they apply the achievement ethic to their own personal development, and set a *goal of reaching the Authentic Self*. This process is doomed to failure, since they have made an ambition of the process, which operates against accepting the various elements within themselves.

Abandoning the Ideal Self

It is useless to try to deny the Ideal Self. That only serves to add to the struggle by creating the goal to be more of the Authentic Self, which becomes another version of the Ideal Self, with even more possibilities of generating self-hatred. The Ideal Self has been constructed and groomed over many years, and should be honoured. Even though the achievement ethic can become a compulsive trap, to abandon it prematurely also leads to fixation without resolution of the whole process.

The Two Aspects of the Actual Self

At any moment, the Actual Self is capable of relating to a situation in two ways. It can *react* with ambitious striving, and thus intensify the self-hatred cycle; or it can *respond* with self-awareness and self-acceptance, to strengthen the self-compassion cycle.[4] The Actual Self has both a self-hating aspect, and a self-compassionate one. People are free to choose at any moment which process they will inhabit. When they choose to react with self-hatred, they become walled in their roles; when they respond with self-acceptance, they are vulnerable and able to establish personal boundaries.

The drive to perfectionism of the Ideal Self is often accompanied by a weighty seriousness; with self-acceptance comes some humour and levity. When people can laugh at themselves with warmth and self-compassion, they often experience a quiet flooding of fullness and strength.

Striving towards perfection in the self-hatred process brings *achievement*; self-compassion permits the ease and grace of *mastery* (see below, "Achievement or Mastery").

Guilt and Shame

When people are caught up in the self-hatred process in creating the Ideal Self, they experience guilt for falling short of the perfection they seek. When individuals accept themselves for the persons they are, they can experience shame that accompanies self-recognition. They will become more full with the revelation of shame.

Self Acceptance: A Delicate Balance

For people to become self-accepting, they need to accept *all* parts of themselves. They must come to know the Ideal Self, acknowledging and honouring it; nevertheless, they do not have to respond to the imperatives of the Ideal Self. Individuals can experience all of the feelings accompanying this awareness, thus opening themselves to new patterns of behaviour and feelings. Then the cycle of self-hatred will gradually lose its potency, and the maturation process can proceed.

Notes

1. J. McKeen and B.R. Wong, *The Relationship Garden* (Gabriola Island, B.C.: PD Publishing, 1996), pp. 11-16.

2. T. Rubin, *Compassion and Self-Hate* (New York: David McKay Co., 1975), pp. 13-17.

3. K. Horney, *Neurosis and Human Growth* (New York: W.W. Norton and Co., 1950) p. 24.

4. J. McKeen and B.R. Wong, *The Relationship Garden* (Gabriola Island, B.C.: PD Publishing, 1996), pp. 111, 112.

Boundaries

Development of Boundaries

From the essentialist point of view, each person is born with an essential "Self" which has a thrust to express characteristics that are unique to that person. At birth, that self is mostly potential. Imagine it to be like a tender amoeba-like being, surrounded by a delicate semi-permeable membrane (a boundary) like that around the yolk of an egg. From the outside, people tend to identify that boundary as the infant's body. However, from the developing experience of the infant, the boundary becomes much more complicated than that; it is a *felt* experience of where the self ends and the other begins. Sometimes, that felt experience of the self occurs at the bodily level; at other times, it occurs in other ways. The boundary is flexible and in constant motion, similar to the pseudopods of an amoeba, alternately reaching out to experience what is happening in the surrounding environment, and then withdrawing closer to the center, away from the environment.

Parents' attitudes to their children are crucial to the development of the youngsters' boundaries. Because adults tend to identify boundaries at the bodily level, children are subtly encouraged to do the same. However, if children do not experience safety and pleasure at the contact boundary, they will locate their boundary deeper within, away from the body. Many believe that at birth all infants are autistic(that is, they are unable to distinguish themselves from their environment), and that mother and child are experienced by babies as being the same. The pseudopods of the newly sensing boundary have not as yet developed the ability to sort out what exists within the boundary and what outside of it. Occurrences at the contact boundary help to determine the nature of the developing boundary.

Pleasure, Excitement and Contact

To the gestaltists, contact results in a state of excitement at the contact boundary. When contact is made, the infant (or for that matter, any person) will be stimulated to a state of vitality which the gestaltists call "the charge of excitement" at the contact boundary. Erving and Miriam Polster describe it this way:

> . . . a charge of excitement exists within the individual which culminates in a sense of full engagement with whatever is interesting at the moment.[1]

We ourselves like to distinguish the word "excitement" (which has connotations of charge and is often related to polarity) from what we call *pleasure of contact* , a readiness to respond to a stimulus.

From the bioenergetics viewpoint, pleasure is a phenomenon of letting go. Discomfort is a result of holding on, and pleasure comes in release. Alexander Lowen, in his book *Pleasure*, describes the phenomenon of pleasure:

> To have pleasure one has to "let go," that is, allow the body to respond freely. A person who is inhibited cannot easily experience pleasure because unconscious restraints restrict the flow of feeling in his body and block his natural bodily motility.[2]

Not all letting go is personal. There is *satisfaction pleasure* that arises in interaction that fulfils desires or drives. For example, an infant experiences satisfaction pleasure in being fed; this is not a personal issue, but rather is organismic. When the pleasure is more personal, we call this *contact pleasure*.

Dialogue and Boundaries

The human organism has the capacity to move beyond simple animal functions of charge and tension, into a genuine human dialogue. This capacity is developed through ongoing relationship, and is the subject of our book *The Relationship Garden.*[3]

It is worthwhile to distinguish between *excitement, satisfaction pleasure* and *contact pleasure*. Excitement has connotations of charge that are different from pleasure. Within the realm of pleasure, there are both organismic (satisfaction) pleasure and contact pleasure. Many report a fuller sense of vitality that comes with personal contact. People experience *excitement* by being stimulated as an organism; they experience *pleasure* in having needs and drives met; and they experience *fulfilment* in the contact with another human.

In a relationship of dialogue, both parties are transformed in the contact. Gordon Wheeler describes the gestalt conception of this transformation as a "creative adjustment" of the organism. He goes on to say that his definition of contact involves a "(re)organization of the self in the field."[4]

The proponents of dialogical psychotherapy have followed up on Martin Buber's thesis in *I and Thou*[5] recognizing that not all episodes of contact are person to person. Richard Hycner and Lynne Jacobs put it this way:

Not all contact episodes are dialogic episodes [6]

They go on to write:

The importance of contacting for our identity as a human being—what makes it so compelling and also so complex—is the way it is different from contacting among all organisms. The interhuman contacting process is the process by which we come to know ourselves and others, to apprehend our human existence and that of others.[7]

This capacity for human contact can move to farther reaches of human development:

When a contact episode is begun, the individual is motivated to finish the episode in the most growth-producing manner, given the current conditions of the organism-environment field.[8]

Hycner and Jacobs believe that "this same principle motivates the individual toward dialogue."

The I-Thou moment is a moment in which we are totally absorbed with another, which paradoxically puts us profoundly in contact with our humanity, with the knowledge of being; in this moment the meaning of human existence is revealed. [9]

Can Energy (and Feelings) Be Transferred?

Most theorists believe in energy transfer, where one individual can make another feel good (or bad) by the contact. We think the feelings of the contact are from the innate capability of the organism to feel pleasure at contact. There is no transmission of pleasure (or discomfort). When a person experiences pleasure, this is a byproduct of the openness, not a phenomenon of energy exchange.

We do not believe energy can be transferred; one can resonate in empathy with another; however, the energy is expressed from within, not obtained from without. We have discussed this elsewhere, proposing a theory of *resonance* instead of energy transfer.[10]

We believe that hurt, discomfort, and lack of pleasure, are a consequence of tightening in the energy body matrix, with a concomitant expression of tension in the body tissues. A person is not hurt (or pleasured) by someone else; instead, that person generates hurt or pleasure in relation to how much tightness or letting go is permitted. This polarity of tension/relaxation is determined by the perceptions and interpretations of that person.[11]

We have a similar notion about feelings and emotions. A core theorem to us is that *feelings are all generated within the person, and are not transferred.* Each person manifests feelings that are organized by their perceptions and interpretations (see above, "A Model For Communication").[12]

Dimensions of Boundary Making

There seems to be an *organismic boundary*, and a *personal boundary*. The developing infant is like an animal insofar as there is a body boundary that is determined by sensory experience. This is not personal, or even distinctly human. The human experience includes the capability of developing into a person (which takes some time to unfold). Morris Berman says that the self is conceived around the beginning of the third year of life, and is birthed around the end of the third year.[13] After this time, personal boundaries can become more definite.[14]

In experiencing everyday life situations, boundaries serve us best when they remain flexible and capable of change, even while maintaining a *consistency* that reflects the nature of the Authentic Self. Throughout the life of a healthy person, the boundaries reflect a tendency to both *contact* and *withdraw*, wherein the person is willing to expand to experience novelty (new experiences) even while tending to contract to smaller, more familiar and secure spaces. Such an expansion/contraction capability produces a wave-like sense of action and movement in life, *so long as the integrity of the organism is not threatened.*

A person has many boundaries that operate at a variety of levels simultaneously. Some of them have been described by Erving and Miriam Polster[15] as the following:

a. *The I-Boundary*: The boundary of what is permissible contactfulness for the person that "defines those actions, ideas, people, values, settings, images, memories, and so on in which he is willing and comparatively free to engage fully with both the world outside himself and the reverberations within himself that this engagement may awaken."
b. *Body-Boundaries*: willingness to be aware of sensation of some parts or functions of the body.
c. *Value Boundaries*: willingness to accept experiences that fall within a range of values determined by the Self.
d. *Familiarity Boundaries:* how much of experience will be allowed within or beyond the realm of what has been previously experienced and established as habit patterns.
e. *Expressive Boundaries:* how much feelings and energy can be expressed in the presence of others.
f. *Exposure Boundaries*: how much of the self one is willing to reveal to others.

Pleasure and Discomfort

If the quality of the stimulus of the parent is pleasing, the child will experience a feeling response consistent with being safe and nurtured, with a desire to repeat that pleasant contact. In this way, the child's boundary is likely to develop in the direction of flexibility, responsiveness, sensitivity, availability, with a movement toward others who are gradually being recognized as separate from the child. However, in life's experience, the course of boundary contact does not always run smoothly. Frequently in small ways, and sometimes in gross ways, the contact is uncomfortable. It can be too little (resulting in fear of abandonment) or too much (with the experience of being overwhelmed). It can be hostile (with resulting fear of lack of safety), demanding or indifferent (with resulting experience of low self-esteem). When threatened, people learn to withdraw the boundary away from contact, closer to themselves. Especially confusing are contacts that are inconsistent and filled with double and contradictory messages.

Walls

When threatened, the person has the option of either withdrawing from contact, or remaining close to contact by defending the boundary. Defending the boundary results in a rigidification and thickening of the organic nature of the boundary. In this way, the boundary is converted into a fortified *wall* with diminished capacities for responsiveness and contactability. The world will seem safer to walled individuals; the cost is that they will likely be less alive and full in their lives.

Any boundary can become a wall. The ego defences and the ego adaptive mechanisms are part of the "I Boundaries." The nature of the personality of the individual is an amalgam of these elements.

Roles

Roles are made up of those walls. They serve the function of survival, regardless of whether they are "good" (acceptable or appropriate) or "bad" (unacceptable or inappropriate) roles. Roles invite others to give attention, through reward or punishment. Attention is often an objectifying substitute for recognition; we believe that recognition is an important aspect of loving, while attention is impersonal.[16] People crave to be appreciated for who they are; being recognized satisfies this desire. More often, they are given attention for acting appropriately in response to expectations, thus ensuring that the needed other will not leave. In this process, the Authentic Self is put into storage and life becomes full of obligations, rules, and judgment-filled morality. Spontaneity, fullness of experience, and the joy of being are all diminished. The vitality of boundary contact is replaced by a constant vigilance to ensure that the expectations of others (and hence the perceived needs of the self) are being met. The person becomes "field dependent" in a way that makes the opinions of others more important. Society at large identifies this process as "maturing" or "growing up"; in this way, order is maintained and achievement is ensured. To adopt roles is a necessary process of *socialization*; however, this is *not self-actualization*. Would it not be desirable to have available both of these processes, without them having to exclude each other?

Relationships

Most people relate to others from their walls (that is, roles), well defended and field dependent. Although that seems appropriate for everyday interactions at work or in most social situations, it frequently leaves people isolated and invisible. This isolation can motivate individuals to seek intimate relationships. This attraction to intimacy is frequently confused with the sexual drive and excitement, as we will later describe (see below, "A Perspective On Sexuality"). The drive toward intimacy involves a craving to be recognized, for the Authentic Self to be revealed, accepted, and appreciated.

In revealing themselves, people first offer others their roles and walls. Those are the parts that first attract others, creating a Romance, an illusion of perfection (see below, "Developmental Stages of Relationships"). As that Romance is dying (and it usually will), the acid test of the relationship lies in the inevitable ensuing Power Struggle. There are a number of choices when the Romance dies:
- often people avoid the struggle by separating
- they can engage in the Power Struggle by trying to overcome the other through being "right" (or its obverse, being "wrong," as some people prefer to do)
- they can fight to exhaustion, and move ultimately to indifference or

apathy
- they can transcend the whole scene in order to avoid it
- they can discovering ways of being creative about the struggle in order to maintain a level of excitement
- they can both find ways of discovering patterns of themselves and responsibly share these revelations with one another in order to deepen the experience of intimacy

In an intimate relationship, each person recognizes his or her own self-responsibility. When there is no blaming and no victim, people can embark upon developing a Relationship Garden, through vulnerability and a willingness to share with one other. In this project, people are willing to expose their walls, defences, and weapons to one another. In this way, each person begins to dissolve the tough hide of the walls, to return to a more innocent and vulnerable state. Then, *real* contact is possible, and both parties can experience the invigoration of fullness at the contact boundary. Encounters can then be fresh and fulfilling—albeit also frightening, sad, and sometimes disappointing.

Survivors of Sexual Abuse

One possible problem that can arise from child sexual abuse is that individuals can lose trust in their own bodies and themselves. Because pleasure is a natural function of the body, children possibly enjoy the original acts. Sometimes that pleasure is confused by a strong wish to please the initiator of the abuse. Frequently, the sexual acts are imposed on children, who experience helplessness and thus are unable to resist. Inappropriate sexual acts are a crossing of a person's boundary, usually by people who themselves have poorly functioning boundaries. Sexually abused children can have a mixture of feelings and responses. They can develop feelings of guilt for having participated, no matter how helpless they were in the situation. By drawing their boundaries closer to themselves they can separate from their bodies, which they believe to have betrayed them (possibly because they felt pleasure in such an unacceptable situation). They could create a myth that their Authentic Self is not appreciated; with a conviction of unworthiness, they could then refuse to reveal themselves to anybody else. Although adult survivors frequently hide behind walls designed to project competence and self-assuredness, inwardly, they often live in fear that they will be discovered as frauds; they might act in a friendly and sometimes even seductive fashion, yet often they dread sexual encounters in which they may have to perform. Any letting go is seen as a threat to their hiding; so they desperately try to remain in control of both themselves and others.

Taking Down The Walls

Once walls have been created, they serve as a prison to the self as much as a defence against others. People find great difficulty in bringing down their walls, to soften them back to their original function as boundaries. Too often, the wall is identified with the body; this gives rise to what Reich dubbed the "character armour."[17] Even if the hardened wall could be removed (as some body therapies attempt to do), that person will still have to develop some healthier means of coping with others and the environment. Experiences that heighten self-esteem and self-assertion can be useful; self-compassion and self-acceptance would be an even better strategy. Learning to explore and discriminate within the environment— how to discern the intention and actions of others—is very important in establishing a sense of safety in relationships and in all social situations. Learning how to relate from a position of responsibility rather than victimhood is important. Ultimately, people can claim themselves and their bodies, realizing that they can choose their own behaviour through agreement ("Yes") or denial ("No").

An Issue For Everyone

Although confusion about boundaries is especially graphic in the personalities of those who have been abused either sexually or physically, the principles are pertinent to everybody. Most people are working through issues related to their boundaries, afraid of being overwhelmed and made helpless. Most individuals offer walls of self-defense, righteousness, judgmentalness, prejudices, and security instead of boundaries of contact with all their excitement, vulnerability, fear, joy, and sadness. People usually believe that in order to be accepted they must perform and succeed, impress, please, control, and manipulate others.

In order to rediscover themselves, individuals must be prepared to take risks, reveal their walls to others, and take ownership of their own feelings by being responsible for themselves. To define one's self-worth through taking care of others, or by remaining dependent, are both equally counterproductive to personal development. In every situation it is important to remember that *people do have choices*; they can risk presenting themselves authentically, prepared to accept the consequences of their choices. Undoubtedly, there will be hurt in revelation—for pain, anxiety, and sadness are as much a part of us as are pleasure, peace, and joy. To know oneself is to know all these facets. By sharing this complexity of themselves, people can discover genuine intimacy with each other:

> *What is asked of us in our time*
> *is that we break open*
> *our blocked caves*
> *and find each other.*
>
> *Nothing less will heal the anguished spirit,*
> *nor release the heart to act in love.*
> —Raymond John Baughan [18]

Notes

1. Erving and Miriam Polster, *Gestalt Therapy Integrated* (New York: Brunner/Mazel, 1973), p. 130.

2. Alexander Lowen, *Pleasure* (New York: Lancer Books, 1970), p. 29.

3. J. McKeen and B.R. Wong, *The Relationship Garden* (Gabriola Island, B.C.: PD Publishing, 1996).

4. Gordon Wheeler, *Gestalt Reconsidered* (New York: Gardner Press Inc., 1991), p. 129.

5. Martin Buber, *I and Thou* (New York: Charles Scribner's Sons, 1970).

6. Richard Hycner and Lynne Jacobs, *The Healing Relationship In Gestalt Therapy* (Highland, NY: The Gestalt Journal Press, 1995), p.56.

7. Ibid., p. 58.

8. Ibid., p. 58.

9. Ibid., p. 58.

10. J. McKeen and B.R. Wong, *The Relationship Garden* (Gabriola Island, B.C.: PD Publishing, 1996), p. 176.

11. Ibid., p. 120.

12. Ibid., p. 142.

13. Ibid., pp. 43, 44.

14. Morris Berman, *Coming To Our Senses*, (New York: Bantam Books, 1990), pp. 32-24.

15. Erving & Miriam Polster, *Gestalt Therapy Integrated*, (New York: Brunner/Mazel, 1973) pp.98-127.

16. J. McKeen and B.R. Wong, *The Relationship Garden* (Gabriola Island, B.C.: PD Publishing, 1996), p. 188.

17. W. Reich, *Selected Writings* (New York: Farrar, Straus and Giroux, 1973), p. 53.

18. R.J. Baughan, *The Sound of Silence* (Boston: Department of Publications UUA, 1965), p. 7.

Achievement or Mastery

Many believe that one of the chief tasks in life is to discover who we are; along with this goes the assumption that infants are born with the potential of becoming the persons they were meant to be.

The Struggle for Survival

When newborns emerge from the womb, which provides an ideal environment of comfort and sustenance, they must experience quite a shock of discomfort! The safe uterine atmosphere is suddenly replaced by a hostile environment with temperature extremes, light and sound stimulation, feeding uncertainties, and a myriad of uncontrollable external factors. Threats to the infants' homeostasis (and hence their very existence) are experienced as pain or discomfort. Satisfaction of needs or the amelioration of the sources of pain are experienced as pleasure. When the satisfaction of those needs becomes predictable, babies experience a comforting sense of certainty; the little ones begin to crave this security, while trying to avoid the experiences that produce insecurity (see below, "Strength and Power"). These basic issues of survival are primary needs that evoke a wide variety of patterns of adaptive behaviours that then become unique to each individual.

As children grow, early survival mechanisms are reflected in later patterns of behaviour. When people have experienced threats to survival during their infancy, issues that might usually be only mildly threatening can provoke overreaction, with undue anxiety and tension.

Children are highly field dependent, first for survival and later to seek significance. Youngsters soon learn that much more pleasurable experiences ensue when they are pleasing to others. Thus, a system of mutual control between children and the people in their environment is established at an early age.

Standing Forth vs Standing Out

Throughout life, many people are obsessed with "making something" of themselves, "being important," accomplishing something that "matters," being "significant" or "counting." Frequently, family and society encourage a view of significance that centres on achievements in the workplace and success in the establishment of a stable and loving family; a respected and economically advantageous role in life is considered to afford the highest status. However, many who have achieved these goals cannot understand their feelings of emptiness or meaninglessness. Their discomfort often goes beyond the accumulation of self-hatred that occurs with the abandonment of the Authentic Self in striving for the Ideal Self (see above, "The Ideal Self: Striving For Perfection"). Perhaps they have confused the existential imperative to *stand forth* (and thus be "outstanding") with a societal expectation to *stand out* (and thus be "famous").

Each of us is born with our own potentials; each of us is unique. Yet we are expected to develop and conform in the direction of the general mass of people, and at the same rate. When we fail, we are met with exhortations (sometimes subtle, sometimes severe) to conform. Always there seems to be an expectation that we "make something" of ourselves, that we become "successful," that we distinguish ourselves by "standing out" and being admired. It is as though we are expected to *construct* a life of significance, rather than to *be* significant. Toward this end, doing becomes more important than being.

Standing Out

Because of our society's pervasive moral loathing of self-involvement (narcissism), individuals are taught to think of others before thinking of themselves; such is the readily accepted ideal of "caring." At the same time, they are expected to stand out, to be distinctive, to be better than others—but without acknowledging that this can only happen at the expense of others. This is a contradiction, a typical "double-bind" situation (as described by Bateson[1]); for the sake of sanity, people must deny, repress, or rationalize this dilemma. Our culture encourages competition without acknowledging that those who succeed do so at the expense of those who lose. Winners are rewarded with authority, which gives them power over the lives of others. They earn a disproportionately greater share of material wealth and are afforded a higher public status than others.

It is obvious that *standing out* provides the individual with praise and many other rewards, economically as well as psychologically. What is little understood is that such attention feeds the Ideal Self but ignores the Authentic Self; it is *not* recognition (to be "known again"). Invisible and unacknowledged, these persons are left with an inner emptiness, and a conviction of worthlessness. They are given accolades, but are isolated from the others to whom they are compared. In reaction, other people often are jealous of those who are given so much attention.

People who stand out make objects of themselves and others. Although they may seem to be very energetic (sometimes hyperactive), they lack a sense of genuine vitality and often do not experience being fully alive. In their striving for success they often experience tension (which they may interpret as excitement) or a high-pressure charge (for example, as can occur with big business deals). They become obsessed with accomplishments, power, fame, and the notice of others; they objectify the people in their lives, who serve to fill their craving for attention and approval. By doing so, they become markedly field dependent, their self-worth tied to the amount of approval given to them by others. Because this emphasis on pleasing others is so common in child rearing, it is no wonder that people commonly have a difficult time giving themselves approval and developing a healthy sense of self-esteem. Abandoning much of their Authentic Self, they concentrate on constructing an Ideal Self, and in the process generate self-hatred. Their sense of pride is inflated, but their sense of self-esteem is low. They become driven to achieve more as they become trapped in a self-hating cycle (see above, "The Ideal Self: Striving For Perfection"). They are given much attention and many rewards for successfully developing and living their roles in life; such roles often provide them with positions of power and prestige. Unfortunately, they can only feel good about themselves when they are doing and achieving.

Because the high achievers develop their sense of importance in relationship to others around them (the field), they tend to feel anxious that others might abandon them, or even that others might not be impressed. Hence, such people become obsessed with *control*. The more they can control the people and situations in their lives, the more secure they will feel and the better they will feel about themselves. This frequently becomes an issue for them at home; so long as their spouse and children are willing to be controlled by them, they feel happy. When other family members take steps toward independence or autonomy, they experience this loss of control as a great threat. In this way, power struggles are common within the families of high achievers.

To stand out requires endurance, vigilance, control, effort, an obsession with details, and constant monitoring of the expectations of others. Such people are often prone to emotional instability and sentimentalism, which Oscar Wilde defined as "having the luxury of an emotion without paying for it."[2] In reacting with sentimentalism, the person disconnects from the experience itself, becoming more involved in experiencing the feeling than in remaining connected with the actual event.

People who stand out become *independent* (rather than *autonomous*), and *individualized* (rather than *individuated*); they remain greatly field dependent, continuing to rely on the attention of others for their self-esteem.

Independence vs Autonomy

At first glance, *independence* and *autonomy* seem to be synonymous. They are not.

To be independent is still to be tied in reaction to whatever one is independent from. Hence, independence is not a true liberation (see below, "Strength and Power"; also, see below, "Rebellion and Standing Forth" in "Distinctions"). Many high achievers become independent, and seem very free and powerful; yet, in their attachment to the approval and attention of others, they remain tied and limited. They are independent, but not free.

When one is autonomous, one has a centre within oneself. This person is free of the constraints of others' judgments, while remaining sensitive to the feelings and concerns of others.

Individualizing vs Individuating

There are great differences between *individualizing* and *individuation*. Even though these concepts seem to be the same, they are very different.

In the process of individualizing (becoming an "individual"), one is not really growing in a free unfettered way. One becomes an individual in reaction to others; hence, the individual is tied to others. Thus individualizing is not a true path of self-realization.

When one *individuates*, one is making free choices, and becomes oneself without reacting to others. The person who is individuating can move past the limitations of achievement into true mastery of life. This person grows into deepening awareness of self and others. We have discussed this elsewhere.[3]

Standing Forth

People who stand forth become *autonomous* and *individuated*. They derive their self-esteem from their own sense of jobs well done, from their own appreciation of their having given a task their best effort, being all they can be. To them, the result is not nearly as important as the quality of the *process* of their doing. They are fully involved in whatever they undertake, and experience life as being full of interesting possibilities for exploration and growth. True, they are self-centred (centred within themselves), but not at the expense of others. They remain connected, sensitive to the needs of others as well as to their own. They have a great capacity for empathy, while rejecting any temptation to feel sympathy (which involves a condescension from an attitude of superiority). They recognize and respect the boundaries of others, yet are always interested in vulnerability and intimacy. They care about others while refusing to take care of them, recognizing everyone's potential for being responsible for themselves.

Only when people fail to be fully who they are do they revert to the irresponsibility of resentment and blame. Hence people who stand forth manifest very little resentment or blame for others.

To stand forth requires the courage to be oneself.[4] Standing forth involves creativity, awareness, presence, and focused attention, without sentimentalism (that is, overreaction or dramatization) or self-pity. Such individuals keep in touch with themselves while entering the world with a fullness; they remain connected with the background from which they are standing forth. They express the best of the human condition, evoking inspiration in others. In such a distinguished presence, people commonly desire to be connected with one another, being reminded of their own potential to be fuller and more of who they are.

Achievement vs Mastery

Those who are driven to achieve often work hard at developing skills that are not an expression of themselves; they achieve competence but not mastery. These people often do not find fulfilment, since they are divorced from their achievements.

In contrast, people who stand forth develop *mastery* of their own skills, which are not so much acquired as they are revealed and exercised. To them, the pleasure is in the doing rather than just in the achieving. Because their skills are their own, they find fulfilment in the authentic expression of themselves.

The Dichotomies of Existence

The following chart outlines the polarities in the human experience of growth and development.

Non-Existence

Pain	Pleasure
Insecurity	Security
Standing Forth *(coming into existence)*	Standing Out *(becoming noticed)*
Self-Reliance	Field Dependence
Revealing the Authentic Self	Constructing the Ideal Self
Mastery	Achievement
Revelation	Strategy
Vulnerability	Control
Recognition	Attention
Strength	Power

Conclusion

People who stand forth are outstanding in the world, in the manner in which they live and create; they fully appreciate the meaning of "coming into existence." They understand, accept, and appreciate the world of objects from which they have emerged, yet they are not controlled by it. Rather than becoming field dependent, they remain in touch with what they desire to do; they follow their hearts. Thus, they become more spontaneous, self-reliant, and self-motivated. They are more in touch with themselves and others, more fully human and fulfilled. Instead of achieving their tasks, they master them (that is, they fine-tune the skills that emerge from within, rather than imposing on themselves the artificial task of acquiring some skill for which they are not suited). They increasingly reveal themselves; so, they enjoy much recognition (as opposed to the attention given to achievers). They experience a spiritual oneness without striving for it or even naming it. As they stand forth, they recognize that they just "are," everything just "is," and this is enough.

> *To venture causes anxiety,*
> *but not to venture is to lose oneself*
> —S. Kierkegaard[5]

Notes

1. G. Bateson, *Steps to an Ecology of Mind* (New York: Ballantine Books, 1972), pp. 271-78.

2. Oscar Wilde, in Edgar A. Levenson, *The Ambiguity of Change* (New York: Basic Books, 1983), p. 33.

3. J. McKeen and B.R. Wong, *The Relationship Garden* (Gabriola Island, B.C.: PD Publishing, 1996), p. 193.

4. Paul Tillich, *The Courage To Be* (New Haven: Yale University Press, 1976).

5. Søren Kierkegaard, *The Sickness Unto Death*, Walter Lowrie, trans. (Princeton, NJ: Princeton University Press, 1941), pp. 43-44.

Self-Esteem

Self-esteem is the measure by which people regard themselves, the value that they place upon themselves, the respect that they have for themselves. Commonly, the development of self-esteem is seen to be related to the mirroring function in personality development. The simplistic idea is that the more value that children see reflected in their parents' eyes, the more they will value themselves; the more positive experiences that children have during their earlier years of development, the greater their possibility of developing high self-esteem. It is difficult to argue with that proposition, since it seems to make sense. Yet, it is rare to encounter people who appear to have achieved such a comfortable state of being. More commonly, people seem to suffer from low self-esteem. Indeed, it seems that most of those who are successful (by the standards of our culture) are compensating for a low sense of self-esteem; it is that very sense of low self-esteem that accounts for the drive toward success. Many such people appear to be happy; or at least they would not want to change their lives.

On the other hand, there are others who do not value themselves beyond the ordinary; indeed, many of them believe that others have many more talents than themselves. They, too, appear to be happy. Their virtue seems to be a true humility, and they seem to be comfortable with themselves and with others. Such people refute the idea that a high sense of self-esteem is a prerequisite for happiness and success.

Because it is a current psychological fashion to fret about self-esteem, many people are striving stoically for that blessed state. Some even believe that it was their right at birth to have been provided with the necessary environment (such as loving, highly regarding, mature parents) to engender high self-esteem. These people believe that this was their entitlement, and because it did not materialize, they feel resentment over having been betrayed and cheated by their parents. Some of them become fixated in the attitude that they are unlovable; that their parents didn't seem to love them is taken as proof of this.

Is that the only way of explaining this phenomenon? Surely some people with even more difficult backgrounds have been able to come to some happier resolution with their families. What is the difference?

The Pleasure of Mastery

First, let us examine the development of self-evaluation. Very early in life, children confuse two very different phenomena—the pleasure of mastery and the pride of achievement. The pleasure of mastery appears to be inherent in the organism; children experience a feeling of fulfilment when they take their first steps or learn to tie their own shoelaces or successfully maneuver food to their mouths. With mastery, children experience the intriguing rewards of discovery; they continue to feel pleasure as their world expands and they become increasingly more self-reliant and competent. Such children become more self-determining, motivated by an inherent desire to fulfil their potential, to actualize that which yearns to be realized, to express an inner drive to grow. In these circumstances, the best thing that a parent or teacher can do is to provide a safe learning environment and some encouraging support for such mastery to blossom and mature.

The Stress of Achievement

Unfortunately, most people have a strong urge to be ideal parents for their ideal children; thus, they are determined to help their children achieve these important steps toward self-reliance through encouragement, bribery, blackmail, threats of abandonment, and any number of other coercive means. This is all done "for the child's own good." Under the watchful eyes of such authority figures, children begin to recognize that what they do is always subject to evaluation, to judgments of good or bad, appropriate or inappropriate, satisfactory or unsatisfactory; furthermore, their behaviour seems to produce pleasure and displeasure in others. These circumstances foster field dependence in these children; the evaluation of others becomes more important than the children's own pleasure of mastery.

Mirroring and Introjection of Authority

Through introjection, the child swallows whole the evaluating functions of the parents (variously called the Superego, the Parent Within, or the Ideal Self), and self-esteem becomes linked with this inner judging authority. The nature of this introjected authority (harsh, easy, inconsistent, or rigid) is closely related to the kind of mirroring provided to the child. Distortions in the mirroring function (such as over-valuing, or under-estimating) can have a radical effect on the child's self-esteem. If children are underestimated by their parents, they will tend to introject an underestimating inner judge, resulting in beliefs of inadequacy, unworthiness, self-doubt, and uncertainty. The natural feelings of pleasure that come with mastery are abandoned in favor of such an evaluating process.

Overvaluation by the authority figure rarely produces a happier situation. Such distorted (convex) mirroring may indeed produce within the child a superficial sense of high self-esteem; but if it does not match an inner sense of mastery, the child intuits it to be false. In such situations, children can develop contempt for the external authority (and then, by association, for all authority); frequently, this is accompanied with self-loathing for having duped those important authority figures. Thus, although parental overvaluation may appear to result in high self-esteem, it is accompanied by a deeper, more dangerous self-loathing and contempt for others.[12]

Underevaluating (concave) mirroring from a parental figure tends to produce within a child self concepts of worthlessness, incompetence, and inadequacy. Children tend to incorporate this mirroring by developing an internal attitude that is critical and unaccepting toward themselves. These children grow to become self-effacing, self-doubting, uncertain adults who may be perfectionistic but are never satisfied with themselves. If parents exhibit uncaring lack of concern, or inability to mirror at all, children will tend to see themselves as invisible, unworthy, and unlovable. It is as though the mirroring process provides a stimulus for an inner tropism toward being; it may be an important factor in experiencing existence itself. Without mirroring, the psychological sense of presence that precedes self-esteem may atrophy, thus dooming to failure any subsequent attempts at increasing self-esteem; such attempts may appear to be successful, but with a lack of true ground, the self-esteem generated will be false and unhealthy. Frequently, such persons become society's leaders and role models, whom the masses admire and wish to emulate—people like political leaders, movie idols, and rock stars. One may wonder why so many people have such a penchant for ideal role models, sometimes even being prepared to abandon themselves in favor of some ultimate authority. The search for such authorities has produced a big business in the psychological, spiritual, and religious fields.

Search For Paternal Authority

It is often suggested that the search for ultimate authority has its roots in the craving for father, resulting from inadequate fathering or some unresolved infantile fixation on the father. We believe that such a yearning *precedes* the father-child experience. It is an algorithm established at the juncture between mastery and achievement, when achievement takes precedence over mastery. In this commonly experienced scenario, people lose pleasure in their own mastery, instead seeking comfort and security through relationships with outside authorities, who must be pleased in order to achieve acceptance. Parental figures are the first such authorities; in a patriarchal society such as North America, the father becomes the ultimate authority, slipping readily into this previously established algorithm.

The crown of ultimate authority rests uneasily on father's head (or that of any leader, role model, or star). Because such a position is usually lacking in the pleasure of mastery (which would be accompanied by fulfilment and true self-esteem), any achievement produces more self-doubt, contempt, self-loathing, and pride (false self-esteem). Power needs become of paramount importance, control over others a goal (albeit subconscious or denied). This unfortunate scenario is reproduced at many levels of society, resulting in the unhappy circumstances of many people basking in the glory and acceptance of father-figures (of both genders), with their (surface) self-esteems apparently intact but their self-loathing growing (leaders as well as followers). History has revealed how often this situation has been doomed to failure, ending with masses of people disillusioned because they ultimately believe they have been betrayed. Recovery from these circumstances offers an opportunity to return to the important junction point of mastery and achievement, to learn from the experience, and to proceed further along the path of self-actualization, beyond achievement. Most people waste this opportunity, continuing to seek other ultimate authorities; their true self-esteem suffers.

Seeking Self-Esteem: A New Striving

In the current psychological climate, self-esteem has become a central goal for many therapists and educators. By making it an achievement that must be reached, they have made self-esteem the new ideal. The dilemma is that such striving tends to reproduce the original problem of the self-hatred cycle (see above, "The Ideal Self: Striving For Perfection"). By trying to *achieve* high self-esteem, people are hating themselves for not being perfect at acquiring self-esteem. In this process, they may attain a superficial sense of high self-esteem, only to discover more self-loathing and self-hatred. They have made an icon of self-esteem, and miss it by trying to achieve it.

We all would do well to devote more attention to developing self-compassion, self-acceptance, and self-love, all as a means of experiencing a fuller sense of love with others. Then we could accept our level of self-esteem, low or high, without producing more disruptive self-hatred.

Self-esteem has become a false cause (although sometimes a useful one). Self-acceptance is the key to undo this error. The four A's (awareness, acknowledgement, acceptance, action) are a most useful method to find enhanced fulfilment in life.

Notes

1. J.McKeen and B.R. Wong, *The Relationship Garden* (Gabriola Island, B.C.: PD Publishing, 1996), pp. 149-50.

2. Ibid., pp. 184-86.

Entitlement

Entitlement is a natural occurrence in child development, in which infants believe that the world around them must provide for their wants or needs. The normal maturation process involves a gradual relinquishing of this position. Although entitlement is important at the beginning, it becomes counterproductive later in life. The early phase of entitlement helps to establish a sense of self-importance in relation to the rest of the world. Later, it is this same narcissistic position that stands in the way of a genuine dialogue with another. We see many people who are fixated in their entitlement phase; such fixation seems to be a phenomenon of this age.

Normal Child Development

In the womb, children experience a fusion with their mothers and cannot distinguish themselves as separate. At birth, babies become physically separated; however, psychologically, children continue for some time to behave as if their mothers and the rest of the environment were part of them. As their perceptual functions develop, infants begin to make out vague outlines, and slowly come to identify one of these shapes as their regular provider (when they develop language, they will call this entity "Mother"). In the same manner, they learn to make out other people and objects. At the beginning, children treat all of these objects as extensions of themselves, not as separate entities. The project of psychological maturation involves distinguishing external objects and people, and assigning names to them. The development of language symbols provides a matrix for children to relate to the external world, and build a relationship with it.

Even when children gradually come to recognize that their mothers are separate from themselves, they still experience a sense of possessiveness. When they are hungry, their mothers are their servants, providing for their wants; when they are cold or wet, the people who are their possessions should cater to them. This is the experience of *entitlement*, which is a normal phase of early child development. Between one and two years of age, babies begin to move away from their parents physically, exploring the world around, constantly checking back to see that the parents are still pleased and under the child's control. As children move forward into the world, they carry a feeling of entitlement. Just as they see their mothers as possessions, subject to their every whim and command, they apply this entitlement to the rest of the world, expecting attention and service.[1]

In "good-enough parenting,"[2] parents provide boundaries, and do not indulge every little whim. When children encounter these boundaries within their parents, they can develop an awareness that the parents are separate and distinct entities, with personal thoughts, feelings, and desires. Children will at first try to rebel against this awareness, attempting to bring parents under their control. If parents are successful in maintaining their own sense of boundaries, their children can continue to mature toward more distinct individuated selves. In the milieu of parental boundary-setting, done in an atmosphere of caring and consistency, children can begin to move from the narcissistic, self-involved world to acquire the capacity to recognize the personhood of another, and can begin to develop a more consistent and fulfilled sense of themselves. This long journey of acknowledging and respecting others' boundaries, and learning to define oneself in relation to others, is called *the separation-individuation project.*[3]

Persistent Entitlement: The Arrested Child

If children are successful in bullying their parents (that is, if parents fail to assert their own individuality and boundaries), they will not learn the valuable lessons that permit the next phase of psychological development. In order to mature beyond the self-involved infant state, young people need to come up against the boundaries of their parents and discover that there is someone separate and distinct from themselves, worthy of respect and acknowledgement. Each time children do not automatically get their own way, they are stimulated to recognize that their parents are separate individuals. Indulged children, who do not encounter parental boundaries, fail to develop a concept of the separate other; as a result, these children maintain their entitled position where they are the centre of the universe. Psychological development arrests, and these individuals remain fixated as *entitled ones.*[4]

Often, parents believe they are entitled to have their children be what they want (the *idealized version* of the child). Parents who have lived in the entitled state have not learned to recognize genuine otherness; instead, such people's relationships are based on self-serving expectations, with little patience for the desires or differences of others. Such entitled parents fail to recognize the personhood of their children; instead, they reward their offspring with approval and attention, and encourage the development of the Ideal Self in their children. Youngsters who learn to seek approval believe that they are entitled to attention and reward when they meet someone's expectations; they are disturbed when such rewards are not forthcoming. Parents can only stimulate development in their children to the degree that they have themselves developed; the task of parenting includes with it an urgent clarion call to "grow up yourself!" If parents did not believe they were entitled to the idealized versions of their offspring, and instead were interested in recognizing the nascent personhood of their youngsters, they could become a stimulus for the children to grow with a separate sense of themselves. With such recognition, children could learn to interact in dialogue, valuing both self and other.

Entitled children grow up believing that the world owes them whatever they wish; when desires are not met, they become victims. They do not develop autonomous initiative, and are dependent upon others. As well, they do not learn sensitivity to others, which would permit the more advanced experience of object constancy, and a later subject constancy.[5] With this entitlement, these persons do not become individuated; rather, they remain arrested tyrants, expecting the world to cater to every whim instead of using their own motivation, will, and imagination. Hence, entitled people are stunted, weakened, and power oriented; field dependent, they are tossed about by the reactions of those they try to rule. They rage or sulk, without any capacity to learn that they will not automatically have whatever they want; thus, learning is blocked, initiative is blunted, and the loving compassion of the mature individual does not germinate. Entitled children grow up to be entitled adults, who perpetuate the cycle. Their orientation is "for me," with limited concern for others; such individuals are often lonely, and have a limited capacity for relatedness and intimacy. Such people's self-regard is maldeveloped, and their personal sense of strength is retarded. Desperately trying to manipulate the world, entitled people remain tied to the others they try to dominate. To exert control, the Ideal Self grows in power, trying to please and gain attention; with this desperation comes a deep self-hatred and lack of confidence (see above, "The Ideal Self: Striving for Perfection").

The phenomenon of entitlement, which is a normal developmental phase, becomes an insidious malignancy when it persists beyond early childhood. Although it is always possible to develop increasing sensitivity to others, and to enter into a stimulating dialogue, the entitled person remains insensitive. This individual is prone to a life of controlling others, adopting an attitude of power and domination. One of the most treacherous aspects is that self-involvement interferes with development of self-initiating functions. This self- absorption is rooted in anxiety about survival; entitled persons are insecure unless they are being attended by servants. Rather than face their anxiety, such selfish people develop their view that the rest of the world should take care of them. The result of this attitude is stunted personalities, insensitive to the needs and experiences of others; these people become autocrats who are out of touch with the lives of those around. Entitled people miss those very people in the field who, if they were recognized, could be stimuli for their personal development.

The Profile of the Entitled Person

The entitled adult, retarded in personal development, remains like a young child, irresponsible and without initiative. The attitude of entitlement is "Take care of me." Entitled people remain as victims, feeling hurt and unhappy in this situation of field dependence. They show little empathy and much dependency upon others in relationships. These individuals are not curious, and thus learn only what serves to facilitate the acquisition of what they see as their "due." Entitled people do not learn well from experience and do not develop a genuine interest or caring about others.

In day-to-day interactions, entitled people show little regard for others. They will stand in a door, oblivious that others might want to go through. Such persons will throw a cigarette butt onto the ground with no qualms that someone else will have to pick it up; in their minds, the rest of the world are servants to indulge their carelessness. In relationships, these people think they are misunderstood when a partner does not agree with them; for them, it is inconceivable that anyone else could have a valid point of view. At a table, they will take the biggest and the best items of food and will not be concerned with taking only their share. They often show a lack of forethought, with emergency last-minute plans that inconvenience co-workers and friends. In general, they demonstrate a lack of consideration for others and a belief that the world should take care of things for them. When things do not work out, they react with blame rather than self-investigation. Hence, personal responsibility is replaced by resentment of the world for not providing for their whims and wants.[6]

With entitlement comes a failure to develop courage. The entitled person operates from power and control rather than from the vulnerability and self-revelation that would facilitate the development of personal strength. Such people live in an objectified world and do not develop a sense of themselves or others. They individualize rather than individuate. Outwardly confident, they often lack simple social skills and live with a chronic deep-seated fear for their own survival. Unable to develop boundaries, they instead construct walls that interfere with genuine dialogue; along with walls come the "boundary illnesses" (asthma, allergies, phobias, and cancer). The control-oriented, entitled person is field dependent and does not develop the self-reliance and initiative that mark the resilient personality of someone who has relinquished entitlement. Entitled people are more prone to dependencies of all sorts (on institutions; on anesthetics such as TV, drugs, or alcohol; and on others who will support the illusion of their importance). Often, work is for security and financial gain, rather than for the sense of satisfaction that comes in collaborating with other humans in a sensitive dialogue of activity and love. Entitled people often experience a profound lack of rest and settling, because they have a poor sense of their location in life. With their inflated sense of self-importance, they are out of touch with their place. They are commonly involved in field-dependent attachments to the images of the Ideal Self, and less in touch with the Authentic Self; hence, they have considerable self-hatred and self-denial. Deep down, entitled people have a profound fear of intimacy; because they do not recognize others as persons, they are suspicious and have paranoid fears of what others can do to them. Because they use walls rather than boundaries, they tend to be rigid, seeking clearly defined roles and expectations; thus, they are prone to a herd mentality and are stifled in their creativity.

Entitlement: A Social Disease of This Era

In recent years, there has been increasing evidence of entitlement as a phenomenon in society. In the decade of the 1960s, a questioning of social values and a search for self-awareness gave rise to the "I am me" generation; the current one is a "give me" generation. It appears that the increased freedom of the 1960s and 1970s brought more fear: people now seem to have recoiled from freedom and closed up in their anxiety. With rapid technological development, society has been providing for the individual; in this era of easy access to goods, people have come to expect that others will provide for them (friends, partners, institutions, social agencies, or society in general). What was a privilege in the 1950s has become a right near the end of the twentieth century.

With this entitlement, there is less cooperation, less consideration of others, more "me" and less "we." Such an attitude explains stopping one's car in the middle of a busy street to chat with a pedestrian, and the pollution that comes from thoughtlessly disposing of waste products (on individual and national levels). The spiritual values that could arise from genuine dialogue with others do not develop. In this era there is more materialism—as a substitute for spiritual values, and to provide a security that is lacking in an isolated world.

In this era of entitlement, people experience more anxiety, since they are not developing their inner resources and resiliency. As they become more field dependent, they are less risk taking, and find less creativity. There is less personal felt meaning and more sociocultural obligation. There is a return to conservative, authoritarian religion, with more morality and less situational ethics. We now have many people who are patterning themselves on cultural expectations; the result is less individual imagination and absence of personal ethics. As a society, we have moved away from being autonomous, individuated, curious, and responsive persons; instead we have become a group of dependent, individualizing, obligation-bound, self-righteous followers. More than ever before, potent forces threaten to restrict personal development and individuation.

Individuation

People who gradually relinquish entitlement become more responsible and experience more sense of themselves, as they initiate rather than looking for others to begin things. This attitude is crucial in moving into more mature relationships: the less entitled people are, the more they can pull their weight in a relationship. As entitlement is relinquished, more advanced psychological functions begin to sprout: imagination, initiative, personal responsibility, honour and integrity are born from the self-reliant, unentitled position. In relationships, the more that entitlement is relinquished, the more personal people can become. In dialogue, people will be genuinely interested in learning about others and themselves. When people are curious about themselves and each other, they can open up to a panoramic sweep of growth, embracing life and all its challenges. Such people are capable of true intimacy, and the self-fulfilment that comes with a thorough engagement with life.[7]

Conclusion

As entitlement diminishes, individuals can grow and develop, and stand forth in the face of the tremendous challenges the world presents. Although their sense of aloneness will increase, their personal strength and self-regard will also grow. A sense of fulfilment comes in feeling self-compassion and self-acceptance. Such persons can move into a harmonious relationship with the rest of the world, knowing their location within it. And most significantly, for the person who has diminished the sense of entitlement, there is the possibility of relating with a genuine sense of the other. *Intimacy grows as entitlement diminishes.* As people's capacity for intimacy deepens, they experience less of the limitations of fixations and conventional malaise. Instead, they find themselves psychologically healthy, buoyant, creative and alive. Once they have given up their entitlements, they can find themselves, free and healthy!

I have taken forty years to make my psychology simple. I might make it still more simple. I might say "all neurosis is vanity"—but this also might not be understood.   —Alfred Adler [8]

Notes

1. J. McKeen and B.R. Wong, *The Relationship Garden* (Gabriola Island,B.C.: PD Publishing, 1996), p. 136.

2. H. Guntrip, *Psychoanalytic Theory, Therapy and The Self* (New York: Basic Books, 1973), p. 113.

3. M.S. Mahler et al., *The Psychological Birth of the Human Infant: Symbiosis and Individuation* (New York: Brunner/Mazel, 1976).

4. J. McKeen and B.R. Wong, *The Relationship Garden* (Gabriola Island,B.C.: PD Publishing, 1996), p. 152.

5. S. Cashdan, *Object Relations Therapy* (New York: W.W. Norton and Co., 1988), p. 44.

6. J. McKeen and B.R. Wong, *The Relationship Garden* (Gabriola Island,B.C.: PD Publishing, 1996), p. 122.

7. Ibid., p. 68.

8. Alfred Adler, quoted in Ira Progoff, *The Death and Rebirth of Psychology* (New York: McGraw-Hill, 1956), p. 81.

Strength and Power

Newborns enter this world with the *potential* to become responsible, fully alive human beings, to flower into a full expression of themselves. The degree of self-realization that people achieve in their lives depends on a vast variety of factors (including family circumstances, the culture, and educational possibilities) that each person will experience, and the choices that each will make along the way. During people's life voyage, the *value systems* of the family and culture have a strong influence on the development of their own personal values.

Root Anxiety

Infants' early experiences of life are contextualized within their organismic helplessness; pervasive feelings of anxiety that accompany this helplessness persist throughout life, and seem to forever influence each person's future choices. No matter how well one does in life, ontic anxiety lurks beneath the surface patina of success (see below, "Anxiety: Friend or Foe?"). In response to the threat of angst, people develop personal attitudes and qualities to prevent themselves from sinking into helplessness.

The Power Solution

Western culture has offered people an education in acquiring *power*, which we define as "the state of having *control over* other people or things." Most people accept this solution, and their lives are thus involved in accumulating and maintaining power and control. Power exists in relationship to the external world, and to the objectified self. Power acquisition serves to cover over and compensate for the root anxiety; the more control that a person has, the more remote is the angst and the experience of helplessness. The anxiety and fear of helplessness are not abolished; they are only moved further away from conscious experience, buried deeper within the person. On the surface, people who have accumulated power seem self-assured and in charge; deeper within lurk the hidden anxieties that even they do not acknowledge.

The Strength Approach

Another possible solution to helplessness, less well known and less valued, is for people to acquire *strength* within themselves. Some refer to strength as "personal power"; we prefer to use the term "strength" to avoid the confusion with the control aspects that the term "power" tends to denote. Strength exists mainly in reference to oneself, *not* to the external world; it involves the capacity to accept oneself with all one's emerging qualities. Rather than developing methods of overcoming the opposition and threat of the outside world, people who manifest strength discover the qualities that they naturally have; they accept these qualities (even in opposition to the expectations of others), and creatively design solutions to life's challenges that fit their own situations.

Political or Personal

To be *political* means to be involved in the use of power and control; generally, there is an investment in a particular outcome or effect. To be *personal* means to be revealed and vulnerable, willing to share one's own viewpoints and feelings without a particular investment in controlling a situation. Thus, in any given circumstance, people always have the option to be political or personal. This is not necessarily either-or; sometimes a situation has aspects of both political and personal. We discussed this in *The Relationship Garden*.[1]

Strength and Power

In any situation, people have the option to approach from a position of power (attempting to dominate the situation), or to find their strength by accepting circumstances as they are. In life, people are involved in both strength and power. It is not that one is better or worse; each has its own contingencies and consequences.

Generally, when people are in strength, they are vulnerable and insecure;

however, they are also open and available for dialogue and personal awareness and growth. When people are involved in power, they are invulnerable and seemingly secure; the trade-off is that people in power are more insulated, isolated, and unable to contact in intimacy (which would permit true dialogue to occur).

The following issues should be helpful in discriminating between the experiences and consequences of strength and power positions.

Pain vs. Pleasure

From early on, life experience is mixed with the phenomena of pain and pleasure. This duality is basic during each person's entire life. From the earliest days, people are encouraged to adopt a power orientation, in an attempt to maximize pleasure and reduce pain: the world is a place to be controlled. When people are willing to accept *both* pain and pleasure, they can develop strength within themselves.

Insecurity vs. Security

The human organism lives amidst uncertainty. Each moment involves unpredictable change. To the infant, who is so dependent upon adult figures to provide care, this uncertainty is accompanied by strong feelings of anxiety, which evidences a basic concern for survival. This existential anxiety is a given for every human being. To alleviate the anxiety, children try to establish security in early relationships with adults; they learn to please their parents in order to gain attention and the assurance of continuing care. This is the beginning of the Path of Glory (see above, "The Ideal Self"). To the child, the parent is a potent figure who buffers against the assaults of life. If the parent is pleased, the child will be safe and secure and will have minimal pain; if the parent were to abandon the child altogether, the child could perish. Thus, the cry of the infant expresses a recognition of the unpredictability of life and the dependence upon external parent agents for protection. This inner experience of insecurity continues into adult life, leading to continuing dependent, power-based relationships. Although people could learn to accept the uncertainty of life, and gain strength in so doing, most usually try to control the external world to maintain a sense of security.

Vulnerability vs. Control

Although the option exists to face all facets of experience, children are quickly taught to control themselves and the environment, minimizing vulnerability. To maximize pleasure and security, they learn to control their parent figures by adopting a pleasing attitude, and moulding their behaviour to assure parental protection. Of course, to control their parents, children must learn what the adults do and do not want, and then modify their behaviour accordingly. Children learn to control facial expressions, emotions, and actions, reading their parents for feedback of appropriateness. In short, they learn to control themselves in order to control others, setting a pattern for the rest of their lives. The prize is an increased sense of security and pleasure; the price is the loss of spontaneous expression, and the forfeiting of much authentic, innate experience. This becomes the prototype for subsequent relationships, and indeed for people's way of relating to all of life. Instead of accepting information from the external world and responding to it (that is, being vulnerable), people generally try to control themselves and their environment in order to gain more predictability. In contrast, if one is willing to be vulnerable, personal strength can be enhanced by one's willingness to *respond* to life instead of resisting it.[2]

Strength vs. Power

Control of both self and other involves power. Whenever people are prepared to experience all facets of life, strength develops. In the power attitude, life is an adversary. In the strength mode, a person is a willing participant in the life process; although there will be pain, uncertainty, and vulnerability, the individual grows ever stronger in the capacity to embrace these, along with joy and pleasure.

Intimacy vs. Isolation

Intimacy involves revelation and sharing, making closeness possible. If one attempts to control the other, a necessary distance and isolation results.

Being Personal vs. Objectification

When one is vulnerable and intimate, the individual person is revealed and personal. Whenever one operates at a distance in order to maintain power and control, both self and others are depersonalized and objectified.[3]

Autonomy vs. Field Dependency

Individuals who control themselves and others in order to have the security of power are *field dependent*.[4] In infancy, everything is done in reference to the fear of abandonment, which would result in the child's demise (see above, "Achievement or Mastery"). Even when people grow up, they generally have not addressed this basic existential fear, and their field dependency (the necessity to please and control others)continues. For these persons, life remains an adversary; they deny their fear in their urgent quest for control of themselves and others. In this mode, people are continually in a state of anxiety, fearing the responses of others. Just as the infant fears the rejection of the parent, the field-dependent adult fears the loss of control of the other. The individual who is willing to face and embrace fear, pain, and insecurity has less need to respond to the vagaries of the others in the field. Hence, instead of "playing to the audience," this person is able to make individual decisions and is self-referential; this is *autonomy*. People in a position of autonomy are resilient, sensitive, and capable of compassion for themselves and others.

Boundaries vs. Walls

Power-based people are willing to barter with life, using themselves as currency. They may appear to be very defined and clearly demarcated from others; however, power-based persons hide behind *walls* rather than living at their *boundaries*. Walls are brittle barriers, defences that keep the outside away; they are based on fear of the other and insecurity about the self. Unfortunately, walls do not only defend; they also diminish the ability to make sensitive contact with the environment and with others. Boundaries, on the other hand, accompany the sense of self that comes with the strength orientation. Boundaries are resilient, mutable, and involve a sensitive relationship with self and other. People become increasingly defined through active choices that contribute to making boundaries (see above, "Boundaries").

Discernment vs. Automatic Reactions

In the power orientation, others are objects to be controlled; in the strength orientation, others are recognized as living beings to be embraced and engaged. The power-based person does not appreciate the world of others, who are objectified as roles (for example, as "my wife"); in power, reactions to others are automatic, dogmatic, and rigid. In strength, there is a subjective, humanizing *responsiveness* with discernment of particulars; thus it is possible to relate specifically to individual concerns. In power, there is a dehumanizing objectifying *reaction*, that obscures specifics, making discernment difficult.

Individuate vs. Individualize

To acknowledge and embrace one's insecurities means one can *individuate*. When people are power-based, they *individualize*; they look very free, and yet they remain tied to the external world by the requirement to be independent of it (see above, "Achievement or Mastery"). Individuating involves the actualizing of authentic potentials, and the referent is internal; individualizing has external referents and has little to do with authentic being. Whereas the individualized person is either dependent (needs to lean) or independent (cannot lean), the individuated person is free to be interdependent (can freely choose to lean or not).[5]

Self-Responsible vs. Victim, Blame

When people are responsible for themselves and all their actions, they develop strength. To achieve power, the dominator must have victims to subjugate; the victim is also tied to a power orientation, with a complementary role to the dominator. Blame can only occur when one adopts a victim role in a power orientation; responsible people gain strength through accepting their own participation in any event.

Faith vs. Hope

Hope involves a dissatisfaction with the present and a wished anticipation of a future change; in hope, people are concerned with dominating events to change them, or remaining victim to external forces that might alter the situation. Thus, hope is related to power and control and is irresponsible; people are less present in hope, and their personal growth and freedom are limited. Faith is *"the felt sense of the assurance of the continuity of life"*; it emanates from within the individual. With faith there is a satisfaction with past, present, and future; fears of both death and life are diminished, and the person grows in strength and presence.[6]

Authenticity vs. Role

In developing the power of the Ideal Self, people learn to play roles, presenting a socially acceptable image to control their surroundings; because they are tied to others, role-players have a weakened sense of themselves. In strength, people are willing to express themselves in a genuine fashion; hence, they reveal more of the Authentic Self, and are more free of the external (see above, "The Ideal Self: Striving For Perfection").

Mastery vs. Achievement

The achievements of power accrue to people devoted to the Ideal Self; although skills and accomplishments are piled up, they have no connection to the Authentic Self. Generally, their achievements are motivated by external referents, and often are not in harmony with their inner nature. With strength, people develop a growing mastery and competence, which is not necessarily praised or even acknowledged by the external world. People in mastery are aware of themselves and the world around them, without investment in a particular effect; in contrast, people involved in achievement and control often are invested in a particular outcome, and show the insensitivity that accompanies power and dominance. Mastery results in genuine skill development (i.e., development that is native to the individual's capabilities), whereas achievement accomplishes arbitrary skill performance (i.e., performance unrelated to the individual's potentials).

Situation Ethics vs. Morality

In power orientations, there is a morality, which involves definitions of right and wrong. Power-based individuals follow a grid of rules and do not question themselves; they can be quite definite and decisive, but from an inhuman position. When people adopt a strength orientation, they remain in touch with themselves and their values, while being sensitive to the concerns and values of others; hence, each situation is open to personal appraisal, in reference to one's own ethical standards. In situation ethics, there are no fixed external rules; instead, individuals are challenged to continually reassess their own values in the context of each new situation, and to apply their values in a way that benefits both themselves and others.[7]

Shades of Grey vs. Black/White

In object relations theory, people in strength are more matured than people in power. When people are in strength, they see the world in personal terms of self and other, rather than in the depersonalizing moral terms of good and bad. For individuals in strength, there are subtle shadings in any situation, with much to consider; by contrast, for those in the power orientation, things are clearly demarcated into the black and white binary motifs of good and bad.[8]

Humility vs. Pride

Pride involves an inflated sense of self, and is a condition of nonbeing. Humility, a being state, involves a sensitive appreciation of oneself and of one's place in the world; humble individuals see themselves as significant but without exaggerating their importance. False humility is a power orientation wherein one sees oneself as lowly and insignificant; this involves a posturing, an unawareness of the uniqueness of the individual, and is a position of nonbeing.

Desires/Choice vs. Shoulds/Injunctions

To listen to one's own desires and to operate from personal choice develops strength and autonomy; to obey injunctions ("shoulds") maintains power through field dependent self control.

Surrender vs. Submission

On the surface, surrender and submission appear the same; yet, they are very different.[9] Submission occurs in a power motif, and involves *giving up oneself* to the control of some external person or thing; this is the other side of dominance, and is tied to it. In strength, there is not submission, but instead surrender *to oneself*. The individual is reduced by submission, and becomes greater in the fulfilment of surrender. This is the spirit of D.H. Lawrence's passage in *Aaron's Rod*: "Give thyself, but give thyself not away." [10]

Presence vs. Absence

Presence occurs with the vulnerability of strength; when one is involved in the invulnerability of power, the authentic person is not present. With presence, people locate themselves at their contact boundaries, willing to respond. Presence is accompanied by alertness, awareness, and fullness.[11]

Recognition vs. Attention

Recognition of another (Latin: re + cognoscere—"to know again") involves a personal closeness; giving attention objectifies both parties, and makes recognition impossible. Thus recognition is associated with strength and fulfilment; attention is associated with power and achievement.[12]

Fulfilment vs. Charge

With strength, one feels an inner sense of fulfilment that is personally nutritive. In power orientations, one experiences a charge that is driven and stressful.

Responsibility vs. Obligations

In strength, people act in a responsive manner, sensitive to the requirements of themselves and their surroundings. In power, people function on the basis of obligations, which are predetermined rules of conduct that do not consider the individual or the current situation.

Care about Others vs. Taking Care of Others

Taking care of others involves a role and a power orientation. Caring about others involves a consideration and concern which might not involve any action. To take care of others will weaken their initiative and maintain a tie to the caretaker; to care about others can involve letting them make their own mistakes and find their own way.[13]

Sensitivity to Others vs. Sensitivity to Being Hurt

Sensitivity to being hurt by actions and comments of others is a very powerful position; anyone who accepts this becomes controlled by the so-called "sensitive" person; in actuality, this is insensitivity, not genuine sensitivity. True sensitivity to others involves being responsible for one's own feelings (especially one's hurt) without blame, and without attempting to control the other; one can be very aware and sensitive to others and still maintain one's own autonomy.[1415]

Trust Self vs. Trust Others

In power orientations, one puts trust (expectation and control) in others; then one can blame others when they do not do what one wants. In strength, there is no place for putting trust in someone else; instead, one trusts oneself and has faith in one's own abilities to discriminate and make choices.[16]

Inspiration vs. Admiration

In admiration, people elevate those they admire, while reducing themselves; obviously, this is a power-based perspective. When people are aware of another, they can come into a fuller sense of themselves, their own potential, and their capabilities—this is being inspired.

Empathy vs. Sympathy/Pity

To feel pity or sympathy involves elevating oneself and diminishing the other; this is a power orientation. To empathize involves feeling close and identified with the other, seeing oneself mirrored in the other; both persons are equal and are responsible for themselves.

Responsiveness vs. Reactivity

In power, people *react* to situations in impulsive, imprecise, programmed ways. In strength, people *respond* with the fullness of themselves in a genuine, spontaneous way.[17]

Self-Compassion vs. Self-Hatred

Self-hatred involves power; self-compassion encourages strength. In the power thrust to achievement, one abandons the Authentic Self, and self-hatred accompanies the stress of trying to live up to the image of the Ideal Self through self-denial and self-control. In self-compassion, people grow stronger in their acceptance of all aspects of themselves, including their imperfections (see above, "The Ideal Self: Striving For Perfection").

Acceptance vs. Blame

To blame keeps one in the power role of a victim, where one is impotent and oppressed by life. To accept oneself and one's situation permits a growing strength and a felt assurance in life.

Shame vs. Guilt

In guilt, people attempt to overpower and subdue themselves, to bring themselves back into line; in feeling guilty, they remain objectified and are not present. In shame, individuals acknowledge themselves and feel the flush of self-recognition; with shame, they can become aware, present and strong (see below, "Perspectives on Guilt and Shame").

Field Aware vs. Field Dependent

In field dependency, one's actions are governed by the reactions of the field; hence, one becomes shackled to externals and does not develop self-reference. When one is autonomous, one can remain aware of the field and take account of responses in it, without being dictated by them; this position is one of strength.[18]

Integration: Foreground and Background

In summary, strength enhances being, awareness, compassion, growth, and life. Power—along with its obvious advantages of achievement, security, status, and control—is associated with nonbeing, unawareness, fixation, self-hatred, stagnation, and (spiritual) death.

The following lists the possible choices that are open to the growing person. Although the qualities listed are opposing extremes, the human experience is a mixture of both aspects. For most people, there is a tendency to choose one, and devalue the other. For example, historically people have chosen power as a means of establishing security, and thus have devalued the strength functions. In recent years, people involved in personal development have tried to emphasize the strength aspects, and devalue or deny the uses of power. The mature individual will be able to recognize how much of each aspect is operative in any given situation, and move more freely between them. To learn about our nature, we need to face both aspects, and acknowledge our relationship to them. In any circumstance, there will be varying measures of both aspects. Be alert to the tendency to choose one side as "good," dismissing the other. To learn about our nature, we need to acknowledge both our power fixations, and our strength orientations. *This is not an either-or situation, but rather one of foreground and background.*

STRENGTH		POWER
Pain	<————>	Pleasure
Insecurity	<————>	Security
Vulnerability	<————>	Control
Strength	<————>	Power
Intimacy	<————>	Isolation
Personal	<————>	Objectification
Autonomy	<————>	Field dependency
Boundaries	<————>	Walls
Discernment	<————>	Automatic reactions
Individuate	<————>	Individualize
Self-responsible	<————>	Victim, blame
Faith	<————>	Hope
Authenticity	<————>	Roles, Ideal Self
Mastery	<————>	Achievement
Situation ethics	<————>	Morality
Shades of grey	<————>	Black/white
Humility	<————>	Pride
Desires, choice	<————>	Shoulds, injunctions
Surrender	<————>	Submission
Presence	<————>	Absence
Recognition	<————>	Attention
Fulfilment	<————>	Charge
Responsibility	<————>	Obligations
Care about	<————>	Taking care of others
Sensitive	<————>	Sensitive to being hurt
Trust self	<————>	Trust others
Inspiration	<————>	Admiration
Empathy	<————>	Sympathy, pity
Responsive	<————>	Reactive
Self-compassion	<————>	Self-hatred
Acceptance	<————>	Blame
Shame	<————>	Guilt
Field aware	<————>	Field dependent

Notes

1. J. McKeen and B.R. Wong, *The Relationship Garden* (Gabriola Island, B.C.: PD Publishing, 1996), pp. 46, 47.

2. Ibid., pp. 190, 191.

3. Ibid., p. 58.

4. Ibid., p. 114.

5. Ibid., p. 193.

6. Ibid., p. 113.

7. Joseph Fletcher, *Situation Ethics: The New Morality* (Philadelphia: The Westminster Press, 1966).

8. D.B. Rinsley, "The Developmental Etiology of Borderline and Narcissistic Disorders," in *Bulletin of the Menninger Clinic*: 44(2), 1980, p. 127-134.

9. J. McKeen and B.R. Wong, *The Relationship Garden* (Gabriola Island, B.C.: PD Publishing, 1996), pp. 169, 170.

10. D.H. Lawrence, *Aaron's Rod* (Harmondsworth: Penguin Books, 1950), p. 200.

11. J. McKeen and B.R. Wong, *The Relationship Garden* (Gabriola Island, B.C.: PD Publishing, 1996), pp. 24-26.

12. Ibid., pp. 137, 142, 188.

13. Ibid., pp. 23, 24.

14. Ibid., p. 148.

15. J. McKeen and B.R. Wong, *In And Out Of Our Own Way* (Gabriola Island, B.C.: PD Publishing, 1995), pp. 128, 129.

16. J. McKeen and B.R. Wong, *The Relationship Garden* (Gabriola Island, B.C.: PD Publishing, 1996), p. 111.

17. Ibid., pp. 111, 112.

18. Ibid., pp. 114, 115.

Distinctions

This section contains a number of paired concepts that are often confused with each other. Avoid the ready trap of seeing the ideas in moralistic terms—do not feel obliged to choose one of the paired concepts as "right" or "true" and therefore "better" than the other. Instead, the process of *discernment* involves seeing the concepts for what they are and investigating your own perspective on them.

The issue of discernment is very important for each person's development. By clarifying these ideas, it is possible for people to locate themselves in life in a way that frees them from the tyranny of moral injunctions. Furthermore, understanding the meanings of these concepts can facilitate communication with others, so that more intimacy can be enjoyed.

Morality and Personal Ethics

The moral code of appropriateness, "rightness," and "truth" is very useful as an organizing principle in maintaining a social order. However, society with its requirements often fails to consider the needs and concerns of the individual. In fitting in, people often lose the ability to think for themselves. Abiding by a culture's moral code without questioning serves to reduce existential anxiety. But reducing anxiety also reduces life, and the spontaneous creativity of the individual is gradually stifled. In this exchange, individuals gain a sense of security, while losing their individual freedom of thought. Morality involves the duality of right and wrong. In a moral position, certain values and actions are judged "correct," "true," or "right"; others are judged to be "incorrect," "false," or "wrong." From a nonmoral position, nothing is ever right or wrong; rather, different situations demand careful scrutiny to determine one's own personal position, determined by one's own value system. To discover one's personal perspective on key issues, it is necessary to relinquish the footholds of conventional moral thinking and decide for oneself. Discernment does not mean abandoning society's moral guidelines; but it does mean thinking for oneself, rather than swallowing, without consideration, the predigested perspectives of the culture at large. To unthinkingly adopt the attitudes dictated by society is to accept a conventional morality; when one applies discernment to make distinctions and arrive at one's personal standpoint, this is the action of personal ethics (see below, "Morality").

Responsibility and Blame

It is a common misconception that responsibility and blame are the same. When people are responsible, they hold themselves *accountable* for participating in any action, either voluntarily or involuntarily, consciously or unconsciously. If a pedestrian is accidentally struck by a car while crossing a street, that person is responsible for being the one crossing the street, perhaps not being fully mindful of the circumstances, perhaps even being in a self-destructive state. From the framework of responsibility, both the driver and the pedestrian have a story to tell that reveals each person's participation in the accident.

The framework of blame presupposes a *morality* of right and wrong; some person is at fault. The evidence is weighed to discover which of the parties is at fault and which one is the victim, who is guilty and who is innocent. From childhood onward, most people's experiences are framed in these terms; so it is difficult to step outside this grid and view experience from a morality-free position.

To take the example of infectious diseases, people are usually seen to be the victims of germs, which are considered to be the perpetrators of the illness. In the framework of responsibility, people are considered to be responsible for creating the circumstances in which the germs grew, and for the state of the body's vulnerability to that particular organism. The illness process need not be seen in light of good or bad; it can be viewed as a manifestation of a great number of processes in which the ill person has participated, consciously or unconsciously, at some level of being. Nothing and nobody is at fault; each person has a responsibility for participation in an event, each with a story to tell, with individual purposes to be served.

The holistic health movement rests squarely on the concept of individual responsibility for states of health and illness. There are no victims; but at the same time, nobody or nothing is seen as at fault. The focus is on the individual's participation in the illness process from beginning to end, on the purposes that are served by such participation, on the story that is being told, and on the metaphor that is unfolding. In the concepts of complementary medicine, while traditional methods of treatment are being applied, attention is given to helping the person discover the reasons for creating, participating in, or supporting the illness. Unfortunately, many subscribers to holistic health become hostile to what help traditional medicine can offer; they sometimes even blame the person (sometimes themselves!) suffering from the illness. This guilt-producing attitude contributes to the perpetuation of the illness rather than furthering the healing process.

Guilt and Shame

Guilt is the feeling of discomfort and tension that is experienced by a person who has broken some imposed rule or law for which that individual has some respect. Guilt is always related to some *external* judgment, or some morality that has been internalized so that the external source need not even be present at the time of the infraction. The bodily reaction in guilt is to tighten up, close down, feel cold, and develop a state of tension. The person experiences being caught, trapped, or in danger of being punished. Neurophysiologically, the experience is primarily mediated through the sympathetic nervous system. Guilt involves the punishment for not living up to the expectations of others (or of an internalized judge). Existentially, guilt a *state of nonbeing*. Guilt involves objectification of oneself; hence, people are not present in guilt. Guilt limits intimacy.

Shame arises as a feeling only in reference to oneself, not to external sources. In shame, people recognize themselves exposed as they actually are; in this recognition, they see that they are not all they could be. Thus, shame is always related to *self-recognition*, awareness of one's own expectations and the image of oneself. The bodily reaction is one of flushing, of filling up with warmth, of being exposed and naked, and of being without defence. Neurophysiologically, the experience is mostly mediated by the parasympathetic nervous system. Existentially, it is a *being state* (see below, "Perspectives on Guilt and Shame"). Shame involves revelation of oneself; hence, people are vulnerable and present in shame. Shame invites intimacy.

Faith and Hope

Faith is the *felt sense of the assurance of the continuity of life*. It involves a sense of confidence without requiring a rational or logical explanation; it is experienced at a level deeper than the intellectual, relating to a profound sense of trust without supporting evidence. Existentially, it is a being state that embraces both being and nonbeing. Faith involves a living acceptance of the present, and a confidence in an unfolding future.

Hope is always related to *expectations for the future* that will satisfy some unfulfilled desire or wish; in this way, hope involves a dissatisfaction with the present, and the nonpresence that comes in waiting for a better situation in the future. Hope involves a denial of the present, and a moving away from life; existentially, hope is a nonbeing state. If some external authority or force shows promise of fulfilling people's desires (to satisfy their hopes), those people will often abandon themselves and follow; this excuses them from having to take responsibility for self-initiation in the present.

Surrender and Submission

These terms become very confusing in relation to sexuality; they also are involved in nonsexual interactions. People often believe that love can be expressed in its highest form through the act of letting go with another; yet, they have been warned against being dominated by somebody else for fear of losing their own identity. This dilemma can be untangled through an understanding of the difference between surrender and submission.

The act of *submission* is related to *power*. One person gives over control to someone else, yielding to the will of another. *The main referent is the other*; the self is diminished in importance. However, as in all power circumstances, both the one who dominates and the one who submits are invested in controlling the other, albeit from seemingly opposite ends of the pole. In existential terms, the exciting charge that is experienced over the prospect of submission is related to the flirtation with nonexistence or death—the giving up (or the taking over) of all responsibility through the ultimate dissolution of the will.

The act of *surrender* is related to giving up of control of the self, and its *referent is only to the self*, not to another. One surrenders (lets go) of oneself, but not to anyone else. In order to survive and be rewarded in society, people need to develop self-control through roles, social conventions and task competency. Such self-restraint is important to the development of one's personality; but at the same time it inhibits spontaneity and involves some loss of sense of oneself. The act of giving up such controls (as in surrender) results in a softening, an exhilaration, a sense of experiencing oneself again, fresh and new.

All relationships involve a dance between submission and surrender of the people involved, with alternating development of personal strength (with surrender) and power (with submission/domination). The relative amounts of those experiences determine the nature of a relationship and the possibility for personal growth within it.[1]

Power and Strength

Power involves the ability to exert control and ascendance over another, and a position of dominance (or submission). On the other hand, *strength* is related to the solidity of the self, independent of others. Thus, power is always related either to an object or person that is external, or to the "self as object," which involves a process of depersonalization. Strength is related only to the quality of endurance of the self, unrelated to another. People with strength require less power, because they are self-sufficient.

Every experience offers opportunities for exercising either strength (as with risk-taking and vulnerability) or power (as with moral and political events). Most relationships are governed by power politics, with strong needs for each individual to be "right." People can grow in strength through sharing feelings, revealing each person's viewpoint, and being vulnerable one to the other (see above, "Strength and Power").

Fear and Excitement

The physiological responses to fear and excitement are similar, perhaps even identical. The heart rate quickens, breathing is increased, the skin perspires and perhaps develops "goose-pimples," the hair seems to lift, the pupils of the eyes enlarge. These symptoms of the "fight or flight" reaction are the same, whether the person is in danger of being beaten up or is experiencing an imminent possibility of winning millions of dollars in a lottery!

The only difference between such experiences is the person's *interpretation* of the situation. With excitement the person wants to be present in the threatening experience (as in a roller-coaster); when the person has not freely chosen to be there, and danger is threatening, the person interprets the experience as fear. Frequently (but not always) people believe that safety has been provided in exciting situations; where they interpret that safety is lacking, they commonly will interpret their feeling as fear instead of excitement.

Cynicism and Irony

Cynicism involves a devaluing of experience and a stepping back from life. The contempt for life in cynicism is self-defeating and involves pride and presumption (as if the cynic actually knows what is best, looking down on the world). Cynicism often accompanies the lack of courage to face life as it is. The contemptuous cynic disapproves of life rather than entering it.

Irony involves a very intimate appreciation and acceptance of life. Irony is involved in a very high form of humour, which acknowledges life as it is. There is humility associated with irony (contrasted with the pride associated with cynicism).

Sacred and Holy

The word "sacred" is used to describe situations that have been elevated to the status of special, important, honoured, inviolate, separate, and better. The term implies a morality, which elevates what is sacred; people make "sacred ground" and "sacred cows," and then do battle to conserve them. In this way, to make something sacred is to separate that item from the rest of life.

The notion of "holy" involves a joining to life. When experiencing something holy, a person participates in a responsive manner. To appreciate each circumstance as connected to all of life is to have an holistic (Greek, *holos*, meaning "whole"[2]) viewpoint and a participation in the holy. People experience the holy aspect of any situation when they recognize its relationship to the rest of life. Unlike the sacred, there is nothing special about the holy; in *every* situation, a person participates in the holy, but does not always appreciate it.

> The wretchedness of our world is grounded in its resistance to the entrance of the holy into lived life. —Martin Buber [3]

Perfection and Excellence

Perfection is related to the Ideal Self, and involves striving, achievement, and denial of the Authentic Self (see above, "The Ideal Self: Striving For Perfection"). Seeking perfection is associated with self-hatred and dissatisfaction with life. Thus, the orientation of seeking perfection is related to nonbeing.

Excellence is a function of the Authentic Self and is related to mastery. Excellence involves an acceptance of life—not a striving for perfection, but rather a standing forth in expressing one's unique potential. Excellence comes with self-realization and self-expression. It is an attribute of being.

Minimalism and Minimization

Minimalism is a philosophy of doing just enough, reflecting a sensitive relationship with life and an appreciation of it. To minimize is to devalue something, diminishing its importance. Minimizing acts against life by not accepting it; minimalism is a life-enhancing attitude, involving only the appropriate use of resources with no waste.

Presence and Intimacy

Presence involves being in the here and now. Intimacy involves a revelation and a sharing of oneself. One can be present and not intimate; when one is intimate, one is also present.

Parody and Mockery

To parody someone involves knowing that person intimately, and then humorously representing aspects of the subject's character; often, parody involves a sensitive appreciation and love for the person and may be accompanied by a closeness or a joining. Mockery is a put-down that involves contempt and derision; often, mockery is used in the service of power and dominance over the other.

Aloneness and Loneliness/Isolation

Aloneness is a condition of human existence that involves separateness and uniqueness. It is neither positive nor negative; it is just a given. Acceptance of aloneness permits people to feel their deepest nature. *Loneliness is experienced when a person does not accept aloneness,* and believes that existence can be different. Such a person walls off from the world, experiencing self-pity for not having a companion; this is often associated with hope. Ironically, people become closest to others by accepting that they are alone. The experience of isolation is most acute when people do not accept the essential separateness of each individual. Aloneness involves self-reliance, acceptance and faith; loneliness arises with field dependence, non-acceptance and hope.

Anger and Violence

Anger is a feeling; one of its functions is to move a person out of the helplessness that arises when that person feels hurt or frightened. Anger can result from a great variety of situations, such as unmet expectations, crossed boundaries, and devalued self-esteem; it arises when love is frustrated and connection is interrupted. As such, anger is neither negative nor positive; it is merely a feeling response on the part of an individual. When anger is shared, it can enhance intimacy (as can any internal state that is shared).[4]

Violence is the act of crossing boundaries without permission. Thus, the key to whether or not a situation is violent is *consent*—with consent there is no violence, regardless of the act. When anger is shared with permission and within clearly defined and agreed upon limits, it is not violence. It is possible to perpetrate violence in the name of love, if boundaries are crossed without consent; this often occurs when parents force children into some activity "for their own good."

Rebellion and Standing Forth

Rebellion occurs when one acts against a situation or another person; there is defiance and field dependency associated with rebellion. In this reaction against something or somebody, one becomes tied and dependent upon that something or somebody. With rebellion or revolution, individuality and independence are attained; these are issues of power and control.

Standing forth occurs when one firmly asserts oneself. This is not done against anyone else; rather, it is an expression of oneself, quite independent of anyone else. This is a process of self-affirmation and growth, which provides for the development of autonomy and individuation.

Hierarchy and Holarchy

Hierarchy involves an ordering of things or events where there is a higher value placed on certain aspects, and lesser value placed on others. The notion of "higher animals" is hierarchical. Generally, hierarchy is used in a moral frame of reference; certain states or things are "better" than others. When speaking of a developmental scheme, hierarchy sees the earlier stages as primitive, to be overcome and discarded. Hence, the notion of hierarchy involves parts of different value.

Holarchy is an holistic concept; one sees the whole and its component parts without valuing one aspect more than the other. In holarchic thinking, one sees the differences in things or events or stages, without placing a value on them. Hence, it is possible to talk holarchically about mosquitoes and humans, without having one more significant than the other. In a developmental scheme, a further stage *transcends and includes* the stages that preceded it. For example, you probably still use basic notions that you learned in early grade school; however, you don't use them in the same fashion as when you first learned them; you have gone beyond the original idea (transcended it) and yet still use certain aspects of the basic notion (including it).

In hierarchical thinking, one must complete grade one in order to get into grade two, which then is superior to grade one. In holarchic thinking, grade two transcends and includes grade one (grade two is grade one plus grade two; grade three is grade one plus grade two plus grade three).

> *Evolution is a process of transcend and include, transcend and include. And this begins to open onto the very heart of Spirit-in-action, the very secret of the evolutionary impulse.*—Ken Wilber [5]

Notes

1. J. McKeen and B.R. Wong, *The Relationship Garden* (Gabriola Island, B.C.: PD Publishing, 1996), pp. 169-70.

2. *Dorland's Illustrated Medical Dictionary* (Philadelphia: W.B. Saunders Company, 1965), p. 684.

3. M. Buber, *Hasidism and Modern Man*, edited & translated by Maurice Friedman (New York: Harper Torchbooks, 1966), p. 180.

4. J. McKeen and B.R. Wong, *The Relationship Garden* (Gabriola Island, B.C.: PD Publishing, 1996), pp. 37-38.

5. Ken Wilber, *A Brief History of Everything* (Boston: Shambhala, 1996), p. 30.

Part Two:
ROOTS

The greatest mystery is not that we have been flung at random among the profusion of the earth and the galaxy of the stars, but that in this prison we can fashion images of ourselves sufficiently powerful to deny our nothingness.

—André Malraux [1]

1. André Malraux, quoted by Maurice Friedman in *To Deny Our Nothingness* (New York: Dell Publishing Co., 1967), p. 17.

Anxiety: Friend or Foe?

For life is at the start a chaos in which one is lost. The individual suspects this, but he is frightened at finding himself face to face with this terrible reality, and tries to cover it with a curtain of fantasy, where everything is clear. —José Ortega y Gasset [1]

Ontic Anxiety: The Anxiety of Being

Nonbeing threaten's man's ontic self-affirmation, relatively in terms of fate, absolutely in terms of death. —Paul Tillich [2]

The very state of being alive is accompanied by a chronic state of tension known as *existential anxiety* (also called "ontic" or "ontological anxiety"—the anxiety of being). This is a state peculiar to humans, who are capable of apprehending their own death; animals do not experience existential anxiety. The difference is that human beings have the capacity to become aware of the contexts within which they exist, along with the complex interrelationships that accompany such an appreciation. This apprehension is vast and incomprehensible, beyond reason and control—hence, the chronic state of ontic anxiety. Anxiety is at the root of our existence. Rollo May said that "animals have an environment, human beings have a world."[3] Existential anxiety is one feature of the human world; this includes the terror of nonbeing. [4]

Thus, the human state is accompanied by a deep sense of uneasiness. Humans are aware of their fragility and finitude, and experience profound anxiety in face of this—ontological anxiety. In an attempt to cope with this anxiety, each person develops a particular life-style. Such life-style patterning underlies the development of family, friends, culture, and the very fabric of society itself. When this life-style patterning does not adequately contend with this baseline anxiety, people then establish behaviour patterns that give rise to more anxiety. They become anxious that their activities do not inhibit the basic anxiety. In a cyclical fashion, such anxiety grows on itself, out of control and debilitating to the person. It is manifested in symptoms involving body, mind, and emotions; such is the pattern of *neurotic anxiety*.

Neurotic Anxiety

Ontic anxiety is rarely experienced in its pure form; generally, people are unwilling to experience much of it, quickly defending against it, or converting it into *neurotic anxiety*. Neurotic anxiety is a reduced version of ontic anxiety, channelled into neurotic defences and patterns that people find easier to handle. Neurotic anxiety is involved in such neuroses as obsessions and compulsions, and underlies addictions and other self-destructive behaviours. Basically, most would rather have symptoms of a neurosis than deal directly with the terror of being. Remnants of ontic anxiety persist in such feelings as isolation, meaninglessness, vague restlessness, discontent, and doubts about life. Ontic anxiety provides a great challenge for humans; in order to face this anxiety and become themselves fully, people must accept profound insecurity.

With ontic anxiety, people often question their purpose and goals. Sometimes they experience a discernible underlying feeling of despair, or a sense of that they are lost, or have been abandoned. Life loses its colour and intensity; in extreme, they can choose the neurotic solution of becoming depressed, where nothing seems worth doing. Sleep disturbances are common. The person experiencing ontic anxiety commonly loses any *reason* to live, and can even lose the *will* to live. This is a dangerous situation; but it is also a challenge to face life courageously, to find a personal meaning, and thus, the will to live.

Not All Anxiety is Pathological

Western traditional medicine has viewed anxiety as a symptom of an underlying disorder, or a cause of many psychosomatic illnesses, and so has devoted much attention to the eradication or suppression of anxiety. An alternative view, such as that of the existential philosophers and clinicians, sees anxiety as a basic phenomenon of life, underlying all change, growth, evolution, and sociocultural achievements. From this vantage, not all anxiety is pathological. Indeed, anxiety is a condition of existence, and without it, we would not be alive and human.

Only when anxiety becomes severe, incapacitating or interruptive to the person's life adjustments, does it take on neurotic characteristics and hence become an appropriate subject for medical intervention. Most people (including most physicians) have some difficulty in discriminating between *ontic* (existential or ontological) *anxiety*, which can be accompanied by many positive adjustments in a person's life, and *neurotic anxiety*, which can lead to many debilitating syndromes.

Frequently, because the differences between these forms of anxiety are not easily appreciated, all anxiety is treated alike. Through the indiscriminate use of tranquilizers prescribed by a physician, or the use of socially accepted chemicals such as nicotine or alcohol, the individual attempts to "cure" or alleviate the anxiety state. Frequently, nonmedical drugs such as marijuana or cocaine are used both for pleasure and for relief of anxiety. We are becoming a people of low frustration-tolerance, unwilling to experience more than a slight level of pain physically or emotionally. Drugs help to relieve the symptoms without attacking the underlying causes. At the same time, they contribute to a blunting of life's experiences, a levelling of the human condition to one of sedation and mediocrity.

We have created peace without progress, tranquility without a sense of meaning. This dilemma is dramatically encapsulated in the play *Equus* by Peter Shaffer, in which a psychiatrist struggles with the moral implications of therapeutic intervention:

> My desire might be to make this boy an ardent husband—a caring citizen—a worshipper of abstract and unifying God. My achievement, however, is more likely to make a ghost![5]

Contending With Anxiety

Humans are offered a variety of standard meanings, activities, and goals to ameliorate, mask, and cope with the *dread* of nothingness, the *meaninglessness* of life. At birth, the child's experience of the world must be confusing and anxiety provoking: how can sense be made of such chaos? From a constructivist point of view, reality is organized through the use of the following intelligences: linguistic (language), logical-mathematical, musical, spatial, bodily-kinesthetic, and personal.[6]

Through the use of these intelligences (see above, "A Model For Communication" and "Constructivism") and by utilizing information provided by parents and others, children gradually develop a sense of themselves in relationship to the rest of the world. This sense of location, of finding their bearings, provides a *grounding* that helps to deal with the underlying ontic anxiety. The more these intelligences are developed, the more secure one will feel. Many people experience great anxiety when they find themselves in a foreign country, unable to make effective use of verbal communication; this is compounded when body language is misinterpreted. Extreme loss of those intelligences is considered symptomatic of mental illness; relative losses result in a state of confusion in which people experience difficulty in making sense of life.

Anxiety in Childhood

From the child of five to myself is but a step. But from the new-born baby to the child of five is an appalling distance. —Leo Tolstoi[7]

The infant feels protected from the threat of death in the arms of the parent. Such a sense of security is important to the effective development of each person. While a child is experiencing meaningful relationships, the core feeling of isolation and dread is temporarily relieved; thus, it is no wonder that people feel compelled to discover and maintain intimate relationships throughout life. The more that people view relationships as a solution to the existential problem, the more dependent, obsessive, and compulsive they will become. Such relationships are immersed in the fear of abandonment, field dependency, low self-esteem, manipulation and control, power struggles, and a fixation on romance. [8]

In infancy, the dependent mother-child relationship is the most common and the most profound solution to ontic anxiety. This pattern of dependency is reproduced in a wide variety of ways throughout the person's life, forming the structure and meaning of all later interpersonal and social relationships. Power, control, and fame are common masks of meaning. Spirituality, morality, religion, culture, creativity, skill mastery, and personal development are some of the more acceptable solutions. Ontic anxiety is ever present, and can be a motivation for all of these activities. A courageous person can flower in face of the constant threat of extinction.

Embracing Ontic Anxiety

When individuals come to terms with ontic anxiety, by accepting rather than repressing it, their interactions become less dependent; then relationships are characterized more by a sharing of two autonomous solitudes rather than a melding of two individuals into one. Then two people can become more, rather than less, of themselves in dialogue! The relationship becomes like a garden, in which each individual thrives, relating to others by free choice. Unfortunately, most relationships are more like a trap, in which each person becomes contracted, attached to the other by fear. When people are autonomous, they deal with their ontic anxiety constructively; when people are dependent, the ontic anxiety is covered over and ignored. Both relationship styles are means of coping with ontic anxiety. Satisfying relationships provide a sense of intimacy that successfully deals with the ontic anxiety. Without satisfying relationships, the individual experiences a relative sense of loneliness that, in the extreme, becomes a feeling of isolation. The less the degree of intimacy, the more likely that people will revert to control methods to compensate.[9]

Morality

Besides having their basic needs provided, children must learn codes of behaviour in order to fit in with others. Early in development, youngsters are taught to distinguish behaviours in terms of "good" and "bad"; this is the teaching of *morality*. These distinctions are designed to help people to adjust to life in that particular society. Conforming to these moral codes provides people with acceptance and value, increasing their sense of security. *Amoral behaviour* exposes the individual to social pressures and ontic anxiety. On the other hand, *antisocial behaviour* serves to provide a sense of meaning to the same extent as does social behaviour, albeit in oppositional ways; rebels define themselves against the culture, instead of in it. Commonly, the most anxious people are prone to seek the strongest kinds of moral solutions, either for or against. Righteous, rigid and fundamentalistic attitudes usually indicate that those people are coping with underlying ontic anxiety; these people seem so sure, and yet underneath, they are so uncertain. When people fixate on morality, they are commonly compensating for their lack of acceptance of their root anxiety.

In most societies, the moral solutions to the ontic dilemma tend to become codified into systems of religion, which provide useful and effective ways of coping with meaninglessness and emptiness. Most often, the conservative religions tend to expect strict adherence to moral codes, thus encouraging a dependency that helps to relieve the ontic anxiety. More liberal religions promote a sense of personal freedom and the development of more individual responsibility and autonomy; although this is a more anxiety-provoking path, it is ultimately a more personally liberating and growth-inducing one. Conservative approaches offer more hope and more relief from ontic anxiety, with less personal risk; so they are more appealing to most people. Everyday attitudes (not only in matters of religion) of righteousness, judgmentalness, fixated opinions, prejudices, rigid morality, a strong belief in right and wrong, intolerance, and an authoritarian control over the behaviour of others all reflect a *moral solution to ontic anxiety*.

Spirituality

Moral solutions (the codes of right behaviour) are primitive manifestations of an underlying, deeper process—the *spiritual* (the sense of meaning in life). Although the drive toward the spiritual is present throughout life, it is not easily appreciated or understood; so, primitive moral solutions are readily accepted in its place.

> *Nonbeing ... threatens man's spiritual self-affirmation, relatively in terms of emptiness, absolutely in terms of meaninglessness.*
> —Paul Tillich [10]

To the existentialist philosophers, human existence has no inherent meaning except for the meaning that each individual creates in a courageous life of standing forth. When people begin to dig deeper into their own nature, and question their beliefs and assumptions, they discover that there is no inherent meaning to life; instead, they find meaninglessness, which is often experienced as an inner emptiness. In order to embrace their being courageously, to find meaning and fullness, people need to face the spiritual emptiness and meaninglessness of their existence.

Spirituality is always a personal experience; it can be shared with other people, but cannot be imposed upon them. When that happens, it takes on the aspects of control, developing into a religion.

Guru Worship

In recent decades, many people have rebelled against the control of western religions. Seeking the liberating truths of eastern spirituality, they often have made another religion of those spiritual paths, worshipping gurus instead of finding themselves. Andrew Harvey notes the pitfalls in guru worship this way:

> *If you are projecting adoration onto someone [a guru], you yourself start to shine with the reflected luster of that projection, so you experience a covert self-adoration. You are now decorated with a little aura of sanctity that you didn't have to earn. This is corrupt, because if you were really to own those qualities that you are projecting, you would have to be responsible for them.*[11]

The authentic spirituality underlying all religions can be discovered on a personal level; but, this takes the courage to face and embrace ontic anxiety. To exchange one religion for another does nothing for self development if personal responsibility is abandoned.

Hope and Faith

Hope involves a dissatisfaction with present circumstances, and an anticipation of better things to come in the future. Faith involves a profound acceptance of life as it is, in the present. Hope, then, is a trap; when people pursue hope, they abandon the possibility of embracing their lives profoundly in the present.

We define *faith* as *the felt sense of the assurance of the continuity of life.* In faith, people become free in the acceptance and embracing of their own lives in the present. Then they are active agents in their own destinies, rather than passive victims of circumstance. [12]

In the quest for meaningfulness, there is always a great temptation to adopt the stable *hope* of the moral (things can be better if I obey the rules), instead of wrestling with life's insecurity which can lead one to experience the *faith* of the spiritual.

Guilt

> *Nonbeing ... threatens man's moral self-affirmation, relatively in terms of guilt, absolutely in terms of condemnation.* —Paul Tillich [13]

Moral solutions to the dilemma of ontic anxiety provide measures of control that further the aims of society. For the individual, the internal experience of ontic anxiety is replaced with an underlying feeling of *guilt*; in the extreme, such guilt is experienced as condemnation, and relief from guilt produces a sense of grace. The moral solutions are provided by the culture; in order to partake, the individual must surrender individual freedoms, and adopt the moral positions of the culture.

Spiritual solutions, by contrast, involve free individuals facing the absolute sense of meaninglessness and the relative experience of emptiness. Rather than diminishing the anxiety, people can learn to embrace more and more nonbeing by facing the anxiety of meaninglessness and emptiness; in embracing nonbeing, being grows. The spiritual solutions are an individual effort, and provide a sense of personal meaning in life. [14]

Collective Meaning

On a collective level, meanings in society are reflected in cultural pursuits such as music, art, crafts, literature, and the performing arts. On a deeper, more primitive level, cultural stories or themes appear in myths that provide a sense of meaning. Each culture has its own typical expressions, although the underlying patterns are similar. Productivity can take on the characteristics of a religion, often at the expense of these cultural pursuits. However, in the end, all such activities serve to deal with ontic anxiety; not all necessarily further personal growth.

Roles and Meaning

First through parental guidance, and then later through mass education, each person copes with ontic anxiety primarily through the development of *roles*. These provide a sense of purpose in life, a direction for the expression of inner energy, and a feeling of power among and over peers. Because roles are so related to the context in which they are developed, they increase the individual's field dependence. The loss of these roles (real or threatened) reveals the underlying ontic anxiety, which is often experienced as a sense of helplessness or depression. This might occur when a mother loses her role as provider and caretaker as her children grow up and leave home, or when a person is fired from a long-time job, or when long-term relationships come to an end through divorce or death. The extent to which the people in each of these cases have defined themselves in terms of these roles will determine the extent of resulting helplessness and anxiety. People who have developed a personal sense of meaning through being mindful of inner authenticity and being true to themselves, in face of the expectations of others, will be able to accept such losses with equanimity and faith.

Embracing Ontic Anxiety

Ontic anxiety can feed the drive toward self-expression and meaning, and be the spice for the enjoyment of life, so long as it remains related to the Authentic Self. When a person becomes more dependent on the approval of others, ontic anxiety is converted into neurotic anxiety, with a threatened loss of power in life. When neurotic anxiety is treated with chemical medications such as tranquilizers, the danger exists that one will concomitantly dampen ontic anxiety, and hence the zest for life. This loss of zeal also occurs in people who abandon their Authentic Selves to adopt their roles in life, afraid to take personal risks in their pursuit of happiness.

To paraphrase a biblical saying, "For what is a man profited, if he shall gain the whole world (security), and lose his own soul (meaning)?"

> When we walk to the edge of all the light we have and take the step into the darkness of the unknown we must believe one of two things will happen—there will be something solid for us to stand on, or we will be taught to fly. —Claire Morris [15]

Notes

1. Ortega, *The Revolt of the Masses* (New York: Norton, 1957), pp. 156-157.

2. P. Tillich, *The Courage to Be* (New Haven: Yale University Press, 1976), p.41.

3. R. May, E. Angel and H. Ellenberger, eds., *Existence: A New Dimension in Psychiatry and Psychology* (New York: Basic Books, 1958), p. 62.

4. R. May, *The Meaning of Anxiety* (New York: W.W. Norton and Co., 1977), p. 208.

5. P. Shaffer, *Equus* (Harmondsworth: Penguin, 1977), p. 107.

6. H. Gardner, *Frames of Mind: The Theory of Multiple Intelligences* (New York: Basic Books, 1983).

7. L. Tolstoi, quoted in E. Becker, *The Denial of Death* (New York: The Free Press, 1973), p. 25.

8. J. McKeen and B.R. Wong, *The Relationship Garden* (Gabriola Island, B.C.: PD Publishing, 1996), p. 19.

9. Ibid., p. 47.

10. P. Tillich, *The Courage to Be* (New Haven: Yale University Press, 1976), p.41.

11. A. Harvey, "Teachers and Seekers," an interview in *Yoga Journal* (July/August 1995), p. 61.

12. J. McKeen and B.R. Wong, *The Relationship Garden* (Gabriola Island, B.C.: PD Publishing, 1996), p. 61.

13. Ibid., p. 41.

14. Ibid., p. 41.

15. Attributed to Claire Morris, source unknown.

Location

Primary Contextual Location

At birth, a child's major challenge is to face chaos and attempt to organize it. In order to survive in an unpredictable world, children must learn to identify all the objects (including people) that come into the sphere of their senses of touch, sight, sound, smells, and taste. Depending on how pleasant or unpleasant their experiences prove to be, they gradually build up memories of *where* they wish to be *in relationship to these objects* By doing so, they begin to make sense of their surroundings and become increasingly capable of identifying their location in relation to those objects. In the presence of a caring environment, children experience that they are wanted, and tend to locate themselves as desired objects in the world. When experiences are mostly negative, they will locate themselves as undesirable and readily abandoned objects in the world. This is the nature of their *primary contextual location*, which will set the emotional tone for the life-journey upon which each newborn embarks. The primary contextual location provides the palette of affective colours (for example, sombre and serious, or bright and joyful) that an individual will use in undertaking life's tasks. These early experiences play an important part in determining which emotions a person will typically feel throughout life.

Location in Time

Infants with their primary contextual location face the world and its opportunities on at least two distinct dimensions, namely time and space. In this configuration, the infant slowly begins to appreciate the recurrent nature of behaviour. For example, when mother disappears from view, she will probably return (sometime in the "future"). At certain times food will appear, ideally closely following hunger pangs. Such regular activity provides the basis for faith within the developing person, and trust of caregivers. With growing memory, children begin to locate themselves in relation to the events along their personal time continuum. Later, they will be able to compare their location in time with that of others; but this comparison will make sense only when they are able to locate themselves on their own time lines.

Dislocation in Time

Any dislocation in time will produce a sense of confusion and disorientation; this can happen in sleep disorders. This disorientation in time is also evident when people regress, and respond in the present as if they were facing past circumstances; these responses and behaviours that are inappropriate to the present time are commonly seen in people who remember abuse in their past. People who suffer in this way desperately attempt to stop time, to resist change and experience less, so that their worlds will become more manageable. In the face of threatening situations, such people quickly revert to attitudes and behaviours of helplessness from childhood, often with feelings of fear; usual solutions include running away, hiding, withdrawing, blaming, and becoming willful, resistant, indulgent, childishly "hysterical," or rebellious. Such behaviours become fixated in time, compulsively repeated, with no movement toward a real solution that could open up their world to promote healthy growth, an expanding personal space, a growing curiosity, an increasing trust in others, and a sense of faith in the continuity of life (see below, "The Walking Wounded: A Way of Life?").

The Docks

Life is like a voyage on a river; the passing of time is marked by events, which can be seen as docks seen as one's boat passes by. Because some docks seem more interesting than others, people tend to tie their boats to those and are reluctant to leave them. But leave them they must: they need to untie themselves from those docks (experiences) to continue their journey in time. Sometimes, if particular experiences are especially significant (either because it is a great pleasure or a great horror), people refuse to untie their rope from those docks; instead, they leave a long rope attached as they continue on. Attached in this way, they become fixated in their location in time, although they continue their journey down the river. When faced with charged, anxiety-provoking experiences, they tend to pull on the ropes to quickly return to the docks in the past. Because they are so often returning to old docks, they become limited in their ability to assess or appreciate the new docks in the present. The question that they must ask themselves is, "What am I getting out of holding on to this dock with such determination?" or "What awful thing would happen if I *did* let go of this experience?"

Certainly, most of us can readily move on the time continuum from the past to the future; but rarely are we *really* in the present. Most of us will quickly regress when faced with traumatic or risky circumstances in the present. Those fixated positions (our *fixated primary locations*) can usually be identified with an earlier age at which we experienced some very significant events—frightening, enjoyable, or both. From such stuck positions, we gaze along the time continuum in the direction of either the future or the past.

Making The World Smaller

People who resist time refuse to change their manners or morals in relation to the present. They wish to keep their lives manageable by not having to relate to changing events; they yearn for the familiar past. Sometimes that past contains traumatic or unpleasant experiences that continue to govern their present; for example, women who had been sexually assaulted in the past often relate to men in the present as though they *all* are going to be exploitative, thus limiting their relationships with men. Such women are handling their anxiety by narrowing their world in order to make it more manageable. To do otherwise would mean having to assess each new male acquaintance in the present. This kind of fixation on the past (frequently accompanied by a tendency to leave the body, or to hate the body and its sensations) arose in the beginning as a means of survival; however unpleasant the effects might be, it continues as a means of making the world smaller and more manageable.

The Space Continuum

Also significant are the individual's experiences along the space continuum. Each person is suspended between "inner" and "outer" space. In early childhood training, people are encouraged to abandon their inner experiences to concentrate on the myriad tasks in transitional (outer) space that are essential to survival (for example, walking, talking, reading, self-care, social niceties and consideration). It is in this transitional space that children meet and learn how to control significant other people in their lives. Of course, people do not locate themselves only in relationship to either themselves (self-reliant) or others (field dependence). Rather, all people locate themselves somewhere along this space continuum, becoming more or less self-reliant and field dependent, in varying (but usually characteristic) degrees. Each individual establishes a characteristic stance in life with regard to space and time, becoming more or less comfortable with inner and outer worlds, as well as past and present time.

Focus On Outer Space

Our educational institutions tend to support a reliance upon outer experiences and other people, with a relative abandonment (and considerable suspicion) of inner space. Science has concentrated its efforts on gaining knowledge of the material world in order to control that world; little scientific attention is directed toward the exploration of inner space. Similarly, people are encouraged to concentrate on controlling their environment and the people in it; they learn to please, to manipulate, to dominate, to be nice, to display only socially acceptable feelings and behaviour. The better they do it, the more acceptance they earn. Those who are adept at this project become comfortable, living much of their time in relation to great numbers of people, and in a great variety of spaces.

Retreating From Anxiety: The Neurotic Solution

Withdrawal from ontic anxiety into neurotic anxiety is *the neurotic solution* (see above, "Anxiety: Friend Or Foe?"). People who are uncomfortable with large, unknown, and uncontrollable spaces react with anxiety; they experience being threatened and uncomfortable. The most direct and undefended form of the inability (or the perceived inability) to handle much space occurs in the neurotic syndrome known as agoraphobia (the fear of open spaces). Even though most people's reactions are usually less extreme, many still relate to the spatial domain with defences that cluster around behaviours and physical symptoms. For example, boundary illnesses such as allergies can serve to control the anxiety or the threatening environment by limiting the scope of one's activity. In a similar fashion, the obsessions and compulsions of everyday life often serve to organize people's time and attention to such a degree that they might never encounter their underlying anxiety. When these defences are extreme, people's lives become handicapped by the necessity to perform repetitive rituals or behaviours (such as addictions to substances or people, compulsive work, repetitive self-destructive actions, or unrelenting repetitive thoughts). When these patterns become debilitating, they are diagnosed as neurotic illnesses.

In relation to space, such people have made their world smaller and thus more manageable. Choices become limited, freedom is curtailed, and the mind is relieved of any need to face the root problems. Furthermore, by being medically sick, such persons are allowed to expect others to take over much of the responsibility for their lives. Others will make decisions for them, will usually supply endless attention, and will support the view that they are helpless victims of families, friends and society. The result of this caretaking is the development of a society in which the helpless begin to dominate the activities of the majority; as so aptly described by Lance Morrow, we are becoming a nation of "busybodies and crybabies."

In the neurotic solution, people become fixated somewhere in the intersection of space and time, losing the freedom to move freely along these axes. They have made their world smaller and thus more manageable, although much less expressive of the vastness of their authentic being. Their present becomes contaminated by the past, and their inner space has less expression in outer space. Although the most common pattern is to be fixated on the past and on internal space, a smaller number of people fixate on the future or on outer space; these are simply variations of the neurotic solution.

Remarkably, a great number of people locate themselves through their suffering. Chronic physical pain or emotional distress, although very uncomfortable, can be quite predictable. Hence, in an ironic fashion, these people can locate themselves, and achieve some measure of security by having symptoms of illness, or some other form of suffering. Their ontic anxiety is obscured by their ongoing relationship with pain. Closely related to this is guilt, a form of emotional pain; some people (or cultures) locate themselves and find security in chronic guilt, and indeed, guilt can become an integral part of their identity.

If people find outer space too dangerous to really enter, they can dedicate their everyday behaviour to obsessions and compulsions and addictions. Instead of developing contactable, sensitive boundaries, these people tend to construct isolating, thick, defensive walls. Behind these walls is the experience of safety; nevertheless, these people are inwardly helpless, fixated in a different time, unable to deal adequately with the present. In the extreme, they might ignore reality entirely; this is what happens in psychotic episodes.

The Psychotic Solution

If the neurotic solution still does not adequately handle the anxiety, people might remove themselves even further from others and the threatening circumstances in the environment, by withdrawing further into their inner worlds. They occupy much smaller spaces in which they have greater control, where they are the unchallenged authorities. They become out of touch with others by becoming emotionally numb, unaffected by the exigencies of a normal life, which seem too much to bear. Because they are masters of that inner space, all seems possible; they can experience themselves as either more powerful or more helpless, unrelated to the measurements of reality. From their vantage point, they are safe; from conventional society, they are pathologically out of touch, and can be diagnosed as psychotic.

Dealing With Anxiety

Currently, it is common practice to treat the anxiety accompanying neurotic and psychotic reactions with drugs such as tranquilizers and energizers. Although these pharmacological agents are useful in allaying the anxiety, they in themselves do not address the underlying personality problems stemming from fixations in space and time. Indeed, these drugs tend to reinforce people's sense of helplessness and encourage development of an addiction to being helped. The individual experiences a loss of faith in inner space, and an increasing need to trust authorities in outer (transitional) space; at the same time, these authorities are commonly hated and feared. It is amidst these kind of ambivalent love-hate relationships that the psychologically impaired person experiences being trapped in both time and space, living a life of restricted pleasure and meaning. It is no wonder that suicide is becoming an increasingly common option.

Finding Freedom in Space and Time

People orient themselves somewhere in the intersection of the continuum of space and the line of time. Healthy, mature individuals (who are rare) would be able to freely move along both of these planes, changing as appropriate to each situation. Such people could play like a six-year-old child with six-year-old children by regressing in time, to really express the energy of the six-year-old within. During play, these persons would freely move from inner space, where fantasies and emotions are abundantly available, to express them in outer space, where they could be shared with playmates. At the end of playtime, such persons could readily come into the present as adults, in order to organize the toys and clean up the mess in the room (outer space) in which the fairies and dragons of inner space had played; they might even prepare for the future by storing the toys in readiness for the next episode of play. Their present has reference to memories of the past, and anticipation of the future, without being fixated.

In order to break away from crippling fixations in time and space, individuals need courage to remain present and in touch. This is easier in an understanding, supportive environment, where they can learn to travel more freely along the time/space axes. In order to affirm themselves, people must directly address the fears that trigger the spontaneous flashbacks to past time and space, and develop the strength to remain vulnerable and in contact with others. If people are to find the safe harbour within themselves, they must learn how to let go of past fixations that have been used to anchor themselves in the caretaking ports of others.

Time

The past is a treacherous whore
entrapping us in the pain of
regrets and lost desires
The future is a romantic boy
lost in the dreamy landscape
of vague imaginings
The present is the living glory
of senses, feelings and affections
alive in wonder and grace

We must find
brave new words
sturdy language
to break free
from the shackles
of mindbound conventions
and habituated vision

to express ourselves
without romanticism
without sentimentalism
without cynicism
without hope

and especially
without regret
                —Jock McKeen[2]

Notes

1. L. Morrow, "A Nation of Finger Pointers," *Time*, August 12, 1991, p. 48.

2. Jock McKeen, previously unpublished poem, 1998.

Nemo: The Abyss Within

Most people seem to be trapped between the desire to let go and the fear of letting go. Being able to let go would offer welcome relief from tension and worry, an experience of pleasure or even ecstasy. If so, why are people so commonly frightened by the possibility? Frequently, they express a fear of "coming apart," of "losing myself," or of "falling into a pit." We believe these statements are expressing people's relationship to the abyss within. Much of human concern and activity is involved in avoidance. Morris Berman describes this avoidance this way:

> The problem of hollowness, then of a-Voidance, is really one of secondary satisfactions, the attempt to find substitutes for a primary satisfaction of wholeness that somehow got lost, leaving a large gap in its place. The British novelist John Fowles calls this emptiness the 'nemo,' which he describes as an anti-ego, a state of being nobody.[1]

The human dilemma is that people experience themselves as empty, or meaningless, or nobody special. Much of human striving has to do with compensating for this experience. Having somehow lost a sense of wholeness, and instead finding a gap within, people try to find substitutes that will fill that gap. John Fowles, in writing about the nemo, puts it this way:

> Nobody wants to be a nobody ... all our acts are partly devised to fill or mark the emptiness we feel at the core.[2]

Stage of Undifferentiation

From conception to birth, the foetus develops in a nearly perfect uterine environment. Some have speculated that during this time, the foetus does not experience being separate from its environment. For very new infants, their mothers are experienced as extensions of the infants themselves, essential parts of them that provide sustenance and comfort. Very soon, this sublime period of primary narcissism (in which everything is "me")

110

gives way to new developments. The infant must recognize that some parts of "me" begin to act beyond the child's control, disturbing the inner sense of peace. The breast, the bottle, mother—these appear to have a will of their own, coming and going at times unrelated to the infant's wishes.

The "Other"

Reluctantly, infants learn that these uncontrollable parts of themselves are separate; they create walls in order to distinguish themselves from "other." At this point, children are still very narcissistic, experiencing themselves as being everything inside the wall; beyond the wall is the "other"—objects that move in the child's space (mother, father, siblings, pets). These objects are *desirable* for the comfort, pleasure, and security that they can offer; they are *dangerous* because they appear to have wills of their own. For both reasons, these objects beyond the infant's walls must be controlled, and subjugated to the child's will.

Transitional Space

In the first few years of life, children's main project is to learn to separate themselves from others. Although they are physically separated at birth, they do not become fully aware of this separation for some time. As youngsters grow, the objects in their space seem to become more uncontrollable. Furthermore, there appears to be an increasing number of them occurring on the periphery of space, coalescing into an ever-growing outer space, separated now by a wall. Defensively, children contract themselves away from those objects, thus creating a vast, empty space between. That space created by contraction becomes the void (transitional space, the abyss, the nemo).

> The actual appearance of the nemo—the vague perception that something is missing, that one is split, or empty—would appear to date from the third year of life.[3]

At this point, children's space is defined by walls; they are separated from "the other" (the first objects in children's space) by the void (nemo). The objects seem to move uncontrollably in this void; thus, youngsters fear the nemo and its contents. Because their parental figures appear to have mastered movement in this void, they are highly regarded and imbued with great power; the friendlier they are to the child, the more dependable an ally they will be, and the more relaxed the child can be. Uncontrollable objects are feared and designated as being "wild."[4] When animals such as pets prove to be controllable, they become strong allies. Inanimate objects such as teddy bears, which resemble the wild but are completely controllable, are the most comforting allies; these so-called *transitional objects* help us to handle the terror of the void.[5]

> So if the world gets sliced up into Self and Other, and the breach can only be negotiated by Transitional Objects, there exists a real danger that intermediate animals and substances could usurp transitional space, without control over which we fear a fall into chaos.[6]

Characteristics of the Nemo

Magic occurs in the nemo; it is the locus of creativity and imagination. However, to the child, therein dwell the forces of darkness as well as the forces of light and creativity. Out of the nemo (which is frequently located under the bed or in a closet) rise the uncontrollable monsters of childhood. But it is also the abode of fairies and angels, elves and trolls. Anything that comes from there or moves freely in it (such as sorcerers and wizards, parents and priests) is imbued with great power. It is the stuff of fascination and folklore, the sacred and the profane. In some cultures, wild animals that can negotiate the nemo are worshipped (such as the snake, bear, and tiger) in order to control their power, or to appease them so that they will not use their power against society.

Managing Terror

Very early in our lives, we become involved in rituals that help us to manage the terror of the nemo. Before the nemo becomes an issue for us, our own bodily excretions are seen as a part of ourselves. We are then as curious about our feces as we are about our fingers or toes. But once the walls of the nemo have been defined, we become nervous about losing our bodily wastes into the nemo. When they leave our defined walls, they pass beyond our control, entering into the nemo and becoming separate objects, changing previously held confidence in ourselves; our human wastes are then treated with repulsion and anxiety.

The False Self

During the first year of life, the individual is separating through the construction of walls and the experiencing of the nemo. During this time, children make a social construction which has been called "the false self." Masterson describes the false self as "a collection of behaviours, thoughts and feelings that are motivated by the need to cling to the object, with avoidance and suppression of individuative stimuli."[7] At this point, the true self has not been born:

> ... there is not at this point any true self. The true self is in a state of limbo or atrophy—it is only a potential. The defensive function of the false self is to rationalize and provide a false sense of identity for those regressive, compulsive behaviors that reflect the adaptive side ... necessary to defend against the abandonment depression.[8]

The Conception and Birth of the Self

According to many theorists, at approximately two years of age, the self is conceived; generally by three years of age, a self is finally born.[9][10] During that important year of life between two and three, children complete the separation of themselves from others and their environment. At about two years, children experience the first awareness of themselves as separate entities; this is the "conception" of the separate self. Between two and three years of age, once the self-concept has occurred, children begin to be capable of creating boundaries along with the walls, to define themselves from within; this is in contrast to the walls that have defined the false self from without, in reaction to the external world. By the end of the third year, this capacity for boundary making and self distinguishing is intact, and the self is born as an enduring entity.

From this theory, the boundary of the self is seen to be inherent to each person, a function of biology and growth. However, parenting tends to encourage the construction of a wall, the development of a false self, rather than permitting the individuation that would come with establishing boundaries. When people do not exercise their capacity to make boundaries through making personal choices, their self-assertion and self-responsibility tend to wither. Most commonly, people abandon themselves very early in life (see above, "The Ideal Self: Striving For Perfection"); fortunately, it is never too late to reclaim themselves, and many people attempt to do this later in their lives.

The Persistent False Self

The task of dealing with the so-called "real" world is primarily relegated to the false self, which has been shaped by the person's interactions with authority figures at home and in society. Control, manipulation, and the use of strategies are all defensive tools of the false self, developed by the maintenance of walls for the purpose of perceived survival needs. The need for approval and the fear of disapproval are issues of this false self, creating an ever-growing field dependence. While the true self is growing behind this wall, it faces much self-doubt as it observes the extent to which others value the false self.

Ultimately, each person must decide which path to follow—either to become more real (and thus more responsible and alone), or to develop the false self (and become acceptable and secure). By the time children are three or four, they already have well-established masks of the false self. In our terminology, the issues of the real self relate to the Authentic Self, and the false self phenomena relate to the notion of the Ideal Self (see above, "The Ideal Self: Striving For Perfection"). Most people elect to continue to hide their Authentic Self, and manifest their Ideal Self. They thus are more and more out of touch with their deep nature, and live more on the surface, presenting masks and roles. Arthur Janov calls the point where the Authentic Self is abandoned the "Primal Scene":

> Whether the rend is dramatic in the form of one major scene or simply the result of the accumulation of minor scenes, a day comes when the child becomes more unreal than real.[11]

Hubris

To the extent that people believe in the walls of the false self and invest emotional energy in them, they are prone to develop *hubris* (the insolence or arrogance caused by inordinate pride; exaggerated self-confidence). When confronted with honest feedback from others that they find difficult to hear, most people will resort to their hubris, defending the false self with a variety of mechanisms, such as rationalization, denial, obfuscation, distraction, and deflection. Remarkably, most people, when given the chance to reveal the true self, instead mount a defence of the false self, unless they have come to terms with their hubris. Originally, that defensiveness was a product of the need for acceptance and survival; later in life, that defensiveness serves only hubris.

Obsessions—A Common Defence

An obsession is a repetitious thought that is difficult to relinquish. A compulsion is a repetitious activity that is dictated by the obsession; the obsession is the thought, and the compulsion is the action that is linked with the obsession.[12] People become obsessed as a way of coping with the emptiness of the abyss. They fill their minds with the same repetitious (and thus, dependable and secure) thoughts; their actions, dictated by the obsessions, are predictable. By this means, people achieve a measure of security; their life becomes predictable amidst the chaos that lurks in the nemo.

Remarkably, most of human life is involved in obsessions and compulsions. People get into obsessive relationships, and have compulsive patterns related to their home and work life. We have written about the nature of obsessions in relationships in *The Relationship Garden*, proposing that people acknowledge their obsessions to an intimate partner, and work their way to more freedom by revealing these sinister thought processes. To become more free from obsessions is double-edged: whoever accomplishes this finds much more energy and creative ideas, but with an accompanying increase in anxiety and uncertainty.[13]

For many people, they do not want to face their ontic anxiety, and obsessions and compulsions are a ready tool for avoidance. Captive to their obsessions and compulsions, their energy is consumed in seemingly important repetitive behaviours. This obsessive/compulsive patterning provides them with a sense of security; they are so preoccupied that they do not have time or thought for the anxieties about life. They have converted ontic anxiety into a predictable neurotic process. Their lives become familiar, although somewhat dull and boring. What they relinquish is their freedom of choice that could come in facing, moment by moment, the uncertainties of their existence.

The nemo is primarily the product of the building of walls. Others exist on the other side of this gap (see below, "Bridging The Gap"), creating the need for control, objectification (see below, "Objectification"), dependence, defensiveness, blame, and victimhood. The false self can be diminished through the dismantling of the wall, and the boundary of the true self can be exercised through the discovery of options and the assertion of choices. Only when these issues are addressed will the true self grow into its maximum potential. For many people, this challenge is simply too great:

> *Many men never give out the whole of themselves, their deepest truth. They live on the surface, and yet, so rich is the soil of humanity that even this thin outer layer is able to yield a kind of meagre harvest which gives the illusion of real living . . . . how many men will never have the least idea of what is meant by supernatural heroism, without which there can be no inner life! Yet by that very same inner life shall they be judged . . . . Therefore when death has bereft them of all the artificial props with which society provides such people, they will find themselves as they really are, as they were without even knowing it—horrible undeveloped monsters, the stumps of men.*
> —Georges Bernanos[14]

Notes

1. M. Berman, *Coming To Our Senses* (New York: Bantam Books, 1990), p. 20.

2. J. Fowles, *The Aristos* (London, Pan Books, 1968), p. 51.

3. M. Berman, *Coming to Our Senses* (New York: Bantam Books, 1990), p. 24.

4. Ibid., p. 81.

5. Ibid., p. 50.

6. Ibid., p. 80.

7. James Masterson, *The Narcissistic and Borderline Disorders: An Integrated Developmental Approach* (New York: Brunner/Mazel, 1981), p. 101.

8. Ibid., p. 105.

9. M. Berman, *Coming to Our Senses* (New York: Bantam Books, 1990), pp. 34, 35.

10. J. McKeen and B.R. Wong, *The Relationship Garden* (Gabriola Island, B.C.: PD Publishing, 1996), pp. 43-44.

11. Arthur Janov, *The Primal Scream* (New York: G.P. Putnam's Sons, 1970), p. 29.

12. J. McKeen and B.R. Wong, *The Relationship Garden* (Gabriola Island, B.C.: PD Publishing, 1996), pp. 138-39.

13. Ibid., pp. 139-41.

14. Georges Bernanos, *Diary Of A Country Priest*, translated by Pamela Morris (New York: The Macmillan Co., 1937), p. 108f.

Objectification

When children are born, they separate physically from their mothers. However, this physical separation is not accompanied by an immediate psychological separation. The newborn child is experientially and psychologically fused with its entire environment; everything is an extension of the child. Because the perceptual apparatus has not yet developed, early experiences are ill defined and all-or-none in their scope. The child experiences global reactions to hunger or satiety, heat or cold, pain or pleasure, dark or light.

Naming of Objects

As perception improves, children gradually begin to make out gross shapes around them, and to attach labels to these shapes. They learn to distinguish one huge shape that comes and goes, seemingly associated with relief of distress; this shape they will ultimately call "Mother"("Mother" refers to whoever functions as primary caregiver, male or female). The first eighteen months of life are involved in rapid perceptual development with accompanying naming of objects. By this naming, children are symbolizing experience and organizing their perceptions into a reproducible reality. Through distinguishing and naming objects, processes which are necessary for their development, children learn to identify the world around them and begin to make sense of it, gradually establishing control over their surroundings.

In naming, children objectify the world around them. Objectification makes the world intelligible, reproducible, and subject to control. Growing children move around in and play amidst this assemblage of objects. They make larger excursions away from their primary security objects, their mothers. As children crawl away, they look back over their shoulders, to make sure that mother is still there. As they become more confident, they will even play in the next room, with periodic voice contact with their mothers. Thus, children assemble a picture of their mothers, known as the "internal object" (see above, "Entitlement").[1] As this object becomes more stabilized, youngsters learn to move in the world with the security of knowing that their parents (and the protection associated with parents) exist. In this way, the symbolization of others is an important method for psychological control and stability.[2]

In the first two years, even as children are naming objects, they do not distinguish the objects as separate from themselves. The "mother" that comes and goes is experienced as an extension of the child. The teddy bear that the child holds is still part of the child, not a separate entity. Indeed, children see all things that they name and objectify as part of themselves; this is the "primary narcissism" of the infantile state. Although they are distinguishing separate objects (and thus honing their faculties of discrimination), they still see the objects as themselves. So, children have a me-mother, a me-toy, and me-food.

Conception and Birth of the Self

As mentioned above (see above, "Nemo: The Abyss Within"), although the physical being separates from mother in delivery, the self is not conceived until about age two—with a flash of *self-recognition*—and is "birthed" generally at about age three, when self-awareness is established.. When conception of the self takes place, the child literally recognizes, "I am here!" During the "terrible twos," children are experimenting with their self-directed wills and establishing a more stable experience of themselves; this culminates in the birth of the self at about age three. From this point on, the person is no longer just a fixed biological entity; instead, the individual's will and personal choices come to the fore, and that individual can embark upon a life of individuation. As we previously discussed (see above, "Strength and Power" and "Achievement or Mastery"), the individuating person is capable of autonomous activity, living in strength, and self-awareness; this is in contrast to the person who individualizes, developing a false self, whose motif is power and who stands out rather than standing forth.

Relating to Objects

This has interesting ramifications for the development of relationships. As Becker described, parents are seen by their children as huge and powerful, protectors against the ravages of the universe.[3] Children experience gratitude, and feelings of security in having their parents on their side. However, the recognition slowly dawns that these parents, who are so powerful, could be a great threat to the children's well-being if ever they became displeased! Thus, children are ambivalent about their caregivers—their parents, who are powerful enough to ward off the threats of the universe, could use this same power to destroy their children. Parents are larger than life, to be revered, appreciated, and feared. Thus, children learn to anticipate what the big people want, and devote themselves to the activities of pleasing in order to take control of the objectified parents. Of course, children are terrified of being abandoned, and want control to assure themselves that they will not be left behind by their caregiver-objects. At first, this pleasing is quite primitive and impotent; the child learns to entice with crayon scribblings and peek-a-boo games. Very quickly, these activities become more sophisticated and are incorporated into a serious process of field-dependent pleasing, in which people quell their own desires in the face of the imagined demands of the external. Children establish the Ideal Self (walled self) to try to get this control, to establish security against the nemo. In this way, youngsters sell out the fledgling Authentic Self. If children choose a pattern of control and manipulation to develop a walled self, they lose contact with the Authentic Self. In this way, most children become arrested in a world of objects, and deny their own autonomy and self-development in exchange for the security of control over the objects in their environment. Thus, no genuine dialogue occurs, since people do not learn to relate to the humanness of others. This is the basis of the "I-It relationship" described by Buber.[4] For an I-Thou relationship to flower, individuals have to face the terror of nonbeing and accept aloneness and lack of control over external objects. In this way, truly personal relationships become possible.

Maintaining Objectification (It-It Relationships)

Objectification, which was at first perceptual, is codified in language. Children develop attitudes and beliefs about the objects around them, and then relate to these concepts. This is the tyranny of the mind, which creates a world of symbols. Language includes the assumption that the objects around us are real and need to be dominated. Also included in language is a moral structure (right and wrong, appropriate and inappropriate), that helps to keep the individualizing person within the moral guidelines of the culture.[5] In Buber's terms, this form of relationships maintained by language are "It-It." The self is an object, and the world around is filled with objects.[6]

Imagined Power Over Objects

Children feel impotent amidst the objects around them; they seem like victims of size and development (and time!). Early childhood fantasies involve a reversal of power, where children become the centre of activity, taking control of others. Listen to a young child playing with a doll or a truck, and you will see a fantasy of power and domination and control! The toys are externalizations of fantasied power reversal, which also occurs in dreams and imaginings of the future. "When I get big and you get little" precedes many youngsters' imaginings of what will ultimately unfold when they accumulate the power they crave. As well, these fantasies provide the matrix for life goals. Many of us have chosen occupations that are consistent with our early fantasies.

Sexual Charge and Objectification

Children cannot actually experience their dreams and fantasies of domination, since they lack the physical size and power to realize them. At puberty, the changes with sexual development bring an experience of vitality and excitement in the body; for the first time, a physical experience of power is felt. This brings the possibility of dominating and controlling others. Often, this sexual power is associated with earlier unconscious fantasies, giving rise to the particular choice of sexual objects. In this way, objectification is a key element in sexual charge (see below, "A Perspective on Sexuality").

Beyond Objectification (I-It Relating)

For an authentic relationship between persons, each would have to become aware of the objectification of the other, to acknowledge the objectification, and in this process accept it. This is the discipline involved in the practice of the communication model (see above, "A Model For Communication"). In relationships, partners can share fantasies even when they involve objectifications of power. Indeed, people don't really usually relate to each other as persons; generally they are relating as It-It, objectifying each other. When people share judgments, they are beginning to move through this objectification, to address the person of the other. To admit the objectification transforms the interaction to I-It.[7]

The I-Thou Relationship: Inclusion

The relationship becomes truly dialogical when both people become aware of the human-ness of each other; this is the process of *inclusion*.

> Inclusion ... is a way of imagining the other in his unique wholeness in the most real way possible. This act involves conceiving what the other, the desired partner of the dialogue, is thinking, wishing, feeling and perceiving[8]

In Martin Buber's terms, the relationship becomes one person relating to another as "I-Thou." We tend to use a more familiar terminology, "I-You." In this dialogue, both parties are experienced as human and persons, not just as objects.[9] In the I-Thou dialogue, Buber spoke of inclusion as "a bold swinging, demanding the most intensive stirring of one's being into the life of the other."[10]

> Inclusion means seeing the definite otherness of the partner and his uniqueness. It means seeing the other concretely without reduction or abstraction.[11]

Uncertain Dialogue

When two people are in different states—for example, one person is functioning in I-Thou, and her partner is operating in It-It—the exchange is fraught with difficulties. In the absence of intimate responsiveness, she remains uncertain of the validity of her awareness of her partner. The interactions are uncertain, and there is a tension and instability related to this. What is the way through this? *Curiosity*. When both partners are willing to engage in interchange with honesty and openness, using the four

A's (awareness, acknowledgement, acceptance, action—see above, "The Ideal Self: Striving For Perfection"), they can overcome the limitations of objectification and become more dialogical.[12]

Objectification is Normal

Objectification is a normal process, and is necessary for psychological development in earlier stages. Unfortunately, people tend to become fixated in the objectifying process, and the further possibilities of intimacy and revealing become blocked. On the positive side, objectification helps to provide security in childhood, and later, generates excitement in the pursuit of power and sexual excitement.

Objectification is not bad; therefore, it is not necessary to stop it. Nevertheless, people should recognize the limitations of objectification. To provide security, social conventions, and day-to-day order, objectification is a very efficient human tool. However, in the domain of intimate relationships, this objectification must be acknowledged as one's own, not as the "truth." In this way, people can share their judgments (objectifications) of each other through the process of the four A's (awareness, acknowledgement, acceptance, action—see above, "The Ideal Self: Striving For Perfection").

In dialogue, anything shared can enhance intimacy—this includes sharing fantasies, judgments, and objectifications.[13] When people take responsibility for their objectifications, acknowledging that they are the ones doing the objectification, they establish personal boundaries. With this acknowledgement, the individual experiences more anxiety, but less objectification. Hence, the world of the Authentic Self opens up, yielding the possibility of genuine communication with the humanness of the other.

At the beginning, people who learn this often think that they should simply stop objectifying. This would only be a denial, which would only fixate them further; by trying to get rid of their objectifications, people remain stuck with them. It is possible for individuals to learn to play with romance and other objectifications without making them their ultimate meaning. In the same manner, they can play with sexual charges, which are based upon objectification, without making them the end-all. Enter the theatre, enjoy the movie, and then go back into the street to continue with life!

There is a spiritual dimension to this. In surrendering to objectifications, revealing them without resistance, people can let go of false ideas of themselves, and can gradually become more in touch with their more genuine nature. By acknowledging the objectifications of the It-It, they move into I-It interactions; when they become curious about the personal world of the other, they transform again, to the domain of I-Thou, which permits authentic dialogue with another to occur.

> *The unrelated human being lacks wholeness, for he can achieve wholeness only through the soul, and the soul cannot exist without its other side, which is always found in a "You." —C.G. Jung[14]*

Notes

1. D. Rinsley, "The Developmental Etiology of Borderline and Narcissistic Disorders," *Bulletin of the Menninger Clinic*, 44(2), 1980, p. 129.

2. J. McKeen and B.R. Wong, *The Relationship Garden* (Gabriola Island, B.C.: PD Publishing, 1996), p. 19-20.

3. E. Becker, *Denial of Death* (New York: The Free Press, 1973), p. 146.

4. M. Buber, *I and Thou* (New York: Charles Scribner's Sons, 1970), pp. 11-12.

5. S. Freud, *Civilization and its Discontents* (New York: W.W. Norton and Co., 1961).

6. M. Buber, *I and Thou* (New York: Charles Scribner's Sons, 1970).

7. Ibid., pp. 53-61.

8. W.G. Heard, *The Healing Between: A Clinical Guide To Dialogical Psychotherapy* (San Francisco: Jossey-Bass, 1993), p. 78.

9. M. Buber, *I and Thou* (New York: Charles Scribner's Sons, 1970), pp. 53-56.

10. M. Buber, *The Knowledge of Man: Selected Essays*, M.S. Friedman and R.G. Smith, trans. (Atlantic Highlands, N.J.: Humanities Press, 1988), p. 71.

11. W.G. Heard, *The Healing Between: A Clinical Guide To Dialogical Psychotherapy* (San Francisco: Jossey-Bass, 1993), p. 78.

12. J. McKeen and B.R. Wong, *The Relationship Garden* (Gabriola Island, B.C.: PD Publishing, 1996), pp. 74-75.

13. Ibid., p. 79.

14. C.G. Jung, *The Collected Works of C.G. Jung*, translated by R.F.C. Hull (Princeton, NJ: Bollingen Foundation and Princeton University Press, 1966), vol.XVI, par.454.

Bridging The Gap

Objectification

Beyond ouselves is nothing but a void, a *transitional space* within which each of us must create our own personal world. We create a world of objects using our perceptual apparatus; what we perceive through our senses are these objects, which we imbue with meaning. The infant will notice that some objects are mobile and others are static; some are useful in satisfying needs and others can be ignored. The useful ones (such as a parent), which provide comfort and pleasure, are experienced with a positive emotional charge; any that produce discomfort or pain are assigned a negative emotional charge. Confusion arises when the same object (such as a parent) is ascribed with both kinds of charges, becoming both desired and feared. This is always so when the object is alive and reactive, with a will of its own (as is the case with a person or an animal). With such beings there is a real danger of being hurt. Transitional space that is filled with objects of desire also becomes land-mined with objects of fear; frequently, they are the same objects. It is no wonder that early in our lives, the issue of control seems so important to our survival.

At the same time as we are wrestling with sorting out our relationship to the many objects in our transitional space, we must determine how much of that space is inner and how much is outer. Where do I end and where does the other begin? How much of transitional space do I appropriate as myself? Where and how do I draw the boundary of myself? Do I remain flexible and in touch with the objects in my world, or do I become overly defensive and build walls instead of boundaries? What is real and what is my imagination? What is the other really thinking and intending, and how much am I projecting upon the other, believing that I know what the other is thinking and intending? This issue is never ending, and is the basis of most of the confusion that people create and experience throughout their lives. It is intimately connected to the ways that we think and relate.

Autologue, Monologue, Dialogue

Thomas Szasz maintains that "thinking is self-conversation"[1] that "occurs in the metaphorical space we call ... 'mind'."[2] As such, all thinking is related to language. Furthermore, Szasz suggests that "reality is the universal experience of talking to oneself."[3] Since such self-conversation (i.e. thinking) is from the self to the self in the privacy of the mind, it is referred to as being an *autologue.*[4]

As children grow in body and mind, so does their experience of the "gap" that separates the self from others. Initially, comfort is provided from others through touch and voice. But as the demands for increasing separation occurs, the child must learn to go it alone, aided by an introjected image of the care provider (a "stable internal object") that is carried within memory (see above, "Entitlement" and "Objectification"). As language skills rapidly develop, this internal object is one of the first images that a child talks to within his or her "mind." By so doing, the youngster feels comforted by seemingly being no longer alone. With advancing years, such thinking is further utilized for a variety of complex functions—including problem solving—that help to deal with the problems of the gap and transitional space (see sections below in this chapter, "Transitional Space" and "The Gap").

Unfortunately, bridging the gap by thinking alone is ephemeral and usually inadequate, often prey to misinterpretations and self-delusion. Early on, the child discovers that the use of language is attention-getting and controlling. Besides using language to *think* (as in "autologue"), *expressing* what is being thought about reaps a harvest of attention in transitional space. Through such expression, children announce their needs, so that expectations can be met from the "objects" (initially the caretakers). Since young children lack an appreciation of the personhood of those others, their expressions take the form of a "monologue." The situation is very similar to an actor on stage, informing the audience about inner occurrences in a character, yet being unable to hear what is going on within the audience members. Since most people fail to develop beyond this level of communication, most interactions consist of *mutual monologues*, which temporarily fill transitional space but provide little or no sense of fulfilment.

The task of moving from a world of "objects" to discover others (and hence the self) as persons involves recognizing and acknowledging those others. To do so requires an interest in the other, and a consideration of the other as a unique, autonomous, self-determining, responsible being whose world of inner experiences can be felt and appreciated. Such is the nature of the quality of "inclusion" (see above, "Objectification"). At such a time, there can be a mutual sharing of inner experiences—true *"dialogue."* In this way is it possible to transform objectified beings into real persons who *live* and *feel* their connection and their location in life; the "gap" then fades into the background.

The infant's early mental experience is pre-language ("protologue"). Early language is autologue, with no recognition of others. When people are involved in monologue, others are objectified. Only in dialogue is the personhood of self and other appreciated.

Transitional Space

Simply stated, everyone is wrestling with transitional space, experiencing a gap between themselves and others, between themselves and inanimate objects, between themselves and institutions (another form of objects), and most alarming of all, between the I and the self. The latter gap is created by another act of objectification. One of the most important projects in life is to become an individuated human through relationships with the objects in our individual worlds. We can choose the extent to which we will objectify or humanize others in our personal worlds. To objectify another is to ignore the personal human qualities of the other; this is done with *generalizations* (for example, "Everybody feels that way") and *politicizations* (for example, "All men have trouble showing their feelings"). People can move past objectifications by being self-responsible, and by *personalizing* (for example, "I feel this way").

Morality

The anxiety associated with the chaos of transitional space seems unmanageable; hence people experience a need to organize and control that space. By doing so, they create meaning; this involves deciding on "right" and "wrong," "good" and "bad." In this way, people create morality to govern the interactions between themselves and others. The purpose of such morality is to provide a continuity and security for the individual and the culture. Unfortunately, the importance ascribed to this morality tends to grow beyond this basic function; the guidelines of morality becoming rigidly codified and invested with meaning beyond their function. This frequently occurs in the creation of religions. In this fashion cultures are formed, with individual pleasure being sacrificed to the continuation of group ideals.[5] Acculturation involves gross objectifications. Throughout history, millions of people have been killed in the service of cultures and moralities. The objectification of people (as "enemies," "infidels," or "barbarians") immediately robs them of life; in war, the actual killing of the body is only a small further step, since the enemy has already been de-humanized. That is why military training devotes so much effort to teaching soldiers how to depersonalize the "foe." A father of several children would find it difficult to kill another father of several children; it is easier for a "soldier" to kill an "enemy," a "conqueror" to kill a "native," a "defender of the faith" to kill a "heretic."

Repression and Denial

Because the chaos of people's inner space is closer to themselves, it is even more frightening than transitional space. Many impulses and feelings that arise from within individuals (such as the desire to kill) are unacceptable to them. The convenient solution is to repress and deny such impulses, projecting them into transitional space, making the outer world even more terrifying than before. The usual repositories for such projections are other people and "wild" animals—the objects that have a will of their own, and are thus less controllable. Most children begin to do this projecting at an early age; this explains why they cling and "make shy" in the presence of others. Security is to be found in the controllable objects such as their mother, or inanimate things such as teddy bears and pacifiers. If people lack effectively controlled objects in transitional space, they are liable to experience symptoms of anxiety, and possibly even panic attacks. What they have repressed is this: the source of fear is their own unacceptable ("bad") impulses rising from within inner space, projected into transitional space. Without an object to project upon, the individual experiences general anxiety; objects that are projected upon become identified as the "enemy," or "wild" or "crazy." In addition to individuals, whole civilizations appear to need these objects of projection, even establishing permanent institutions to service them.

The Gap

Thus, individuals create a gap between themselves and others in transitional space. Whatever is unknown is interpreted as uncontrollable—and thus viewed with suspicion, as a prospective enemy. This is the manner in which many women and men, cultures and societies, religions and institutions view one another. In relationships, this is the process by which children and parents become alienated and partners become separated. The gaps are maintained by the establishment of morality; somebody always needs to be "right," making others "wrong." By sustaining the gaps, grudges are held and punishments required. To relinquish the gaps would mean giving up the convenience of having objects to project upon; then individuals would have to face the horror within, to contend with the unacceptable impulses and feelings that well up from inner space, and ultimately to be *responsible* for themselves. In the same manner, institutions could become responsible, rather than blaming and persecuting other institutions or individuals. However, responsibility is quite uncommon. The magnitude of the fear and anxiety that would accompany such responsibility explains why persons and institutions desperately cling to a rigid morality of rightness, making others wrong, instead of opting to let go of control and experience happiness.

The gap is frequently of little concern for those in power and control, who judge themselves to be "right." It is usually only seen as a problem by the disenfranchised; banished from institutions and family, they are unable to participate in many decisions that affect their actions, their life styles, and their livelihood. In this process, the institutions and family members who are in control lose the input of the marginalized, who, because of their "wildness," are frequently the most creative resources in society. Equally regrettable is the tendency of the disenfranchised to create an "enemy" of the institutions or family members in power, wasting much creative energy and resources in the maintenance of a feud. Frequently, the people who lose the most in such feuds are those not directly involved in it, rather than the embattled opponents. During marriage separations, the children usually suffer more than do the litigious parents. In the battle between institutions, the clients are deprived of a greater variety of services, many of which could benefit their health or happiness. In wars, often more civilians than soldiers are slaughtered.

Disowning the Body

Even more remarkable is the gap produced between the self and the body. Because the self is so identified with awareness and consciousness, it is usually thought to be the mind itself, independent of the body. Because so much that occurs within the body is unconscious and uncontrollable, people often relegate the body to a position outside of themselves in transitional space, and relate to the body as an object. Because their bodies are always with them, people can use their bodies as handy screens upon which they can project their anxieties, fears, anger, hate, and love. Thus, many make enemies of their bodies, disowning them and being distant from them. Nevertheless, it is always possible to befriend one's body, taking ownership for feelings and processes, and being intimate with one's physical being. The more alienated people are from their bodies, the more frightened and defended they become. The more split off from their bodies they become, the greater the distance they experience with others. Thus, the gap widens. In this separation from the body, many illness processes can take root and grow, seemingly beyond the person's control.

Bridging and Healing

In bridging between self and others, a person can learn to come to terms with the gap between the self and the objectified self. In healing a rift with someone else, people tend to heal the split within themselves too. It is tempting to believe that before you can love another, you must first learn how to love yourself; but it is more likely that you will learn to love yourself *while* you learn to love another. By bringing yourself forward and revealing yourself to another (an act of intimacy), you will discover how distant from others you have been, and how split off from yourself you have become. The awareness of those splits offers an opportunity to heal both gaps. When people reveal themselves to others, they become aware of the objectifications they have wreaked upon themselves; both self and other are recognized in such an intimate encounter.

From Dependency to Self-Responsibility

The most primitive aspect of loving is taking care of another; the infant desperately needs caretaking, and the mother expresses her loving by taking care of the child. In a similar way, adults take care of others, especially the helpless and the wild. By so doing, they can ignore their own internal helplessness and wildness. The person in need of help faces issues of trust—can the other person be relied upon to deliver what is needed? Furthermore, the helped person comes under the control of the helpers, and thus, the helpers appropriate more transitional space to themselves. In keeping people attached to them, helpers and caretakers further objectify them, and thus widen the gap.

Recognition is an aspect of a more mature kind of loving, in which people acknowledge, respect, and accept the life and uniqueness of themselves and each other. When everyone is seen as responsible, people are not so prone to the objectification inherent in taking care of each other. In this state of loving, people realize that the gap between them is an unnecessary self-made construction. Their strength and self-assurance grows. Increasingly they find personal faith (the felt sense of the assurance of the continuity of life)—faith in their own inner resources, in their own location in the world, and in their own existence in the face of nonexistence.

Home Together

Once we recognize that the gap is of our own creation, and we acknowledge all the ways in which it has served us well, we can begin to become responsible for our own lives. Instead of being focussed on another across the gap—looking to see what the other can provide, how much the other can be trusted, or how dangerous the other might be—we can begin to have faith in ourselves as full expressions of life, complete in ourselves. We can then recognize and accept the existence of ourselves and others, being curious about each other's uniqueness, learning what we each can contribute toward the creation of a transitional space in which we all can flourish together.

We can then respect all beings and things, because when there is no gap, *they are us*:

> *If all the beasts were gone, we would die from a great loneliness of spirit, for whatever happens to the beast, happens to us. All things are connected. Whatever befalls the earth, befalls the children of the earth*[6]
> —Chief Sealth

Notes

1. Thomas Szasz, *The Meaning Of Mind* (Westport, Connecticut: Praeger Publishers, 1996), p.2.

2. Ibid., p.5.

3. Ibid., p.11.

4. Ibid., p. ix.

5. Sigmund Freud, *Civilization and Its Discontents*, James Strachey trans. (New York: W.W. Norton and Company, 1961), p. 42.

6. Chief Sealth, quoted in Morris Berman, *Coming to Our Senses* (New York: Bantam Books, 1990), p. 63.

Morality

Much of the information in this chapter has been previously discussed (see above, "Anxiety: Friend Or Foe?" and "Bridging the Gap"). This material will serve as a summary for this most important topic.

Anxiety of Existence

Humans are born in ontological (ontic) anxiety; this terror of nonbeing is at the root of our human nature. According to Paul Tillich, all other anxieties are varied expressions of this basic anxiety.[1] On the spiritual dimension, people experience anxiety in facing the inherent meaninglessness and emptiness of life. Most are too afraid to experience either the ontic or the spiritual dimension of existence, and generally conduct themselves in reference to the moral. On the moral level, people exist in a tension between the absolutes of grace and condemnation; their day-to-day experience is one of guilt. In short, instead of facing the terror of nonbeing, or the emptiness and meaninglessness of life, people generally choose to live in the context of moral codes to cope with the basic anxiety. In so doing, they live limited existences, with guilt and reduced vitality as the consequence.

The Moral Code

Morality involves a system of right and wrong. Certain behaviours and attitudes are right, and others are wrong. People are good to the degree that they live within the "right" code, and bad when they live by the "bad" choices. Since individuals can never fully live within these codes of behaviour (or are afraid that they might slip), they frequently live in a state of guilt.

Morality assumes a dichotomy of correct and incorrect, true and false. Whenever people say "This is true (*or false*)", or "This is right (*or wrong*)," they are exhibiting a moral stance.

The moral position is depersonalizing and objectifying. I am an object when I see myself as either good or bad; I do not appreciate you the person when I say you are right or wrong. To move into a personal intimacy, people must relinquish the temptation to see things in moral terms. Unfortunately, this will open them to the anxiety of their inner emptiness, aloneness, and impotence. However, if they take the courage to do so, they also have the possibility of experiencing themselves and others authentically.

The Black and White World of the Infant

The newborn infant is structured to function in a moral grid; the world of the infant is split into opposing poles of all or none, black and white, pleasure and pain, good and bad. Object relations theorists say that the child tends to experience one of these poles at a time, in all-or-nothing fashion.[2] "Good" describes the pleasure of a dry diaper, warmth, and satiety; "bad" applies to pain, hunger, and excess of cold or heat. For the very young infant, experiences are "all good or "all bad." The mother is all good when she does the child's bidding, and all bad when she does not. Children see themselves in this same light; they are either all good or all bad. Early on, children are fused with other people in their environment; hence, the infantile self-other symbiosis is experienced as either all good or all bad.

As children learn to separate themselves through the process of objectification, they can label themselves and others as good or bad. Hence, the mother might be good and the child bad (or vice versa). This paradigm is often replicated in interactions that come later, in adult relationships. When you disagree with me, I am inclined to think that I am all right and you are all wrong. This is just infantile thinking using a moral grid of good and bad.

The Life Choice: Individualize or Individuate

Between the ages of two and three, the self gradually "hatches" as a separate autonomous entity (see above, "Nemo: The Abyss Within" and "Objectification"). With self-awareness come bodily feelings, and the development of the kinesthetic body, as described by Berman.[3] At this tender age, each has a major life choice to make. Youngsters can either face anxiety and separation, and surrender to life, or they can try to control the surroundings, to avoid the pain and anxiety of separation. Most children choose to control, to make the situation manageable and to overcome fear. Of course, their parents also probably have opted for a life of conformity and individualizing to avoid their own discomfort; hence, children probably do not have a role model of individuation to follow. Thus, people develop the walled self by means of approval seeking, manipulation, external focus, and field dependency (see above, "Boundaries," "Strength and Power" "Bridging the Gap" and "The Ideal Self: Striving For Perfection"). At this stage of development, objects are seen as "not me"; these objects must be controlled to protect the walled self.

The Functions of Morality

With the establishing of the walled self (false self), morality becomes a convenient tool for providing a structure for behaviour. Morality also gives a sense of security; all that children need to learn are the appropriate behaviours to fit in, in order not to be abandoned. Thus, rules and guilt are potent controls, maintaining a strong inclination to be a "good boy" or a "good girl," which persists even in adult years. Many dedicate their entire lifetime to living out the roles, rules, and conventions that are aimed to please others. Most choose a life of secure conventions through external orientation, rather than facing the risks of developing their authentic natures. Individuals build up distinct codes of behaviour to perpetuate this pleasing of the external, and struggle to live up to the mandates of these codes in a desperate attempt to survive. In this framework, *guilt* is important for people to punish themselves when they transgress their code of morality. Guilt is an internalized police structure, a way of keeping the false self in safety. No wonder people so readily want to feel guilty: they then can feel the security of knowing they are paying for sins as they go, and thus won't be summarily turfed out from the kingdom!

Guilt and Shame

The Ideal Self is a expression of morals—rules, prescriptions, and restrictions. The process of externalization in field dependency involves an abandonment of the Authentic Self in favour of the Ideal (false) Self. Self-hatred is the price of this rejection of one's essential nature; power is the pay-off. Thus, the Ideal Self functions with guilt and self-recrimination. Shame accompanies one's recognition of oneself. Shame is an entrance to the Authentic Self; in shame I am revealed as I am. Guilt operates against the revelation of the Authentic Self, and serves to perpetuate the masquerade of the Ideal Self.

Coming Home

Strangely, the body is often seen as "bad," and people frequently have lost the experience of their kinesthetic nature. For many people who have lost touch with themselves, the path "home" is a process of becoming familiar with sensations and feelings *in the body* that either have not developed or have been forgotten. With this comes the delight of one's own feelings and awareness; however, one is also acutely aware of being separate from other beings, and of the anxiety of nonbeing called ontic anxiety (see above, "Anxiety: Friend or Foe?"). The more people become autonomous, the more they recognize that they are alone, facing the dark dread of nonbeing. Also, the more they sink deeper into the experience of physical sensations and emotions, the more they are faced with guilt and anxiety.

Personal Ethics That Transcend Morality

Society is held together by rules of "right" and "wrong"; laws represent a codification of morality, providing guidelines for appropriate behaviours and attitudes. This code of rules is not personal; citizens are not called forth as persons in the moral code, but only have to obey the conventions. To become personal, one has to transform morality into personal situational ethics; this is done by making personal ethical decisions in each situation, rather than falling back on the requirements of the law. When people begin to think for themselves and question laws, conventions, and established roles, they become alienated from the social order—they are more in touch with the Authentic Self, but they are less conditioned as moral beings. Mature people who are in touch with the Authentic Self will make ethical decisions based on a sensitivity to themselves, to others around them, and the entire social context. Thus, this is not insensitive selfishness; such an ethical stance involves a highly evolved sensitive relationship with life.[4]

This does not mean that an authentic person does not have principles. Indeed, such people, in dialogue with their surroundings, will constantly be making sensitive decisions based on personal ethics. To mature into deeper resonance with the Authentic Self, they must relinquish the easy, conventional rules of conduct and replace them with situational ethics, where they are called upon to decide with their entire beings, using only the guidelines of their own personal conscience and code of honour.

Religion and Spirituality

Both religion and spirituality are means to deal with the emptiness and meaninglessness of life. Religions generally have established codes of behaviour, and hence are moral. Spirituality is the search for a personal experience of universal principles. Spirituality is amoral, and requires the presence of the authentic person.

Political or Personal

Politicization is the objectification of experience, involving the imposition of one's morality upon other people. When an individual makes someone else "wrong," or blames another, this is *politicization*. When people share their feelings (positive or negative) and do not insist that the underlying judgments are "true," they are being *personal*. People have the option in any interaction of being personal or political. Whenever people insist that they are "right" (or "wrong," feeling guilty and blaming themselves), then they succumb to the moral. The moral can be a cowardly way of stepping back from life; to be personal involves courageously advancing into the unknown, responsively interacting with other people and with one's surroundings.

Blame and Righteousness

Blame operates against responsibly being oneself. When people blame others, or blame themselves in guilt, they are stepping back from life. When they accept others and themselves without having to force agreement, they can then enter into life-enhancing dialogue. To engage with others, people have to relinquish their need to be "right." And of course, they want to be "right" so that they will not have to face the terror of nonbeing. Many political causes initially rooted in the feelings of individuals soon lose sight of the lives of other persons and are reduced to warlike fervour: where there could have been dialogue, joining, and learning, there is only blame and fault-finding. Righteousness is the enemy of life in the living moment. We lose ourselves and each other in trying to be "right." There is a tremendous arrogance in believing that I am "right," or that I know what is "true"; the arrogance of righteousness involves a tightness and a lack of acceptance that operates against vital dialogue. Righteous people generally have disdain for others who do not agree with them, believing them to be lesser, or simply wrong; in this disdain they move back from life, becoming prone to more illnesses and to less fulfilment. Blame makes an object of the other, and the opportunity for dialogue is lost. Unfortunately, for most people, the following generally applies:

People would usually rather be right than happy. —Bennet Wong

Notes

1. Paul Tillich, *The Courage to Be* (New Haven: Yale University Press, 1976).

2. D. Rinsley, "The Developmental Etiology of Borderline and Narcissistic Disorders," *Bulletin of the Menninger Clinic*, 44(2), 1980, pp. 127-34.

3. M. Berman, *Coming To Our Senses*, (New York: Bantam Books, 1990), p. 34.

4. Joseph Fletcher, *Situation Ethics: The New Morality* (Philadelphia: The Westminster Press, 1966).

Part Three:
FEELINGS

Each of us knows he is alive, and each of us seeks to be more alive, for each knows that far too often he is not as alive as he could be, as he really wants to be. Yet that is the way it is with us. Some days we are so alive, and some days we feel ourselves slipping under the death tide that is inexorably gathering within us. It is the great tragedy of the human experience that time and again we are blind and deaf to the opportunities for fuller living.

—James Bugental[1]

1. James Bugental, *The Search For Existential Identity* (San Francisco: Jossey-Bass, 1976), p. 1.

Guilt and Shame

The concepts of guilt and shame are commonly misunderstood and frequently confused one with the other. Yet, guilt and shame are very different experiences, with distinct consequences and significance. It is important to be specific about the definitions of each, so that they can be more readily distinguished and understood.[1]

The psychological and philosophical literature of the western world has dealt almost exclusively with guilt, and has given very little attention to shame. The main trend in western theology and religion has also followed in this vein: guilt is seen as a common human condition, and shame is rarely mentioned. When shame is recognized, the tendency is to value it negatively: shame is a condition that one would rather not have. The popular admonition "Shame on you" speaks of our sociocultural bias against this phenomenon; when people are displeased, they wish shame on one another, like a curse.

Valuing of Guilt and Shame

The phrase "Shame on you" involves a misuse of terms. When people say this, they usually mean "Guilt on you." Guilt is seen as a social necessity. Nietzsche suggested that guilt is a payment one makes in a debtor-creditor situation; the currency of guilt holds the fabric of society together.[2] Although Nietzsche himself did not prize guilt, he recognized that the culture at large does tend to value it in a positive light. If one does something that disturbs another, one can expiate one's shortcomings by the feeling of guilt. Guilt is a currency by which one makes reparation for wrong-doings against another. Much of western culture is founded upon guilt as payment; indeed, this frequently occurs in nonwestern cultures as well.

Remarkably in some classical Asian cultures, shame has been seen as a highly prized state, one that is very important and valuable. In Buddhism, shame is seen to be one of the wholesome states of consciousness, along with faith, mindfulness, scrupulousness, selflessness, and empathy.[3] Although there is some cultural heritage in the orient that prizes shame, modern times have brought westernization to the east, and guilt is highly valued there as in the west. Generally in the modern world, guilt is valued highly, and shame is devalued.

Defining Guilt and Shame

We define *guilt* as a complex of feelings involving regret, self-recrimination, depression, anxiety, and fear of punishment, arising from having transgressed some code of behaviour originally defined externally. *Shame* is defined as a feeling involving embarrassment, exposure, remorse, and anxiety, arising in the recognition that one is not all that one could be. Jean-Paul Sartre put it this way:

> I am ashamed of what I am. Shame therefore realizes an intimate relation of myself to myself. Through shame I have discovered an aspect of my being . . . Shame is by nature recognition. I recognize I am as the Other sees me.[4]

Guilt arises in reference to the external, and is depersonalizing. In feeling guilt, one is defining oneself as a transgressor of some moral code; so, guilt involves a deadening of the personal self, and a self-objectification. Shame, on the other hand, arises within the person in the recognition that one has fallen short of what one could be. In shame, one is vulnerable, exposed, and very present. This condition is similar to what the existential writers referred to as existential guilt; shame is in reference to the self, and is highly personal. In guilt, one is cold, withdrawn, objectified, and not present; in shame, one is warm, flushed, present as an authentic person.

Thus, *guilt is impersonal and shame is personal*. In shame, the individual is present; in guilt, one's genuine nature is denied. Guilt is a social convenience; one feels guilty in order to avoid responsibility for what one has done. It has been said that guilt is just an excuse to go on doing exactly what you have been doing without awareness or desire to change; guilt then is a cop-out. By saying "I'm sorry," the individual can pay for the transgression, and avoid any further insight into the situation. Shame involves a recognition of the self, and thus is a condition where change is possible. In summary, shame involves personal responsibility; guilt avoids personal responsibility.

These definitions of guilt and shame are very different from those proposed by John Bradshaw, who maintains that abuse produces "toxic shame," a condition of having been made wrong and feeling bad about it.[5] From our definition, what Bradshaw calls "toxic shame" is probably merely another form of guilt.[6]

Ontic Anxiety

Existential writers have proposed that humans ultimately deal with being in the face of nonbeing (the ontological or ontic condition): in being alive, we are faced with the inevitability of our own death. The ontological issue is *being confronted by nonbeing*; this is the absolute condition, the underlying stratum, of our human existence. Because of this, we have at the root of our existence a mammoth, all-pervasive feeling of anxiety (often called angst or dread or existential anxiety). In relative terms, this is experienced as our facing our fate. (See above, "Anxiety: Friend or Foe").

Spiritual Anxiety

This root anxiety is basic to our existence; yet it is too awesome and huge to face minute by minute. Instead, humans convert this basic anxiety into more manageable forms—into spiritual anxiety and moral anxiety. As a spiritual concern, people experience anxiety as a profound sense of emptiness in recognizing the apparent meaninglessness of life.

Moral Anxiety and Appropriateness

Commonly, people do not want to face either nonbeing or meaninglessness, and choose to live their lives on the moral dimension of right and wrong—the realm of appropriateness. As a moral concern, the root anxiety is experienced in terms of good and bad, right and wrong. We feel anxious (guilty) when we believe we have done wrong; we feel less anxious when we believe we are in the right. At the root of this moral position is a fear for survival.

People learn this early. When children feel insecure or uncertain (ontic anxiety), they encounter their fear of abandonment. The parent figure who protects the child seems to stand between the little person and powerful threatening forces. If the parent is pleased, the child can continue to feel secure in the protection; a displeased parent could leave and the child might perish. In simple terms, children endeavour to please parents in order to assure continued support and protection. In this way, youngsters initiate a life-pattern of trying to live up to the expectations of others, and begin to develop field dependent attitudes and behaviours. In this process, people shift their focus from inside themselves to external authorities. If children can please their parents, then they will not be abandoned by the parent, and hence will survive. This attitude of pleasing others is carried on into adulthood, expressed as pleasing behaviour. The root of this appropriateness is in a desire to be secure. Thus, at the root of appropriate behaviour, there is a life and death issue: one wants to be acceptable in the eyes of others in order to avoid being abandoned to the perils of existence.

The Ideal Self

As children grow, they gradually build up a picture of the parents' expectations; this is internalized as "the superego introject" (in psychoanalytic terms), or what we call the "Ideal Self" (see above, "The Ideal Self: Striving For Perfection"). This internal voice becomes a harsh taskmaster, an internalized judge that the individual carries around. This inner authority usually becomes even more demanding than the original parents. When the internal judge is displeased, it harshly criticizes, and "beats up" on the person. The judge's reprimands tell people that they are bad and need to be punished. The form of punishment is guilt. When people feel guilt, their taskmaster is satisfied that the slave is subservient. Thus, guilt functions to keep individuals under control, to be directed by the internalized Ideal Self. The individual has been depersonalized, objectified; the personal experience fades, and the objectified prisoner must pay for misdemeanours with guilt.

Guilt is Depersonalizing and Objectifying

Guilt is an expression of nonbeing, a denial of the self. Even so, people often would rather feel guilt for having been wrong (moral dimension) than face up to emptiness and meaninglessness (spiritual dimension) or encounter the nonbeing that accompanies the being in life (ontic dimension). Guilt involves submission to the power of authority, and a depersonalization. In this process people lose touch with their beingness (because this includes the anxiety that they are unwilling to face) and become identified as objectified roles who are either in the right or the wrong.

Physiological Aspects of Guilt and Shame

The feelings of guilt and shame are mediated through the autonomic nervous system, which governs the vegetative functioning of the body. In general, guilt tends to be a closing, contracting activity. Because it is an expression of condemnation and self-objectification, the physiological correlates to guilt include tightening, contraction, and dulling of feeling. Shame, on the other hand, is an opening of the self, with an accompanying self-recognition. A very personal and vulnerable state, shame involves a flooding of the physical being, a flush. The simple question, "Do you feel hot or cold, tight or relaxed?" will help to distinguish between the two. With guilt comes a tightness and a coldness along with a sense of isolation or withdrawal or distance, and a sensation of weight or discomfort or numbness. In shame, the person is hot, flushed, and experiences being vulnerable and exposed. Embarrassment is a form of shame. In shame, individuals are aware of what they have done, and in this self-recognition are responsible for having participated.

Psychological Aspects of Guilt and Shame

With the objectification and self-condemnation of guilt, the self is obtunded and depersonalized. In guilt, one is separated from one's environment, and is in a relative state of nonbeing. In shame, the experience is highly subjective and personal; the self is exposed and is in a state of being. Guilt occurs on the moral plane; shame involves one's very being.

Referents in Guilt and Shame

When people feel guilty, they have placed their centre outside of themselves, and are trying to live up to a moral code in order to belong. In guilt, the focus is outside; the other is the referent. When people experience shame, they inhabit themselves; the self is the referent. In guilt, people are condemnatory of themselves; in shame, there is self-recognition.

The Garden of Eden

The philosophy of our western culture has been organized around guilt, devaluing shame. The story of the Garden of Eden provides a mythological underlay for much of our attitude. The usual interpretation of the Book of Genesis has Adam and Eve as wrong-doers. They were bad for following the advice of the snake, who represented evil. God, in his goodness, had laid down a law, which Adam and Eve broke. God exacted a punishment in banishing them from the Garden. Adam and Eve were guilty. As prototypes, they had set the tone for human experience wherein each human being must live amidst the guilt of the original sin. God is good, and a just judge who exacts retribution; Adam and Eve committed the wrong-doing in listening to the snake, who represents evil. From the moralistic viewpoint, Adam and Eve had to pay for their wrong-doing by feeling guilty.

However, there is another way to view the story. In the beginning, Adam and Eve felt, not guilt, but shame in their *recognition* of themselves. They felt guilt only later, in contending with the punishment of the wrathful God. In other words, they felt shame in reference to themselves, and guilt came later only in relation to another. In shame, they acknowledged themselves and were vulnerable. When their shame was converted into guilt, they became field dependent and objectified as wrongdoers. Their shame, which was personal, became impersonal guilt. This prime myth of our culture has cast us into field-dependent, depersonalized conditions. Each person has the challenge to wake up to shame, and move beyond the original sin (guilt) of the Garden.

Theological Aspects of Guilt and Shame

In guilt, there is separation from the self; this is the realm of sin (literally to be apart, from the Latin *sine*, meaning "without").[7] In shame, there is no sin, but rather innocence; this is the condition of union. Christopher Ricks put it this way:

> *A blush is a very important spiritual experience.*[8]

Guilt and Shame in Relationships

Guilt in interpersonal relationships generally represents a control mechanism. It does not enhance closeness or union; rather, it operates to separate. It does tend to heighten the sexual charge related to dominance and power; however, it does not serve to bring intimacy. Guilt can be seen as an attempt to carry on doing what one is doing without any attempt to change. Guilt is the currency of debtor-creditor situations, and hence is associated with power and control.

Shame arises in a condition of self-awareness, when the self is very present. Hence, shame should be revered when it occurs. If people are to be close to one another, guilt is an expensive indulgence that must be relinquished. In an intimate relationship, shame can be celebrated as a rare gift; when people feel shame, they are present and revealed to one another.

Guilt can be used to start the process of opening to shame, by *revealing and sharing* the guilt. The usual course of guilt involves withdrawal into separateness and objectification; by sharing, this process is reversed, and the guilty person can become present in shame.[9]

When people are in guilt, they are generally trying to control others; they are offering an objectified role, rather than themselves personally. When people are in shame, they are vulnerable and self-responsible. Pride (and accompanying despair) occur in guilt; in shame, there is the possibility of experiencing humility and enhanced self-awareness and self-acceptance.

Consequences of Guilt and Shame

In guilt one is fixated, and no growth is possible; with the self-recognition in shame, growth can occur. Guilt promotes dependence on the external; shame fosters a feeling of freedom and self-reliance. Guilt is usually followed by depression; shame brings remorse with a fullness of feeling about the self. Guilt operates by obligation; shame involves being self-responsible. Guilt invites punishment, retribution, and forgiveness from another (and hence fosters dependency); shame invokes repentance and permits freedom and personal growth.

Notes

1. J. McKeen and B.R. Wong, *The Relationship Garden* (Gabriola Island, B.C.: PD Publishing, 1996), pp. 30, 31.

2. F. Nietzsche, *On the Genealogy of Morals*, translated by Walter Kaufmann and R.J. Hollingdale (New York: Vintage Books, 1969), pp. 64, 65.

3. Lama Anagarika Govinda, *The Psychological Attitude of Early Buddhist Philosophy* (New York: Samuel Weiser, Inc., 1974), p.121.

4. Jean-Paul Sartre, *Being and Nothingness*, translated by Hazel E. Barnes (New York: Washington Square Press, 1966), pp. 301, 302.

5. John Bradshaw, *Homecoming: Reclaiming and Championing Your Inner Child* (New York: Bantam Books, 1990), p. 47.

6. Ibid., pp. 79-80.

7. J. Traupman, ed., *New College Latin and English Dictionary* (New York: Bantam Books, 1966), p. 288.

8. C. Ricks in C.D. Schneider, *Shame, Exposure and Privacy* (Boston: Beacon Press, 1977), p.109.

9. J. McKeen and B.R. Wong, *The Relationship Garden* (Gabriola Island, B.C.: PD Publishing, 1996), pp 107-108.

Depression

Energy

Humans are the expression of energy in a multitude of forms, including spirit, mind, emotions and the body. These various dimensions of being include an extensive inventory of such things as sensation, judgment, imaging, thinking, speaking, actioning, loving, and so on. Holistically, each form is coupled with the others, and expresses all of them, as well as the entire universe. This is consistent with the Taoist view, which is similar to other naturalistic philosophies; this perspective suggests that humans and nature are in relationship with each other, and that there are correspondences between nature's expressions and human experiences. Each form of energy is a transformation of the others (each form of energy *is* the others, in different configuration) . The behaviour of the energy of the human is characterized by cycles, such as birth and death, expansion and contraction, heat and cold, light and dark, loud and quiet, order and disorder, close and distant, and so forth (see below, "Empathy, Resonance and Energy"). These correspondences are often ineffable:

> *Nature is a temple where living pillars*
> *Let sometimes emerge confused words;*
> *Man crosses it through forests of symbols*
> *Which watch him with intimate eyes.*
> —Charles Baudelaire [1]

Sadness

Feelings are to a person's inner world what temperature variations are to the external world. Just as there are cycles of temperature changes in the outer environment, so there are cycles of shifting feelings and moods within. Usually the range of experiences falls within a bipolar pattern. The heat and brightness of summer correspond to the expansive warmth and optimism of joy. The damp coolness and crispness of winter correspond to the isolation and the storage of feelings in a contracted state. Just as the spring is filled with fresh growth and eruption of new life forms, so is the inner world of a person full of anticipation, hope, movement and sometimes aggression. In the fall, as resources are being collected for the ensuing year's growth, there is a sadness in the air. This is similar to the sadness within people that is so natural and sweet, providing the experience of depth and felt meaning.

The inner cyclical seasons of sadness are unique to each individual. Personal growth and development involve a continuing series of new achievements, while letting go of older acquisitions. It is those episodes of letting go that are accompanied by feelings of sadness—the feeling of sadness is organic, existential and inevitable. Just as the mood of the seasons changes with the quietude of fall becoming the buoyancy of spring, so people's feelings will transform, bringing re-invigoration—into action, meaningfulness and shifts of growth—unless the individual loses faith, becomes anxious and wants to hang on. When people lose faith, they commonly embark on the path of "neurotic" solutions; choosing these neurotic solutions lays the ground for the future development of depression.

Depression

According to psychoanalyst Melanie Klein, the necessity of letting go is inevitable, forming "the central position in the child's development" which constitutes the ubiquitous "infantile depressive position." The accompanying "pining" for the love object must be "worked through and gradually overcome" to accomplish integrative growth.[2] Sadness is a natural experience that accompanies the experiences of letting go.

Difficulties can arise early in development. The newborn needs stimulation (human touch, sights and appropriate sounds) to foster growth. Without such stimulants, infants will withdraw into an *"anaclitic depression"*[3] (depression related to infantile dependency[4]), and fail to thrive. Should these children survive, they will likely carry this nuclear sense of emptiness and helplessness into adulthood, colouring all experience; future relationships and personal decisions about life and work can hinge upon this pervasive sense of desolation and impotence. In these cases, their development can be seen to be fixated at the "infantile depressive position"; they might even withdraw to an earlier (Kleinian) "paranoid-schizoid position,"[5] with concomitant anxiety related to ideas of persecution.

When there is inadequate resolution of these phases, anxieties or fixations may give rise to immediate childhood symptoms of depression; or more frequently the anxieties and fixations are repressed and later expressed in adulthood. The most common childhood symptom of depression is a tendency to cling, or not to attach at all to parental figures. Both situations reflect a "field dependency"; if relationships are attempted at all, they tend to be symbiotic in nature—the "other" is made a part of this person's life. Such dependent relationships are characterized by a need to please and conform, a desire to "take care of" the other, a wish to succeed or to be perfect, a low sense of self-esteem, a lack of spontaneity and creativity, a tendency to obsess and compulse (basic elements of addictive personalities), a lack of curiosity about the personhood of the other (even though much attention is devoted towards pleasing the other), a craving for attention and praise, and a low frustration tolerance.

People fixated in a "depressive position" may make adjustments and compensations in their personal and work lives so that they superficially appear to be happy and successful. However, closer examination would reveal signs of the fixation; they might be driven at work, or unable to experience being loved by another, or overly dependent upon a partner for emotional nurturing, or manifesting obsessive-compulsive symptoms of person or substance abuse. Such behaviours often mask an underlying depression. Commonly, such people don't recognize this deep malignant process until their life circumstances (such as a separation from a partner, a loss of employment, a forced retirement from work, a business loss) reveal the poverty of their inner resources. Only at this time might such a person experience the characteristic symptoms of depression.

Qualities of A Depressive Episode

A depressive episode involves a contraction of life energy. The depressed person loses interest in what previously had much meaning, whether it be a job, a partner, family members, recreational activities, social functions, or participation in social affairs such as church or school. In the words of Shakespeare's Hamlet:

> *O God! O God! How weary, stale, flat, and unprofitable seem to me all the uses of this world.*[6]

In this person's world, there is little joy, no spontaneity, a flattening of feelings, a gloomy pall on all experience, a loss of hope and optimism, a strong sense of isolation, difficulty in finding meaning and a chronic state of boredom. Energy level is low, so all tasks appear to be enormous, unattainable or not worth the effort. Frequently, sleep disturbances dominate—either in being unable to sleep, awakening early and being unable to return to sleep, or wishing to sleep all the time. Sometimes, there is a resurgence of previously experienced compensatory mechanisms such as eating disorders (with either extreme loss or gain in weight) or an increased amount of addictive behaviour. The overall effect is a progressive withdrawal from life.

Understanding Depression

In the psychological field, much controversy rages around the issue of the etiology of depression. Currently, the most popular hypothesis is that depression is *organically based.* The assumption is that all moods and feelings are directly determined by neurology and neurochemistry. According to this view, some people inherit, through their genetic endowment, a makeup that is destined to express a depressive episode at some particular time in life. This view is highly deterministic, very mechanical and sees people as helpless victims. People who accept this position can abandon self-responsibility, seeing their depressions as an inevitable result of their genetic inheritance.

That the neurology and neurochemistry are important aspects of this problem cannot be denied; however, instead of seeing them as primary factors, we assume them to be secondary to the person's active (though mostly unconscious) *choices* in life. We believe that the genetic component provides a predilection towards certain choices; but the final common pathway is the self (the will and feelings) of the person. Thus, the organic factors may create a tendency towards depression; but individuals create the circumstances that will stimulate the organic components to respond in the neurochemical way. In this view, the neurochemistry follows choice and behaviour; it does not determine it.

Indeed, personal choices and genetic predispositions are always in dynamic interplay. Although these two factors are always interactive, the organic approach sees the self as secondary agent while we tend to see it as more primary. It is not a matter of either one or the other; to us, the important question is where in the process would it be most *effective* to intervene? Modern medicine offers drugs to shift the neurochemical balances of such compounds as serotonin or norepinephrine that determine the moods of the individual.[7] We recommend that the person learn to *face the issues* for which inadequate or inappropriate life choices have been made; many depressed persons that have done so have enjoyed a natural shift in their neurochemistry, evidenced by their movement out of the confines of their depressive straitjacket. Helping them to do so necessitates a broad understanding of the psychodynamics of depression.

The Psychodynamics Of Depression

This is a very complicated and little understood topic. Attempting to cover it fully could certainly lead to confusion and obfuscation. Presenting it in a simplistic fashion carries with it the danger of contributing towards misunderstandings. We shall risk the latter approach with an accompanying caveat for the reader to refrain from arriving at any rigid or partisan conclusions.

Need For Stimulation

We believe that fundamentally, at a basic level, people are always connected to one another and to all of the universe. However, individuals do not always *feel* that connection; such a situation leads them to judge that they are isolated and alone.[8] Existentially, this is the situation for the foetus and the newborn. Filled with anxiety, the child faces one of life's earliest and most important decisions—to bond or withdraw. Should the caretaker provide adequate stimulation *appropriate for that child*, there is a positive attraction towards establishing an *experienced* sense of bonding between those persons. Note that we do not postulate that children need "love," but rather, they require *stimulation* that is uniquely desired by the child. This would explain the lack of apparent bonding that sometimes takes place with some "autistic" or "failure-to-thrive" children; often, the same caretaker can be involved with another healthily bonded child that is offered the same quality of parental care and stimulation.

Anaclitic Depression

As previously described in reference to the "anaclitic" situation noted by Spitz, some children appear to lack stimulation, while others are unable to accept the emotional and physical stimulation provided by their caretakers. As with plants that will go to seed when lacking the essential ingredients of sun and rain, these children tend to contract and withdraw behind a shell-like wall to protect themselves. Lacking this early vigorous growth creates a handicap that these people will carry on into adulthood. Such a "failure-to-thrive" child will grow into a "failure-to-thrive" adult who is lacking in energy, expansiveness, enthusiasm, spontaneity, resilience and psychological robustness. In old psychiatric jargon, they were variously diagnosed as "inadequate" and "schizoid" personalities. If they were better adjusted persons, they could achieve superficially effective relationships and employment, although their anaclitic core structure kept them inadequate to the task of living entirely fulfilling lives. Commonly, these people describe their feelings in terms of "emptiness," "shallowness" or "hollowness," lacking excitement and joy. Sometimes, to avoid this emptiness, they become involved in substance abuse in an attempt to experience some "highs" in life, even if they must pay later with ensuing equivalent "lows." The highs provide the simulacrum of aliveness.

The anaclitically depressed person is in desperate need of receiving, and being able to appreciate the stimulation of another's feelings. Being taken care of would not be enough; in their developing years, they usually have already had that. Instead, they are in need of an authentic "I-Thou" transaction, a truly dialogical experience. The self that has been in hiding requires a reason to stir and come forward beyond its own walls. But first, someone must find a way through those walls, to experience what it is really like for such a defended one, through the process of inclusion (see above, "Objectification" and below, "Empathy, Resonance and Energy").

Self-Hatred Depression

Most identifiable depression is related to self-hating. This form of depression is a result of a self-perpetuating cycle of feeling bad about the self for having abandoned the true nature of the self (Authentic Self) in order to be ideal; further self-hatred occurs when the goal of perfection proves impossible (see above, "The Ideal Self: Striving For Perfection"). From a psychoanalytic perspective, a relentlessly punitive superego is punishing the ego for desiring the expression of unacceptable impulses (including the impulse to abandon the self). Unlike the anaclitic situation where the self has been abandoned or buried, in this self-hating situation the self is loathed and judged to be in need of punishment. Being kind to a person dominated by this kind of self-directed loathing (and anger) only makes matters worse. In face of kindness and understanding, these people tend to further hate themselves for having duped the other; with the belief that kindness must be reserved for *worthy* individuals, their inner sense of unworthiness dictates that they be further punished. Thus, kindness and understanding can aggravate the depression, rather than helping to alleviate it.

Although these types of depression must be dealt with in a totally different manner, people in both conditions can be approached with empathy and understanding. Ultimately, the goal for both is self-acceptance. The issues for each are radically different. The kind of emotional support that is important for the person mired in an anaclitic depression is generally ineffective with those wrestling with a depression involving self-hatred; indeed, such an approach may contribute to worsening the situation. Unfortunately, most processes of depression involve a combination of these two broad types, necessitating a constant shifting of attitude and approaches as the person's process shifts.

Differentiating The Types of Depression

Ambivalence is a core issue that differentiates these two kinds of depression. The anaclitically depressed person is convinced of the inadvisability to invest feelings in others; past experiences with people have been unsatisfactory, even possibly hurtful or dangerous. There is no ambivalence in anaclitic depressives; they are deeply convinced that contact is unwise.

The self-hating depressed person has been deeply involved with others, but has been confused by a wide divergence of experiences, positive and negative. A typical scenario would involve a child who has a strong attachment to a parent who is either unstable or unpredictable in emotional responses; sometimes that parent is strongly ambivalent about that child. A more pernicious situation involves superficially "sweet" parents who deny the expression of negative feelings both within themselves and with their children. Since these children did not receive support for expressing negative feelings, when they do experience such negative feelings in themselves, they find nowhere to direct them except against themselves. A healthier environment would allow a constant clearing of these ambivalent feelings, minimizing the tendency to self-hatred depression.

Depression and Loss

When healthy, autonomous people lose a loved one through a separation for any reason (eg. divorce, death, or children leaving home), their emotional reaction will be a sadness of missing the other. More commonly, relationships have been more embroiled with ambivalence and unexpressed emotional transactions ("incomplete gestalts"); the involved parties have failed to differentiate into autonomous beings. Sometimes, on the surface they may appear to be ideal—never arguing, always being reasonable and logical, perhaps even appearing to take good care of one another. Although they have been deeply involved with one another, much has been repressed. At the time of a separation, the positive feelings that must be withdrawn ("decathexis") are accompanied with feelings of sadness. However, the unexpressed negative feelings produce a serious complication. Sometimes these can be directed outwardly as an anger against the world, or as a blaming and rejection of others. More often, people direct the unexpressed negative feelings against themselves, giving rise to the symptoms of depression.[9]

Physical Manifestations of Depression

When the self-directed hostility is denied or ignored, the depressive process grows underground. Frequently, it finds expression in a myriad of physical illnesses (including headaches, arthritis, cardiovascular disorders and cancer) through a process of somatization. Other common directions of expression are in obsessive and addictive behaviours (eg. work, substances, food, people), allergies and phobias, failures at work or in relationships, a variety of disturbances (learning, sleep, and eating), loss of sexual desire, and a general state of boredom. Without taking appropriate action, these can develop into full scale clinical depressions.

Working Through Self-Hating Depression

The goal of working through a self-hating depression is to bring to closure all of the incomplete experiences ("gestalts"). The focus would be on all of the feelings (both positive and negative) that have been previously unexpressed. Anger is of particular importance. That anger is typically self-directed is evidenced in some cultures in the practice of beating of the chest or pulling of the hair. In western culture, the beating of the self is a central element of the grief process, progressing to the extreme in the killing of one's self (suicide). This is the pattern of the self-hating process previously described (see above, "The Ideal Self: Striving For Perfection"). Fueled by curiosity, it is possible to interrupt the self-hating cycle through awareness, acknowledgement, acceptance and action (the four "A"s).

Cyclical Depressions

Currently, much attention has been given to a commonly diagnosed group of depressive syndromes that are described as being "cyclical." The most severe form is identified as a "manic-depressive" syndrome (even though the manic phase may never be acted out). Current thinking holds that these cyclical depressions are primarily genetically and organically determined; thus, they are treated almost exclusively with medications.

Some practitioners tend to see the most serious depressions as being some form of this cyclically expressed, organically determined syndrome. To them, other less significant depressions are "reactive" in nature, related to psychosocial factors that will ultimately settle down in some spontaneous fashion without the necessity of clinical attention. Because of this attitude, many depressions are ignored, leaving people to suffer needlessly. Eventually, more serious illnesses or social disruptions may result; by then, interventions may be too little or too late.

An Educational Approach To Depression

From an educational perspective, it is possible for people to understand and take charge of their own algorithm (pattern) of depression, no matter how organic the origins may appear to be. Carefully prescribed medications may be helpful at first, but they should be time-limited and viewed only as aids in crisis intervention. Eventually, depressed persons must come to terms with the *internal process of depression creation*. They can learn about themselves and their life style choices, and discover their own participation in the process of depression. With such a self-responsible attitude, people have greater possibilities for choosing for themselves more appropriate solutions to their nuclear life issues.

Notes

1. Charles Baudelaire, "Correspondences" in *Selected Poems of Charles Baudelaire*, G.Wagner trans. (New York: Grove Press, 1974), p. 23.

2. J. Mitchell, *The Selected Melanie Klein* (Harmondsworth: Penguin Books Ltd., 1986), pp. 150-151.

3. R. Spitz, *The Psychoanalytic Study Of The Child vol.2* (New York: International Universities Press, 1946).

4. "Anaclitic" defined in *Dorland's Illustrated Medical Dictionary* (Philadelphia, W.B. Saunders Company, 1965), p. 75.

5. J. Mitchell, *The Selected Melanie Klein* (Harmondsworth: Penguin Books Ltd., 1986), pp. 191-193.

6. W. Shakespeare, *The Complete Works* ((London: Oxford University Press, 1957), p. 873.

7. Michael Lemonick, "The Mood Molecule," *Time*, Sept. 29, 1997, pp. 56-62.

8. J. McKeen and B.R. Wong, *The Relationship Garden* (Gabriola Island, B.C.: PD Publishing, 1996), p. 11-16.

9. Ibid., pp. 116-18.

Anger

Responsibility For Feelings

All feelings generated within a person are based upon that person's interpretations of reality (see above, "A Model For Communication"). Nobody can make me happy or angry; I become (make myself) happy or angry over what I perceive and interpret others as doing. In this way, I alone am responsible (but not to blame) for all my feelings. When I fully understand this, I can step out of the victim role and take charge of my emotional life, developing a strength that furthers my personal growth. In that process, the power inherent in the victim role is abandoned in favour of effective communication.

Variety of Feelings

Feelings are the colours, flavours, and tones that accompany experience; they depend on related past associations and experiences. Favourable feelings, such as pleasure and joy, tend to motivate the person to reproduce those experiences. Unpleasant ones, such as fear and repulsion, serve as signals for self-preservation and tend to motivate the person to avoid what causes them. If these become confused (as when people are driven to reproduce behaviours that result in negative emotions such as pain or fear), people will likely lose trust in themselves as well as in others.

Genesis of Anger

In working with people, we assume that there is one primary underlying drive in human experience—the drive toward unity and joining, to return to the sense of oneness that ended at birth (let's call this "love"). In human life, the experiences of separation, accompanied by a basic primordial fear of annihilation (see above, "Anxiety: Friend Or Foe?") cause people to have deep anxiety and feelings of aloneness. This motivates them to establish meaningful relationships, in which they might re-experience that sense of union which is referred to as "love." When that is interrupted or unfulfilled, they experience frustration, fear, helplessness, or some variety of emotional pain, which motivates them to act. Infants often wish to control those upon whom they depend to meet their basic physical and emotional needs; infantile behaviours are often carried on into adulthood. For children, crying and the myriad other forms of complaints are common ways of attempting to bring caretakers under control. If these do not readily work, they experience frustration, more fear and helplessness, and then *anger*! Anger is a final attempt to overcome the helplessness that can arise as a result of prolonged frustration. Often, the anger is directed against the person or persons who are interpreted as the source of frustration of the need. If this does not work, people might direct the anger against nameless others or against themselves.

Anger and Violence

Within society, many moral judgments proscribe anger because of its reputed negative effects upon others. However, a closer look will reveal that the anger itself is not dangerous or destructive. What produces problems is the use of anger for control. When that happens, the anger is expressed in ways that *cross the boundaries* of others; this we refer to as *violence*. Such violence occurs even when positive feelings are expressed in ways that violate those personal boundaries, without the agreement of the recipient. Many parents "love" their children in violent ways, forcing them to do many things "for their good." For example, parents can do violence in the name of love by insisting that the children take music lessons when the youngsters vehemently do not want to do so. When people reveal that they are afraid of anger, it is often because in their earlier experiences anger was often accompanied by violence (not only physical violence, but also sometimes mental or emotional violence).

Sharing Anger

If people can share their anger in an open and responsible fashion, without blame or control, they stand revealed and vulnerable; this could be an opening for intimacy. In relationships, such sharing involves an engagement between the persons, an intimate contact with an accompanying sense of aliveness and excitement.[1] However, to be effective, this requires the establishment of some fundamental guidelines:

- There must be an agreement to absolutely no violence; that is, everybody's boundaries must be respected so that nobody will be hit or hurt in any physical way.
- There must be no physical damage to material things, other than those designated and agreed by all parties concerned (for example, pillows that can be punched or sheets that can be torn).
- Either person can call a stop to the proceedings at any time, especially out of fear or concern for either party.
- The boundaries of location and time (for example, for fifteen minutes, in the living room) must be agreed upon before starting. Extensions can be negotiated at the end of that time.
- The inclusion/exclusion of third parties (for example, the children or other members of the household) must be agreed upon beforehand.
- The use of blame, foul language, put-downs, and so on can be allowed in the beginning (if the parties agree), with the proviso that at the end these will be owned in a responsible way. These can be negotiated in specific cases, should they deviate from a person's baseline of acceptable behaviour.

The above agreements remove the possibility of using anger to control one another through violence; instead the anger can be shared, to deepen the intimacy in the relationship. It is important that at the end of such sharing, the parties spend time in clarifying the issues that lie beneath the generation of anger, being careful to use clear responsible communication (see above, "A Model For Communication"), avoiding blame and righteousness. Each person must accept the responsibility for his or her own feelings in order for this to work.[2]

Anger Is Not A Primary Feeling

From this point of view, anger is never seen as a *primary* feeling; usually, it masks a *hurt*. This hurt commonly arises when expectations are not met; the person with the expectations may experience disappointment, and possibly much emotional pain. Instead of experiencing that pain, which would contribute to a feeling of helplessness, the person might unconsciously convert the pain into anger. Anger provides an energy that fills the individual with a sense of power, overcoming the desperation of helplessness; at the same time, the anger can be used to bully or manipulate the other person into living up to the expectation. This usually works, because people are so ready to accept blame for other people's hurts. Also, many people are intimidated into compliance because they have had childhood experiences in which anger was accompanied by violence.

Anger, Assertion and Violence

Some people confuse assertion with anger and violence.[3] When people stand firmly behind their convictions about themselves, without condemning others' viewpoints, they stand forth from the crowd; this is not to be confused with self-righteousness, where a person with rigid moral values sees others as being wrong. When people are assertive, they neither apologize nor succumb to soliciting the approval of others. Because such people tend to stand forth rather than blend in, they are often seen to be intimidating, angry, and rebellious when they are merely expressing their own position. It is important to know the difference; if people are rebellious, they remain tied to others, perhaps becoming independent, yet missing the opportunity to be autonomous (see above, "Achievement or Mastery"). The rebel is violent, reacting against the authority of others, wanting to cross those boundaries. Self-assertive persons confirm their own being independent of the wishes of others; at the same time they remain sensitive to the rights of others, as well as their own.

Indirect Anger

If anger is not expressed directly, it comes out in a great variety of indirect ways. A hostile person can be smiling and friendly, while manipulating events to try to hurt others. Negative gossip that is not reported directly can be an expression of repressed anger; so too can the process of undermining another's authority or credibility. Sometimes anger is masked by over-niceness or over-attentiveness; these are often attempts to compensate for negative feelings. When anger is not expressed directly, it wears on the individual in the form of psychosomatic symptoms such as headaches, peptic ulcers, colitis, teeth grinding, hypertension, and sleep disturbances (including nightmares). When people direct their repressed anger against themselves, they can move into depression, addictions, and a wide variety of other self-destructive behaviours.

Transforming Anger

Instead of repressing and masking anger, it can be transformed, and expressed in socially acceptable and self-enhancing ways. Participation in aggressive sports and competitive games are two examples of such a strategy; even these can be destructive when the pleasure in the sport is converted into an obsessive need for dominance. Anger can also be used to ignite the aggressive drive of the crusader and political critic, who serve to keep society informed about its shortcomings. Anger can provide the energy so that people can rise out of conditions of poverty and helplessness through education or advancement in employment.

In all of these examples, the constructive element of such transformations is lost when people become insensitive to the rights and boundaries of others; when anger is expressed insensitively (as in revenge), it becomes destructive and opposes growth. When people mix anger up with blame, treating themselves as victims, they then can become involved in a malignant pattern of seeking revenge. Their anger then becomes obsessive and hateful, breaking up relationships and tending to leave the person isolated and more insecure. Rather than increasing the person's vitality in life (as occurs when anger is shared), such expression of anger wears out people's bodies and feelings, rendering them less effective in life.

Anger can serve a useful purpose by providing energy, so that people can mobilize themselves into action. Invigorated, they can lift themselves out of a state of helplessness and sometimes depression, and move toward resolution of a problem. Anger is an integral part of life experience; don't exclude it, either from yourself or others you love.

1. G. Bach and P. Wyden, *The Intimate Enemy* (New York: William Morrow and Company, 1969).

2. J. McKeen and B.R. Wong, *The Relationship Garden* (Gabriola Island, B.C.: PD Publishing, 1996), p. 37.

3. Ibid., p. 38.

Part Four:
RELATIONSHIPS

For one human being to love another . . . is a high inducement to the individual to ripen . . . a great exacting claim upon us, something that chooses us out and calls us to vast things.

—Rainer Maria Rilke[1]

1. Rainer Maria Rilke, quoted in John Welwood, *Journey of the Heart* (New York: Harper Collins, 1990), p. xiii.

Developmental Stages of Relationships

In her books, Susan Campbell described five reproducible stages of relationships.[1] We have written extensively about these stages in *The Relationship Garden*, renaming her stage of Stability to our stage of Integration, and adding more items to the model.[2] This brief summary is just to provide a context for relationships issues that are discussed in this volume. For a more complete exposition, see our companion book.[3]

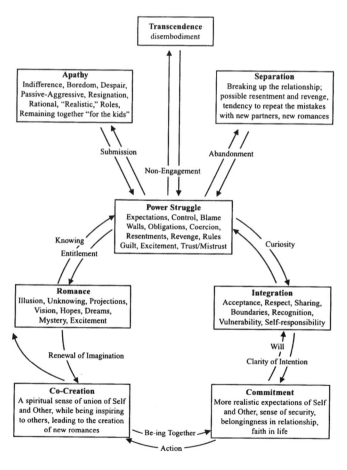

The Romance Stage

At the beginning of a relationship people are unknown to each other. They largely function with the illusions that they will find satisfaction of needs and some enhanced security and meaning in life through being together. They objectify each other, assigning roles and labels (such as a "boyfriend" or a "business partner"). They project onto their partners an objectified version of hopes and expectations—the real persons are unknown. On the positive side, people's imaginations are very alive in this phase, with visions of what could be possible. Mystery, excitement, anticipation, and enthusiasm and hopes are all part of this stage, before actual knowledge of each other begins to develop. The Romance stage can be one of "temporary insanity," with a loss of logic or reason. Romance can be maintained only by remaining ignorant of the genuine personhood of the partner.

The Power Struggle Stage

As people come to know each other, they frequently experience considerable disappointment as their partners fail to measure up to expectations. Often, resentment and blame build as each tries to alter the other to fit expectations through coercion, blame and guilt, often by assuming a victim position. Walls (rather than boundaries) are built through pride and defensiveness. This is a stage of high energy, tension, arguments, hurt feelings, and excitement. In sexual relationships this can be a time of intense amorous fervour. In the Power Struggle, jealousy is common, resulting from a perceived threat of loss of the other; at this period, jealousy is most frequently used to control each other's behaviour. In order to resolve this stage, each of the parties must commit to remaining engaged in the struggle, with established guidelines (such as no violence or blackmail allowed). Each must learn how to share anger, rather than using anger as a means of control over the other. By struggling through differences and unmet expectations, people can learn more about themselves and each other, opening the door to the stage of Integration.

Avoiding the Power Struggle

If partners do not engage in the struggle, they sometimes establish a passive-aggressive distance, resulting in anxiety, depression, and often boredom and uncaring in a state of indifference, which can degenerate further into *apathy*. In this way, they might maintain the form of a "good" (apparently unconflicted) relationship, although they will have limited intimacy and growth; instead, they are prone to increasing secrecy, and underlying resentments. Another way of avoiding the Power Struggle is simply to *separate*, and look for another Romance. A different form of avoidance of the Power Struggle can be accomplished through *transcendence*—literally "rising above" the turmoil, and disengaging.

The Stage of Integration

Integration (unlike apathy or indifference) results from a true recognition and acceptance of the other, with respect and support shown for the growth of each individual. People move out of the Power Struggle stage when they give up the need to be right, and begin to be *curious* about the process in which both of the parties are involved. Through *dialogue*, they find increasing revelation and vulnerability. In this stage, people share in order to engage, rather than because of obligations or expectations of a return for investment. Individuality, creativity, fullness, a shared aliveness, and an interest in both self and other are characteristics of this stage. In Integration, jealousy and anger can be *shared* as expressions of valuing the other, rather than as a means of control.

The Commitment Stage

Having achieved some degree of Integration, people then are able to make a solid commitment, to themselves and to the relationship. The Commitment phase is marked by an expressed intention to remain with one another during Power Struggle issues, which inevitably recur from time to time. In the Commitment stage, partners have a confidence about the relationship, and an assurance that they can deal with differences in a respectful, responsible manner. They know each other, and thus the commitment is informed by their history and experiences together. A deeper, new level of trust and intimacy develops. In primary intimate relationships, partners are able to commit to stay while each is exploring the more frightening and difficult personal issues (sometimes childlike, and frequently related to early family dynamics). Expectations are now more realistic because the other is better known. Each is prepared to declare clear intentions in regard to the other. Commitments made in earlier stages may now have to be revised.

The Co-creative Stage

The understanding, love, growth, creativity, and knowledge that have been developed within the relationship now have inspirational effects upon others outside of the relationship, through the expanded sharing that is now possible. A spiritual sense of meaning and union characterizes this stage. Now there is a materialization and realization of what was imagined in the Romance stage, albeit in a modified, more realistic form. In this, as in all the other stages, a new Romance may develop and the cycle will renew itself.

The Spiral of Development

Note that these stages tend to develop in an *opening spiral*, a circular order that returns to each phase with the experiences of the previous ones included. So, in a way, there is a return to a phase by cycling back to it; at the same time, the return is different, since the experiences have been accumulated. This is illustrated in the diagram above by the arrow that moves from Co-Creation out past the Romance phase. The stages can occur simultaneously and sometimes develop concurrently. Also, people can be in different stages in different facets of their lives; for example, someone might be in Romance with a new baby while being in a Power Struggle with a partner. These stages can occur in all kinds of relationships: parent/child, husband/wife, business partners, friends and lovers.

> To love means to open ourselves to the negative as well as the positive—to grief, sorrow, and disappointment as well as to joy, fulfillment, and an intensity of consciousness we did not know was possible before.
>
> —Rollo May [4]

Notes

1. Campbell, S. *The Couple's Journey* (San Luis Obispo, CA: Impact Publishers, 1980).

2. Campbell, S. *Beyond the Power Struggle* (San Luis Obispo, CA: Impact Publishers, 1984).

3. J. McKeen and B.R. Wong, *The Relationship Garden* (Gabriola Island, B.C.: PD Publishing, 1996).

4. Rollo May, *Love and Will* (New York: W.W. Norton, 1969), p. 100.

Intimacy

An intimate relationship is a loving shared by two solitudes.[1]

Power or Intimacy in Relationships

Any relationship can be maintained from either a position of control or a position of vulnerability. In *power-based relationships*, people try to maintain security by controlling themselves and their partners. In the process, each plays a series of roles (e.g. good provider, competent mother, successful businessman). They submerge the Authentic Self beneath the myriad expectations of the security-based roles, and often experience a sense of dullness or deadness. The roles are effective but depersonalizing; hence, intimacy is restricted. Although seemingly more secure, relationships based on power are often characterized by episodes of jealousy, anger, and anxiety when security is threatened.

The more that individuals are prepared to share all aspects of their inner world, including doubts, insecurities, pains, and fears, the more known to others they can be. Revealing is the cornerstone of an *intimate relationship*. Through vulnerability—being revealed to one another—increasing awareness of self and other becomes possible. The individuals in the relationship gain a sense of personal strength by revelation of the Authentic Self. An intimate relationship is based on sharing rather than on need and security. The person-to-person exchange fosters increasing recognition of each person. Each remains compassionate and sensitive to the feelings of the other, without rushing in to try to take them away. Thus, each partner is met with respect in a caring and sensitive manner, and can flourish in the dialogue of individuating separatenesses. Embarking upon such an intimate relationship can arouse anxiety, possibly excitement, and often fear of losing control. The rewards can be individuation for both parties, discovery of more of the Authentic Self, and a richer experience of life.

The Experience of Intimacy

Intimacy is the condition of being known, one to another, through a close personal connection or experience. In interpersonal relationships, such "knowing" can occur in a number of ways. In usual circumstances, one person opens to the other in a conscious act of *revelation*, offering vulnerability. This vulnerability is usually accompanied by anxiety, related to the fear of being exposed and possibly hurt. On a social level, the issue for the individual is fear of rejection; on a psychological level, it is fear of loss of ego boundaries (experienced as loss of independence); on an ontological level, it is fear of death of the self.

The desire for intimacy and the motivation for offering oneself in face of such awesome hazards arise from a yearning for the experience of connection with another person. Beneath social masks, people crave to overcome a deep sense of loneliness, the experience of being invisible (unseen, or not understood), and possibly a conviction of worthlessness.

Intimate Relationship or Intimate State

When another person has an interest in reciprocating that knowing, an atmosphere of mutuality and acceptance is fostered. This encourages further revelations, more vulnerability, and hence the development of an *intimate relationship*. When only one of the persons offers revelations and vulnerability (as occurs in traditional medical and religious practices), the more defended person retains a position of power; this is an *intimate state*. This intimate state occurs in many interpersonal relationships (often interpreted as "one-sided" relationships); this is seen in interactions where there is more dependency and caretaking, for example between parents and children, or between authorities in social agencies and their clients.

In the intimate state, on person *takes care of* the other; in an intimate relationship, the people *care about* each other. In an intimate state, people are faced with issues of authority, dependence, obligation, possessiveness, jealousy, and privacy. The intimate relationship fosters self-development, growth, respect, acceptance, and responsibility.

The Intimate State

The intimate state, as in the parent-child relationship, operates by the acceptance of roles and the fulfilment of obligations. Most children are taken care of by their parents, but not *known* by them. Many adult relationships are similar to parent-child relationships in this way. Many people desire this intimate state; partners often interpret this as being "intimate" with each other. In this situation, caretakers are not vulnerable or personal; instead, they are hidden in conventions and expectations. Rules and obligations become a way of life, usually with the development of efficient roles and a sense of security.

The Intimate Relationship

In the intimate relationship, people are willing to be vulnerable to each other, no matter how threatening that might be. With open, honest revelation, they develop deeper knowledge of themselves and each other. This is a person-to-person sharing, an I-Thou encounter in which both partners grow. Both persons are *responsible* for themselves, owning of all the feelings that arise from their honest disclosures. There is no room for blame or victims. Partners in an intimate relationship value individual growth and respect for each other. Sensitivity to each other is a significant element in an intimate relationship.

Familiarity Is Not Intimacy

Unless there is openness, there is not intimacy. Familiarity occurs when people study and experience each other intently, without being open or revealed. Often family members learn much about each other by living together for a long time; unless they open with each other about deeper feelings, they will not be intimate. Athletes in competition can become very familiar with one another by studying and experiencing their opponents. In war, combatants often have a deep understanding of one another. Some interpersonal relationships maintain a level of excitement through challenge and control, developed through an appreciation of each other's strengths and weaknesses. In these situations, much is known about each other with little self-revelation. Although there is a quality of closeness in this familiarity, the relationship is not intimate; revelation a prerequisite of any intimate relationship.[2]

Sharing

Intimacy involves *sharing*; anything that is shared can serve to enhance intimacy. Sometimes, what people have to share is their desire to help one another, or their craving to be helped. It is important to be able to ask for help from each other when this desire occurs, acknowledging the extent of helplessness. Although leaning on one another could operate against intimacy if it became a fixed pattern, the acknowledgement of a desire to lean can also be a sharing that enhances intimacy. It is important to be able to be able to lean for a while, and not forever.

The question of power must be examined in all relationships. In the intimate state, the vulnerable person must rely on trust and self-assurance; the withholding person exercises control (often unconscious) over the other. In an intimate relationship in which both persons are vulnerable, one does not control the other; both have their own individual strengths. For example, people often demand that their partners alter their behaviour to appease the hurt of jealousy. In an intimate relationship, sharing of hurt does not involve such control; instead, being responsible for their own feelings without blame enables both to experience and appreciate the pain. In an intimate sharing of hurts, it is possible that either or neither will alter their behaviour.

Creating and Maintaining an Intimate Relationship

- The *welfare of the individual* is more important than the welfare of the relationship. The relationship is not the goal; rather, it serves as a matrix for *individual growth*. The relationship is the garden; the individuals are the plants in that garden.

- Intimacy grows as partners *reveal* themselves to each other. In that revelation, they can discover more and more about themselves and each other. By moving out of roles, each becomes more individuated, making possible an increasingly person-to-person relationship (I-

Thou). They become more visible and present. Rather than *acting* in the world, they are *being* in the world.

- The tools of revelation are *honesty* and *openness*. Both individuals must agree to reveal their processes, ideas, and feelings to the other as spontaneously and quickly as possible. When either decides to censor anything, this should be acknowledged (for example, keeping the details of the partner's birthday celebration a secret). Censoring restricts intimacy; but, since both parties are free to choose, they can accept some degree of censorship.

- Both persons are fully *responsible* for themselves. One person cannot be blamed for the other's feeling; there are no victims in an intimate relationship. Although neither is responsible for the feelings and experience of the other, each can be sensitive to the other's pain, anger, jealousy, and sadness. Although one party does not cause the feelings of the other, each can have caring and compassion for the other's feelings. Neither person should be controlled by the feelings of the other.

- When feelings are freely expressed and *shared without blame*, intimacy can develop. At first, it is often necessary for some feelings to be expressed with blame, in order to purge the energy that accompanies those feelings. After the blame is expressed, both persons can then reassess the interaction, and both can take responsibility for their individual parts in the exchange.

- To maintain intimacy, feelings should *not be used for control*. A person's motives may be questioned by asking, "What is your intent in doing this?" It is important to check out suspicions, rather than assuming that they are facts. For example, it is preferable to responsibly ask, "I find myself controlled by your tears (anger, laughter, etc.); is this what you intend?" rather than "Your tears (anger, laughter, etc.) make me feel guilty!"

- In a *primary intimate relationship*, partners agree that their relationship is the main focus of their intimacy. Intimacies shared with others are secondary to that primary relationship. Anything shared with others must be acknowledged in the primary intimate relationship, so that there are no pockets of experience that are not included in the primary relationship.

• In establishing an intimate relationship, *many immature reactions and feelings* will emerge (such as jealousy, fear of abandonment, threatened loss of self-esteem, anger over unmet expectations). These can be shared in even their most unsavoury forms (including blaming); in order to move toward intimacy—from controlling to sharing—both partners must then assume responsibility for their own responses and feelings.

• *Any experience that is shared can enhance intimacy.* For example, anger, which is often used in more dependent relationships as a form of control, can be shared without blame in order to enhance intimacy. When partners are vulnerable and revealed to each other, a mutual deep knowing becomes possible.

• *Clearing* is an important ingredient in the development and maintenance of this level of intimacy. Defences and blockages will frequently emerge from one or both parties. The process of clearing—wherein each *acknowledges* judgments, feelings, and intentions—creates an atmosphere wherein each can be revealed without blaming. A clearing is not complete until the person who has expressed asks for the experience of the other; without asking about the other, the one-side expression is a *dumping*, not a clearing.

• The act of *objectification* of the other is counterproductive if not shared. The tendency to objectify is deeply rooted in the early development of each person. Examples of objectification include the tendency to view the other as a possession ("my husband"), as an object of desire ("my lover"), as a burden ("my obligation"), or as a purpose ("my reason to live"), instead of as the person that he or she is. Revealing the process of objectification is an excellent way to personalize the other, in order to move closer. At the same time, revealing objectification can be a source of excitement and challenge.

• An intimate relationship will encourage and nurture all experiences that are necessary to the *maturation* and fuller expression of each person. Frequently, what stimulates growth in one is threatening to the other. When one person is threatened, this can be shared without controlling the behaviour of the other.

- As intimacy deepens, people become more visible to themselves and to each other, and they develop a quality of *presence*. Intimacy is enhanced when each person agrees to be as present as possible in the company of the other, sharing all feelings and thoughts.

- *Expectations* of one another are not forbidden (contrary to some interpreters of the human potential movement). However, partners should reveal their expectations, and find agreement about them. Neither person is entitled to have expectations met. Often, power struggles arise when one partner has an expectation that the other person has never agreed to meet. We hold expectations to be of great value in an intimate relationship. When little importance is attached to another, expectations can be quite low; whenever another becomes more important, expectations of that person will be raised. Meeting mutually agreed upon expectations can be a challenge to the growth and development of both partners. However, it is important to remember that expectations should never be used for control; partners might voluntarily wish to live up to such expectations, but would have to freely do so, not through intimidation or threat. When one person decides not to live up to an expectation, the other might experience some hurt; in an intimate relationship, that hurt will be shared by both.

- Each becomes defined by setting *boundaries* and limitations. Each becomes present and revealed as desires and expectations are expressed.

- *Sexual charge* and intimacy are separate phenomena. Although they can be brought together in one relationship, there is a tendency for the sexual charge to diminish as intimacy increases (see below, "A Perspective On Sexuality"). This can be a creative challenge for couples who wish to keep sexual excitement alive.

- *Guilt* interrupts intimacy. When people feel guilty, they tend to withdraw from the contact boundary, indulging in self-recrimination.

When guilt is acknowledged and shared, intimacy becomes possible again. *Shame* involves self-revelation, and tends to enhance intimacy.[3]

- *Pride* maintains distance; letting go of a prideful stance permits more intimacy.

- Having to be *"right"* results in an invulnerability that is destructive to intimacy. When both parties can have their own unique points of view without one or the other having to be right, then their intimacy can flourish.

- Whenever a conflict bogs down, either party can call *"time out"*—a period of time without processing—in order to find some breathing space, to gain a more balanced perspective. When either calls "time out," the request should be respected.

- *Curiosity* facilitates intimacy. When both parties are curious, they can work through the prideful, righteous stances that keep them at a distance.

- *Blame* kills intimacy. Whenever one person blames the other, no intimacy is possible.

Two Solitudes

The path of intimate relationship is not for everyone. Indeed, it may be inappropriate for many. The rewards of intimacy include personal growth, the experiencing of authenticity and personal freedom, the sharing of aloneness, and a sense of fulfilment. The prerequisite is *courage* in two whole persons. To be intimate, both partners grow strong in their own separateness, sharing without depending.

The following poem illustrates this sharing:

Loved

The path to healing is one which leads into discomfort
There is no easy way to open old wounds
    without allowing them to bleed
And pain is so often the price of awareness, wisdom and love

Warriors may choose to walk alone
    experiencing life's dramas with power and fortitude
    crying in silence, dying in isolation
They become the heroes—the glorified
    but rarely the loved

Love comes in sharing
    watching, feeling and allowing
    my pain to mix with yours
It is in these shared experiences I find my strength .
    to face life's dramas with faith and confidence

For I am not alone
Your tears have become my strength,
    my courage to let go of my own
I treasure the tears we have shared
    just as I treasure our joy
It leads me down my path
    less afraid to bleed

Taking the steps to healing
    not dying in isolation
No hero
    worn and torn
        . . . . LOVED!!
                        —Susan Clark

Notes

1.   Bennet Wong and Jock McKeen, from a public lecture.

2.   J. McKeen and B.R. Wong, *The Relationship Garden* (Gabriola Island, B.C.: PD Publishing, 1996), pp. 31-32.

3.   Ibid., pp. 30-31.

Developmental Stages
of Loving

Man's creative struggle, his search for wisdom and truth, is a love story.
—Iris Murdoch [1]

Love: A Confusion in Meaning

The three most confusing words in the English language are surely "I love you." The child who says, "I love you, Mummy" cannot mean the same thing as the mother who responds with, "I love you too." Twenty years later, that same child who says to that same mother, "I love you, Mother," has quite a different picture of what that now means. Undoubtedly, the mother's response, using the same words, now means something different than it did twenty years previously. What has changed?

A young woman's "I love you" directed to her father has a considerably different meaning than those same words directed to her husband. Aside from the obviously different sexual connotations, there are usually other qualitative differences between these two. What is even more confusing is that twenty years later, those same words expressed by that same woman to that same husband now can have an entirely different overlay of meaning. Sometimes, each of the parties is unaware that the other attaches a different meaning to the phrase. Yet the words remain the same. What, then, has changed?

A man says, "I love you" to his lover; a child says the same to a pet cat or a doll; the same words are used between friends. During the 1970s, flower children said the phrase to everybody, even their enemies; now that they are older, a majority of the flower children have become like their previous enemies, and their expression of love has taken on a different meaning. Christians are exhorted to love others as themselves, which is easy to do

185

until their own lives or livelihood is threatened; then the words "I love you" seem more fitting to intimate situations. Again, the words remain the same. What has really changed?

In all of the above instances, although the words "I love you" remain constant, the *meaning* is different in each situation. Most people are confused by the many faces of love; the word "love" is used with different meanings in different contexts. Furthermore, with time, although the situation may remain fairly consistent, each person is likely to change. With changing needs, increasing maturity and understanding, heightened awareness and more experience, the meaning a person attaches to such words as "love," "independence," "need," and "commitment" changes.

The Growth of Love

A person grows through a process of change—physically, emotionally, mentally, and spiritually. As this occurs, the meanings of words will change within each individual. Words, like the people who use them, are also in a process of change. If people are to reach deeper levels of communication with one another, they must understand and accept that process. Love is recognized as one of the most essential of feelings that humans communicate to one another. The meaning of the word "love" changes as people mature, reflecting the stages of growth that they have achieved.

Love As A Commodity

Much confusion arises from seeing love as a commodity, something that can be exchanged in transactions. In this economic approach, a person seems to have only so much love to give, and must be a shrewd investor in order to ensure a healthy return from an involvement with another person. Love seen in this bartering sense can often lead to mistrust and conflict; partners are viewed as adversaries or competitors, to be approached with great caution.

Children are often regarded as empty vessels that must be filled up with love so that they can later give this love away to other people. According to this view, people can become depleted of love and need to refuel from someone else. Parents, children, and lovers become fixated in the pattern of exchanging love as if it were a commodity that can be used for barter and control of one another.

Dynamic View of Loving

If people manage to move beyond the restrictive concept of love as a currency, they can begin to see a dynamic quality to loving. When loving is more of a *state* than a commodity, the lover and the beloved are immediately freed from dependency and the fear of loss. From a dynamic view, loving is a *feeling in action*, in movement between people. It is a natural function of being human. Although loving is most easily recognized when there is an object of the loving, an object is not necessary; it is possible to just exist in a *state of loving*. Even if there is an object of loving, the love need not be returned.

This is a rare perspective. Most people generally choose to see the objects of their loving as investments; then, they are afraid to be vulnerable for fear of losing their love objects. The pain of loving often occurs when people's expectations for return of their love are not realized.

Approaches to Loving

People are capable of being loving; they are able to choose the object of their loving, or to have no object at all. This choice is based on individual factors, which are often neurotic in nature. Many people attempt to compensate for what they believe to be unmet needs from their early developmental history. It is possible to go beyond those needs to create a state of loving. Some people advocate a *transcendental* approach (i.e., going beyond themselves) to accomplish this. We ourselves prefer to remain more emotionally involved in the interpersonal personal growth project we have dubbed "the Relationship Garden." Thus, we advocate a *transformational* approach, wherein people grow and change the forms of expression of themselves, while accepting the immutability of some basic structures (see below, "Is Change Possible?"). Neither viewpoint is right—the approach is a matter of personal choice.

The Loving State

The loving state is one of *transparency*, without defence or covert intention. In being loving, people open to reveal their authentic nature; they accept being exposed and vulnerable, even though they might face rejection or judgments from others. People find self revelation is easier with others who value them as they are, not as someone to meet their expectations. When others respond with their own revelatory loving, there develops a *loving relationship*.

Each of us always benefits from our loving. In the presence of loving, others can choose to benefit in whatever ways they find suitable. We believe that the greatest benefit comes from returning that loving with similar self-revelatory loving— authenticity invites authenticity. By so doing, people can participate in a regenerative growth process.

The Developmental Stages of Loving

Our companion book, *The Relationship Garden*, has a long chapter on this topic; hence, this section will merely summarize the developmental stages of loving.[2] Love is *not a thing*, object, or noun; it is an *action*, a verb, involving emotions. It is the moving *energy of union*, involving an *empathetic* process, in a live *state of being*. Through loving, people are able to *locate* themselves in the scheme of things. Loving is a way people can *illuminate* and *reveal* their deepest nature (the Authentic Self), both to themselves and to others. Each person can experience loving as a *process*, in a variety of ways and on many possible levels; the earlier ways persist as felt possibilities, even as the individual progresses in age and experience. The following ways are arranged in rough order according to the maturational process; they are cumulative, but not necessarily serial in nature.

- **Loving is Supportive** At birth, helpless dependent children experience that they are loved when others take care of them. As they grow, people carry remnants of infantile insecurity for the rest of their lives, even though they generally become reasonably self-reliant persons capable of looking after themselves. Deep down inside there remains the fear of being abandoned (which to the infant would mean death); to be loved in a supportive way seems to provide some temporary relief. A person arrested in development at this stage will be emotionally field dependent, requiring the approval of others and needing to be needed by others. Often, on the positive side, such people become caretakers, or religious or political leaders; on the negative side, they can become socially, emotionally, and medically helpless. Characteristically, they become placating, manipulating, controlling, and sometimes openly threatening. Loving, supportive people (both positive and negative) *need* one another to find security and meaning in life.

- **Loving is Enstrengthening** As children mature, they become interested in mastery of their own life, beginning with crawling, walking, and talking. As they experiment with these skills, they constantly monitor their parents' reactions, seeking approval for their newly discovered independence. If the parents have a need to be needed, they will often be overprotective, subtly discouraging their children's explorations. More secure parents will encourage their children's ever-increasing steps toward independence and autonomy. Similarly, in adulthood, loving persons take pleasure in witnessing their loved ones becoming more of themselves as persons, full of their own strength and less needy of the approval of others.

- **Loving is Enlightening** The individuation process involves an ever-increasing self-awareness and self-knowledge. Loving interactions involve direct mirroring, providing information, experiences, encouragement and feedback in a caring way. Too often, responses are not offered lovingly; when people are critical, disapproving, and controlling, they foster compliance and contribute to the impairment of the individual's self-esteem.

- **Loving is Valuing the Person** Loving sees the other as an autonomous being, separate and whole, *not* as a possession or an object. Unfortunately, most children are raised in objectified roles (e.g. "good son," "successful student," "loving daughter") without having much experience of being valued for the persons they are. Thus, they tend to objectify themselves and lose touch with their authentic nature.

- **Loving is Pleasuring** Loving people find pleasure in the pleasure of others; they take delight in witnessing the spark of life that is ignited in the joy of another. One person does not cause or provide pleasure in the other; nevertheless, the pleasure one person feels can contribute to the situation in which the other finds delight. *The pleasure is in the loving itself*, not in any commodity exchanged.

- **Loving is Recognition** In loving recognition, the being of one person is witnessed by the other. When people are vulnerable and open, they are able to be revealed to each other; in recognizing each other and sharing together, they come to be known more fully to themselves and to each other.

- **Loving is Being Vulnerable and Intimate** During the developmental years, most endeavours are for security and survival. The process of education promotes defences such as roles, achievements, and compliance. Etiquette and morality are taught in the home and at church. Each person learns how to control emotions, overcome impulsiveness, and manipulate others. Although these are all necessary to achieve success as a responsible member of society, people often lose themselves in being trapped by these conventions. In intimacy, people share themselves with each other by shedding those defences (by now a difficult task). To present themselves authentically in a vulnerable (defenceless) way is risky and often anxiety-provoking; but to do so is an essential aspect of loving. Without vulnerability, relationships become entombed in roles, and the persons remain strangers to one another. Personal growth becomes possible through vulnerability, in an intimate dialogue.

- **Loving is Accepting** People remain hidden in the roles of the Ideal Self; underlying this process is self-hatred, which helps to maintain the self-objectification that keeps them defended. When people embark upon a developmental process of self-compassion through the *four A's* (awareness, acknowledgement, acceptance, action), they can become in touch with their deeper authentic nature. They become more loving as they accept themselves more; as they experience more self-compassion, they are more open to love others by accepting them too.

- **Loving is Sharing** Between people, whatever is shared can enhance intimacy. To be loving is to offer to share whoever and whatever we are and whatever we do, our own space and time, our knowledge and understandings, our histories and experiences, our concerns and personal hurts, our fears and excitements, our possessions and our needs, our sadness and joy. The more we do so, the more of ourselves we reveal and know. Even anger can be shared to enhance intimacy, when it is given boundaries and not used to threaten and control the other (as is too often the case). When persons share in this way, they express more of themselves and become more individuated through establishing an *interdependence*. When sharing is impaired, as it is in most families, the children often need to rebel to become independent and individualized, but not individuated. Sharing helps to establish boundaries and autonomy; in contrast, caretaking and obligations establish walls and dependency.

- **Loving is Co-Creating** When loving is shared, people experience a *spiritual bond*. In this state of mutual sharing, caring, and revelation, people become more of themselves, more authentic and more fully present to one another. In this loving state, people emit an energy of wholeness, light, and peace that is easily discernible to others. Such people involve themselves in co-creative projects, sharing their loving with others in inspirational ways.

- **Loving is Eternal** Persons who love and are loved become part of a dynamic relationship in which each is *transformed*. The presence of each is indelibly etched in the ever-developing pattern of the other, and can never be lost. The essence of loving is forever.

A Loving Life

Loving is a vital aspect of each human life. We are each challenged to develop our capacity for loving, and engage with others in communion.

Notes

1. Iris Murdoch, quoted in *The Spirit of Loving*, edited by E.H. Sell (Boston: Shambhala , 1995), p. 22.

2. J. McKeen and B.R. Wong, *The Relationship Garden* (Gabriola Island, B.C.: PD Publishing, 1996), pp. 175-99.

Sexuality

Much confusion exists in the area of sexuality—because the topic is emotionally highly charged, because of lack of agreement on definitions of terms, and because of a scarcity of well-researched knowledge about the subject. In our presentations about sexuality, we find that people frequently become fixated on one aspect of the subject, reflecting a deeply personal bias for or against a particular point; they then stop listening, failing to recognize the whole picture that is being addressed. In this chapter, we divide the subject of sexuality into a number of component parts; nevertheless, it is important not to lose sight of the overall perspective. Sexuality is an important and compelling part of life and relationships, and warrants much attention and understanding.

The Romance of Sexuality

The most exciting time in a relationship is often the beginning period (the stage of Romance), when not much is known about one another, but much is imagined. People's dreams, fantasies, and hopes for the future contribute to their romantic vision. This vision is highly personal, containing within it the individual's past history and life experiences, positive and negative. New partners project upon each other, with the exciting prospect that, at last, their romantic vision will become a reality! When one person's romance fits the other's, the relationship becomes even more compelling. The concomitant anxiety that the romance will not become a reality—and that rejection is a definite possibility—serves to heighten the excitement. Often, people anticipate that a sexual experience will be the ultimate expression of that romance. In the stage of Romance, people are not intimate, since they are relating to mutual image projections.[1]

The End of Romance

Given two people who have discovered mutually satisfying romantic visions and who enjoy a relationship that finds expression in shared sexual excitement, what could possibly go wrong? In North American society most couples come together in this romantic fashion. Within five years the majority of those relationships have ended in separation or divorce. In most instances, these endings are accompanied by bitterness, anger, or depression, with the experience of failure and low self-esteem. For many, the intrusion of reality destroys the initial flush of romance. As people become more known to each other (an important aspect of intimacy), they find increasing difficulty in fitting their partners into the romantic roles that they initially expected. Finally, they realize that the romantic dream was impossible. Although their capability for finding intimacy has increased, most people tend not to value that possibility. Instead, their focus remains on seeking more romance, and they become fixated on the lack of heady excitement and thrills that characterize the early stage of Romance. For many people, when the romance goes, the relationship dies.

Romance Or Intimacy

Obviously, romance and reality tend to be mutually exclusive—one interrupts the other. Since intimacy is the expression of shared authenticity (the reality of the persons), it seems that romance and intimacy are also mutually exclusive. Because sexual excitement is often based on romance, is it possible that sexual excitement and intimacy are also mutually exclusive? That proposal deserves further consideration.

Intimacy and Sexual Charge Are Different

A major area of confusion lies in the use of the word "intimacy" as a euphemism to denote sexual intercourse. Often, when people refer to an "intimate relationship," what they mean is a sexual relationship. Throughout this book, the word "intimacy" is used specifically to represent the state of vulnerability, openness, and sharing that can exist between two people. Certainly, sexual experiences can be intimate; but, in our findings with people, usually they are not. In our view, *sexual excitement and intimacy are separate phenomena*; they do not naturally or readily fit together. Indeed, in common experience they tend to work

DIMENSIONS OF SEXUALITY

	Biological	Sensual-Erotic	Sexual Charge	Romantic	Aesthetic/Mythic	Trans-personal
Location	Physical	Physical	Mental-Emotional	Mental	Deeper Nature	Higher Self
Motivation	Relieve Tension	Relieve Tension	Overcome Helplessness	Relieve Anomie	Emotional Spiritual	Meaningfulness
System	Endocrine	Diencephalic A.N.S. (prim. parasymp.)	Cortical A.N.S. (prim. sympath.)	Cortical A.N.S. (prim. parasymp.)	Cortical R.A.S. (limbic system?)	Higher Self (pineal gland?)
Mode	Ejaculatory	Stroking	Penetration/Fenestration	Image Management	Meaning Management	Ecstasy
Purpose	Reproduction	Pleasure/Pain	Domination/Submission	Control	Meaning Attribution	Union
Means	Organic	Sensory	Symbolic	Symbolic	Sensory/Symbolic	Ineffable (Inarticulate)
Intimacy	Impersonal	Impersonal	Impersonal	Impersonal	Impersonal	Impersonal

against each other—as intimacy develops, sexual excitement tends to diminish. George Bernard Shaw seemed to think so, when he wrote *Man And Superman*; in one section of the play, a man and a woman discuss sex and intimacy:

> Don Juan: *Do my sex the justice to admit, señora, that we have always recognized that the sex relation is not a personal or friendly relation at all.*
>
> Ana: *Not a personal relation! What relation is more personal? More sacred? More holy?*
>
> Don Juan: *Sacred and holy, if you like, Ana, but not personally friendly. Your relation to God is sacred and holy; dare you call it personally friendly? In the sex relation the universal creative energy, of which the parties are both helpless agents, overrides and sweeps away all personal considerations, and dispenses with all personal relations.*[2]

Categorizing Sexuality

For the sake of discussion, the large topic of sexuality will be considered under the following six headings: Biological, Sensual-Erotic, Sexual Charge, Romantic, Aesthetic/Mythic and Transpersonal. The chart "Dimensions of Sexuality" summarizes the qualities of each aspect. We have discussed these distinctions at length in *The Relationship Garden*.[3]

Biological Aspects of Sexuality

The biological aspects of sexuality are generally taken for granted, even though there are many gaps in our knowledge of this very important subject. A common assumption is that the sexual drive is biologically determined, mediated by a complex neurohormonal network that affects the mechanisms of behaviour. Simply stated, people are genetically patterned to produce the appropriate hormones to prepare their bodies for the characteristic sexual functioning and behaviours that drive them toward consummation in the act of sexual intercourse with a person of the opposite sex. The *telos* (purpose) of this is, of course, continuation of the species.

If the above assumption is correct, the natural history of sexual behaviour would go something like the following. The male animal has a relatively stable hormonal balance, offering a preparedness for—but not a drive toward—sexual activity (contrary to popular belief). The female of the species has a complex inner rhythmic cycle of events, a delicate orchestration of hormonal balances. When ovulation is uninhibited, it occurs approximately once a month. In order to enhance the chances of fertilization of the ovum at that time, a subtle chemical intoxicant (a pheromone) is emitted into the atmosphere; if that pheromone can make contact with the male, it will stimulate his sexual neurohormonal apparatus, and he will seek out the female. Sexual intercourse would be the result—but only once a month! This is "natural" (i.e., according to nature) sexuality, determined by human biology. From this point of view, all other sexual behaviour is considered "unnatural" or "perverse" (because its aim is something other than reproduction). Some religions have adopted a moral position based on biological assumptions, claiming that only what is "natural" is morally acceptable. The logical extension of this thesis is that all sexual intercourse other than at the time of ovulation is not only "unnatural," but also immoral! Obviously, biological sexuality involves pre-human drives, and hence is *not personal* to the individual; if there is a personal aspect to sexuality, it is not to be found in the biological domain.

The Sensual-Erotic

The next level of sexual interest to discuss occurs in relation to the organization of the nervous system. The body's neurological apparatus is excited by different stimuli, providing a wide variety of pleasant and unpleasant experiences. Some specific areas (the erogenous zones), when touched or stroked in particular ways, stimulate an excitement or arousal that is described as "sexual." More specifically, *it is a sensual arousal to which sexual meanings are attached.* Stimulation through touch (stroking, texture, warmth, and so on) is only one of many possible perceptual arousals; for example, stimulation is possible through vision (colour, form, size, darkness), hearing (music, sounds of breathing, silence), smell (body odours, perfumes), and taste (body tastes, food, drinks). Such arousal through sensual stimulation constitutes the sensual-erotic aspect of sexuality. This is largely mediated through the parasympathetic nervous system, which produces relaxation and a general feeling of well-being.

The sensual-erotic aspect of sexuality is valued to varying degrees by different people. To some, it is the most important aspect of sexuality; to others, it is only the means to a more exciting end. A wide variety of tactile stimuli can be eroticised, ranging on a pleasure-pain continuum from tender caresses and gentle massage all the way to rough handling, pinching, biting, and hitting. The characteristic pattern of western civilization is gentle caressing and fondling. The sensual-erotic arousal is not necessarily related to any specific person or object; stroking of the senses is all that is necessary to produce the pleasant, erotic experience. In this way, the *sensual-erotic is essentially impersonal*; the specific person that provides that stroking is secondary.

Sensual-erotic experiences are basically physical, mediated through the neurological sensory apparatus. In the brain, the centres chiefly responsible for integration and experiencing of the stimuli are in the diencephalon, which functions below the level of the thinking brain. Since these brain structures are common to all higher animals, not only humans, these experiences are basically naturalistic, and hence *impersonal*.

The Sexual Charge

Sex is engaging in the first rounds; what sustains interest in the long run is power.—Madam Jiang Qing[4]

The sensual-erotic experience can be poetically described as soft and rounded, pleasant, but not compelling. There is another kind of sexual experience that is sharper, more highly charged, more acute and immediate, more urgent and driven—the sexual charge. Sexual charge is largely mediated through the sympathetic nervous system (which has been described as the "fight/flight/fright" system). The sexually charged experience is *impersonal*—generally in relation to a sexual *object*. The specific person is secondary, as in the sensual-erotic experience. Unlike the sensual-erotic, which is biological and sensory, the sexually charged experience is primarily stimulated by *symbols*. The process is basically a mental one, involving the cerebral cortex, which functions with symbols. Objects (including language and objectified people) are assigned particular meanings that are then related to specific and highly personalized feelings. The process of symbolization is important to the development of civilization and its culture; at the same time, however, it tends to turn us away from our natural roots and tendencies. It is a learned process, determined by the interaction of the individual with the culture.

In the symbolic, charged form of sexual excitement, each individual reflects a combination of influences involving the culture (the cultural romance) and his or her personal history.[5] From an existential point of view, underlying both of these influences are unresolved childhood issues—an ongoing fear of helplessness and annihilation, ruminations of worthlessness and self-doubt, and, ultimately, a fear of abandonment by others that (for the infant) could lead to death. The solution offered by society is for each individual to master survival skills and to control the environment—especially the people in that environment—making life predictable. Thus each individual is caught in a struggle for power. At the same time that one wants to control others, there is a desire to submit, to give over and have someone else take charge. This craving for domination and submission becomes the main theme that underlies the sexual experience at the symbolic level; it is what fires the excitement for the sexual charge.

The chief means of expressing the domination/submission theme in sexuality is through sexual intercourse. The desire is for either penetration or fenestration (being entered or penetrated), which are opposite sides of the same coin. The underlying theme is control—both the dominator and one who submits feel triumphant in being strongly desired and needed by the other. Both experience validation and temporarily lose their fear of abandonment. To varying degrees, all interaction between people can be seen as embodying this domination/submission theme. There is a sexually charged excitement in the pursuit of a loved object in the romantic stage of any sexual relationship, on the dance floor or at a cocktail party. There is the thrill of domination when the other person fully agrees, verbally or behaviourally, to do one's bidding. The possibility of failure, of being rejected, only serves to heighten the excitement. There is equal power in submission; many people experience a thrill in being the object of desire or of domination. After a time, the excitement diminishes when the surrender and domination have become commonplace and taken for granted; this occurs in the majority of committed relationships within five years.

Sexual Charge and Objectification

The sexual charge involves a sexualized version of an early fantasied power theme, which often involves a reversal of childhood victimization. In the sexual charge, and choice of partner to dominate, there is a retelling of a life story (see above, "Objectification"). People do not experience a sexual charge with everyone. There are thousands of components that go into making up the sexual charge (gender, age, size, shape, colouring, voice tone, attitudes, and other personality attributes). *One is not sexually attracted to a person; rather, one is attracted to an object* that most closely fits the elements in a now unconscious childhood fantasy.[6] The elements in sexual attraction are the components of a theme of power and domination that is seeking realization. Individuals are not attracted to just anyone; they are attracted to someone (their "microdot") who most closely fits the elements of a character in their fantasy; by so doing, they are attempting to compensate for earlier experiences of victimisation, traumas or simply a sense of inadequacy. Thus, in every sexual charge there is a story; in the "microdot" is a condensed object-icon that contains elements from earlier life needing reparation. They did not succeed in dominating in their past; hence, they now seek to dominate objects and images that reflect upon their past.[7]

In many ways, the sexual charge involves a revenge theme; individuals choose, not a person, but an object to dominate and control, to symbolically repair the problems of childhood powerlessness. This is largely a mental phenomenon—although it is experienced physically as a charge, the experience is mediated through the brain, in the unconscious fantasies of the cerebral cortex. This thesis denies the romantic myth that a sexual charge is for a distinct person. Indeed, from this perspective, the sexual charge is not personal at all; it has to do with the manipulation of a symbolized object that represents earlier unresolved incidents and traumas.

The Sexual Charge of Pornography

In the domination/submission theme there is always a symbolic victim. Depending upon one's point of view, the victim is either the dominator or the one who submits; actually, both are victims! All pornography graphically expresses that theme. Because most men are primarily visual in their sexual stimulation, the theme is represented in the ambience of the poses so readily found in pornographic magazines designed for men. Each posed model, through the positioning of the body and the look in the eye, offers both an invitation and a challenge. It is a good question to wonder who is the victim and who is in control—the model in the magazine, or the person who is driven to buy and view the pictures. Most sexually charged excitement carries this pornographic theme, even though morality often tries to deny and camouflage it. For most women (whose sexual charge tends to be less visually oriented than for many men), the theme runs through the *Harlequin Romances* in which the sweet young woman heroine typically tames and captures the wild, unmanageable hero. Rather than being stimulated by pictures, many women become charged with the fantasy of the domination/control plot or story. Both men and women crave to capture the consciousness of the other.[8]

Romantic Sexuality

As mentioned above, for some people the most exciting aspects of their relationship are involved in romantic activities. For them, the actual act of intercourse is less compelling than the events that lead to the bedroom. They enjoy flowers, candlelight dinners, soft music and conversation. Greeting cards, and telephone calls heighten their experience of being valued and cherished. They find a quiet dominance in having their partners satisfy these emblems of their ardour. These romantic expressions *represent* the importance that romantic lovers ascribe to each other; in themselves, they are *symbolic*, hence *not personal*.

Aesthetic Sexuality

For some people, their main attraction is to pursue beauty and form and grace; they experience pleasure in the *aesthetic*. For them, the human body and activity are most attractive as art. They become full of pleasure and excitement in appreciating dance or painting or sculpture. Their attraction to a partner is largely on the basis of that person's beauty. In this attraction, they are relating to the form, rather than the person; hence this form of sexuality is also *impersonal*.

Mythic Sexuality

Myths are stories that express deep patterns of existence. In the interplay between mythic characters, universal processes are described and enunciated. When these myths relate to the relationships between the sexes, and to the dynamics of masculine and feminine forces, they describe some common underlying themes in human sexual interactions. In day to day sexual expression, these universal aspects are largely unconscious; nevertheless, in many partners' sexuality, one can recognize these deeper elements in operation.

Transpersonal Dimensions of Sexuality

Experiencing a deep sense of loneliness, most people desperately attempt to join with others at numerous levels of interactions and relationships, including the sexual. When power and control are the aim, people seem doomed to endless repetition of acts of domination and submission, in a vain attempt to possess their partners forever.[9] Through *recognition* of each other in vulnerable sharing, people become personally *intimate* with each other, *revealed* and open. Sometimes, when people recognize their *union* with another (and the universe) they engage in a transpersonal experience.

Rarely in sexual engagements, individuals can profoundly let go, relinquishing personal limitations, to discover their unity with the rest of the universe. This is not an engagement or an act of joining with the other; it is *recognition* of the state of being *already joined* with the other. To experience that sexually requires moving beyond the fear of aloneness, and coming to terms with the fear of death. This involves a surrender *of* the self (not *to* the other, as in the case of *submission,* which is related to domination). In surrender, one is prepared to *die* in the arms of the other. Herein lies the *divine,* the *state of grace.*

The transpersonal dimension of sexuality involves letting go of individual concerns to experience *beyond oneself;* hence, transpersonal sexuality is *not personal.*

Individual Uniqueness in Sexuality

What is called "sexuality" is much more complex than people generally realize. Sexual interest involves elements from a variety of domains (here we have named six dimensions). Individuals value the various aspects in a unique, idiosyncratic manner; hence, everyone's sexuality is particular, and highly individual. From this point of view, what is called "sexual pathology" is often only individual uniqueness. Each person expresses sexual preferences, excitements, and practices that reflect individual life themes. Sexuality is the personal diary of each person's history, containing all the hopes and fears, the fantasies and experiences—indeed, the very meaning of that person's existence. It is no wonder that one's sexuality is so carefully guarded, even from one's self-awareness!

There is no area that adult partners cannot explore, provided there is *consent* between them. Sex therapists today are often much too mechanical in their ideas, advocating exercises and practices that would promote easier and more effective functioning of the sexual apparatus; what is missing is appreciation of the *meaning* of individual sexuality at the various levels. Instead of a therapist, often people need an understanding facilitator to pique their curiosity about the deeper meanings of sexual interest and activities, and to help them discover ways of sharing them.

Making Personal the Impersonal

In each of the dimensions we have named, sexuality is chiefly impersonal. The challenge in ongoing relationships is to uncover the sources of excitement (which are mostly impersonal) and then bring these into the intimate sharing of the relationship, *making personal the impersonal.*[10] Removed from the moral perspective, no act or desire is intrinsically wrong; what can be faulted is insensitive expression of a particular desire. The important word is *consent*: for growth and mutual benefit to occur, the participants in the relationship must agree on each aspect of the interaction. To transgress consent and personal boundaries converts the sexual experience into an act of *violence* (as in rape). Each person should be able to explore the meaning of particular desires and impulses in a context where no one is disadvantaged.

Decline of Sexual Excitement

When couples share their sources of excitement, they become more vulnerable and known to each other, enhancing their intimacy; as this happens, they objectify each other less. As they become more intimate, they have less fixation on domination and submission with each other; hence their sexual excitement tends to wane as they interact less symbolically, and more personally. Often, sexual experiences become more fulfilling, which for some has an excitement of its own. This "intimacy charge" relates more to excitement over surrendering than to submitting. Some people call this their sexual excitement, and are content with it.

Rediscovering Excitement

Those who are obsessed with domination/submission might become dissatisfied with the loss of such a charge, and seek therapy or want to change partners. When people want to rekindle sexual excitement in their relationship, they often need to explore creative ways of rediscovering domination/submission themes together. Fantasy, play-acting, stimulation of the senses, and exploration of pornographic stories and movies together are all possible approaches. Seeking experiences outside of the relationship is a common solution, but, because of the threat to the primary relationship, it is a risky one, and is generally not recommended.

Exploring Sexuality In An Intimate Relationship

Through sharing their unique sexual interests together, couples can enhance their intimacy and find a deepening understanding of themselves. In an ongoing relationship, partners can experience more freedom in discovering all the dimensions of being involved in sexuality, ranging from the profane to the divine. With this exploration they can find growth, self-discovery, appreciation of themselves and each other, an ever-growing closeness, and most of all, a greater personal sense of meaning in life!

Notes

1. J. McKeen and B.R. Wong, *The Relationship Garden* (Gabriola Island, B.C.: PD Publishing, 1996), p. 56.

2. G.B. Shaw, *Man and Superman* (Baltimore: Penguin Books, 1952), p. 163.

3. J. McKeen and B.R. Wong, *The Relationship Garden* (Gabriola Island, B.C.: PD Publishing, 1996), p. 154-74.

4. Madam Jiang Qing, quoted in *Time* March 21, 1977.

5. R. Stoller, *Sexual Excitement* (New York: Pantheon, 1979), pp. 13-14.

6. J. McKeen and B.R. Wong, *The Relationship Garden* (Gabriola Island, B.C.: PD Publishing, 1996), p. 165.

7. R. Stoller, *Sexual Excitement* (New York: Pantheon Books, 1979), p. 166.

8. J.M. Russell, "Sartre's Theory of Sexuality," in *Journal of Humanistic Psychology*, 19(2), Spring 1979, p. 41.

9. Ibid., p. 41.

10. J. McKeen and B.R. Wong, *The Relationship Garden* (Gabriola Island, B.C.: PD Publishing, 1996), p. 168-69.

Part Five:
HEALTH, ILLNESS AND HEALING

Healing

I am not a mechanism, an assembly of various sections.
And it is not because the mechanism is working wrongly,
     that I am ill.
I am ill because of wounds to the soul,
     to the deep emotional self
and the wounds to the soul take a long, long time,
     only time can help
and patience, and a certain difficult repentance
long, difficult repentance, realisation of life's mistake and
     the freeing oneself
from the endless repetition of the mistake
which mankind at large has chosen to sanctify.

—D.H. Lawrence [1]

1.   D.H. Lawrence, *The Complete Poems of D.H. Lawrence*, edited by V. de Sola Pinto and W. Roberts (New York: The Viking Press, 1971), p. 620.

Individual Responsibility in Illness and Health

Disease is nothing but life under altered conditions.—Virchow [1]

In earliest times, well-being was related to survival; individuals stayed well by avoiding physical dangers and hostile environments. Threatened and uncertain, humans developed superstitious beliefs in powerful spirits and gods that could do harm to individuals, sometimes just for sport. In recent centuries, scientific investigations have discovered a great number of causative agents (bacterial, viral, and chemical) that could negatively affect a person's well-being. Superstitious beliefs have developed around these entities too; they are our modern spooks and goblins.

Invasion By Illness

Thus, humankind is cast into an adversarial role in relationship to the environment. Healthy survival depends upon how well the environment is controlled. For example, if we are not careful to shield ourselves from the possibility of a viral attack, we will likely succumb to a cold; we become "victims" to some invading forces that lack respect for our integrity and well-being. Excessive worry about these forces could cause us to avoid all sources of possible contamination, including other people, as well as set off a campaign to clean up the environment, way beyond any reasonable standard. This paranoid attitude seems more and more common; with this view, people need to be vigilant in order to avoid ill health. They fortify their defences to protect them from these ever-present noxious invaders; in so doing, they also produce an increasing separation between themselves and their surroundings.

The Alternative: Responsibility

Yet, many of these "enemies" are omnipresent, living in harmony nearby, perhaps even comfortably ensconced somewhere within our bodies. A simple example is the cold virus, which probably lives in most of our throats much of the time. Why then, do we come down with a cold only at certain times? A common belief is that the virus has been waiting for the opportunity to "invade" our bodies, perhaps when we get overly tired or when we eat the wrong things. Another possibility is that sometimes a cold can be useful, that the helplessness it produces might serve us. Certainly, as children we learn that helplessness provides us with many secondary benefits—we get attention, we get excused from chores, school, or work, and perhaps we even receive special foods. Is it possible that when we grow older, we are not above reaping the benefits of a cold? Perhaps having a cold provides a rationalization for a much-needed rest which we otherwise would feel too guilty to take? Certainly, in the climate of our current times, the helpless receive much more attention and assistance than do the competent.

The Meaning of Disease

The idea that we are responsible for our own illness patterns might explain some hitherto inexplicable behaviour—why the obese continue to overeat, or alcoholics continue to drink even though their actions are ruining their lives, or people with heart disease or emphysema continue to smoke. Although these people would like to believe that they are helpless victims of their addictions, it seems likely that they benefit in some way from their symptoms. Perhaps the obese person is attempting to pad the body as a means of avoiding intimacy; perhaps the alcoholic is afraid to face the possibility of failure, and drinks so that nobody will expect much; perhaps the smoker is keeping feelings under control because to express real emotions (such as anger or passion) might drive others away. Whatever the requirement, the body cooperates with symptoms of an illness process that serves the person's particular needs. Thus, whenever a person has symptoms, or a diagnosed illness, there is an underlying *meaning* of these symptoms to be discovered. The body will speak what the mouth cannot, or *will* not!

Fixations in *Qi* Energy

The ancient Chinese conceived of life force energy, which they called qi energy (pronounced "chee"). Their hypothesis was that this life-force energy comes into the being at the time of conception, exists in the individual throughout his or her lifetime, and departs at death. During the person's life, the qi energy continually flows through meridian pathways; the pattern created by this flow constitutes the energy body matrix (energy body), which is the essential pattern of that being. This energy body is radiant, and manifests on various dimensions of a person—spiritual, emotional, physical, intellectual and environmental. In the view of the ancients, if the energy flow in the matrix is balanced and harmonious, the organism functions freely, without illness. To the extent that fixations arise within the energy body, there will be a disruption in the harmony and balance at the level of essence, which is manifest as disturbance or disease in the various dimensions of the person. Everyone has some degree of fixation; these are the holding patterns that underlie the particular personality characteristics. When these fixations become severe, or persist for a long time, they can manifest as diseases. These fixations cause the energy to deviate from the healthy state into illness patterns that are manifested intellectually, physically, emotionally, spiritually and environmentally. Since these fixations are a product of people's life style and attitudes, each individual is *responsible* (but *not* to blame) for illness. The fixations may be generated and maintained by subconscious processes; nevertheless, even though they are often not aware, at some level the individual is the one that maintains the patterns that manifest as diseases.[2]

Emotional Fixations

By withholding the expression of emotions, a person produces obstructions in the energy body matrix, which contribute towards illness patterns in the essence energy. These constricted patterns can manifest on the other dimensions of being as illness (physical disease, mental disorder, spiritual distress, environmental disharmony or more emotional problems). The mechanisms to inhibit emotional expression include *withdrawal*, *repression*, and *denial*. Emotions are held back through very limited breathing; when people learn to breathe more deeply, filling their lungs, they can find more ready expression of their emotions, and become more in touch with themselves. By becoming aware of the nature of these mechanisms, one can overcome them and learn to express emotions instead of repressing them. The more the individual can let emotions flow, the more the life energy can run freely and the more that healing and awareness can develop. Often the individual encounters a great deal of fear overlaying the blocked emotions. By refusing to flee from the fear, people can allow the emotions to emerge; instead of contracting, they can open to more learning, and growth can occur.

Physical Fixation

Illness is also created and sustained on the physical level. Lack of exercise engenders sluggishness and dis-ease. Certain exercises done in an ambitious, goal-oriented way tend to tighten the physical being into a particular pattern, producing restriction and lack of flow. These physical limitations correspond to a rigidly patterned energy body matrix. Goal-oriented athletic pursuits often maintain the rigidity; note that it is the goal-orientation that engenders the limitation, not the exercise itself. Expressive exercises, such as free-form tai ji and creative dance, are probably better for fluid energy flow than are tightly disciplined activities. In fact, any exercise done creatively for self-expression can help to open up the person; any activity that is goal directed will invite contraction. And yet if certain people are goal-oriented types, they are unwise to simply deny their tendency; instead, they can learn to become more fluid, even in the midst of striving.

The maintenance of the open healthy state is also determined by what one ingests. A well-balanced diet engenders healthy functioning and growth, whereas an inadequate diet fails to provide the necessary nourishment. The use of alcohol, nicotine, and other drugs can also sustain blocks, limiting the natural self-expression.

Spiritual Fixation

Illness can manifest at the spiritual level; as well, fixations on the spiritual dimension can create illness. Victor Frankl said that "Man's search for meaning is a primary force in his life."[3] In creativity, people express meaning beyond their self-limitations. Frankl quotes Nietzsche: "He who has a *why* to live for can bear almost any *how*."[4] When this sense of meaning is lost, illness patterns may substitute for it; frequently, the illness becomes the meaning. To find personal meaning in life and to channel energy into creative activity aids the spiritual rebirth that generates health, well-being, and growth.

Overly disciplined spiritual activity can also result in blocks to free expression. Excessive involvement in yoga, meditation, special diets, and other similar pursuits can limit the individual rather than expand awareness.[5] Inherent in excessive discipline is *spiritual ambition*; literally, the individual wants to get somewhere spiritually. In this ambition and the compulsive behaviour that results, a tightening occurs in the energy matrix, expressed as a contraction in the person. In a paradoxical way, the ambition to become spiritually expanded results in a contracted state. The first step in overcoming this contraction is often through the awareness that excessive spiritual discipline can induce it; this awareness may facilitate greater expansion and freer self-expression.

Intellectual Rigidity

Intellectual openness and fluidity sustain health and growth. Fixated intellectual patterns restrict the being; illness can result from such limitation. The intellect performs the symbolization of life experiences; one of its main functions is communication. Investment in specific concepts to the exclusion of others constitutes a rigidification into a judgmental attitude. Such an attitude is reflected in the contraction in the energy state that underlies many illnesses. Acknowledging rigidity and working toward more intellectual flow and grace promotes healing and growth. With the awareness that one's attitude contributes to the creation and maintenance of illness, one can use symptoms as biofeedback, to alert one to the possibility of attitudinal rigidity. By this process of awareness, one can deeply affect the condition of the energy state.

Individual Responsibility

All of us create our own life situations and are responsible for our state of health or disease. Wherever illness is present—spiritual, emotional, physical, intellectual, or environmental—people are responsible for the creation and maintenance of the patterns that the illness reflects. Once again, *this responsibility is not blame*; it merely acknowledges the individual's *participation*. By accepting responsibility for sickness and health, one can move through and beyond illness patterns, into states of well-being and openness. In the process, one can learn about motives and fixations, and discover more of the hidden aspects of one's life.

MindBody Unity

Central to Chinese energy theory is the notion that the various dimensions of being are actually a unity. Complementary medical approaches speak of "mind/body" unity. The full descriptive term should be "body/mind/emotions/spirit/environment" unity. The apparent separateness of mind, body, spirit, emotions and environment is an expression of our unique human viewpoint (which occurs in normal maturation and development); at a fundamental level, our various "parts" are integrally related to each other, they are each other. An illness on one level will show on the other levels. For example, from this perspective, there is no such thing as a physical illness separate from mental distress. Spiritual ailments are reflected in the mental state, in the body, and indeed in the environment. It is possible for an illness state to be primarily on one of these dimensions; nevertheless, the process will also occur throughout the other dimensions, since they are a unity.

Various Manifestations of Illness

In this book, we have concentrated on a limited number of illnesses—depression, allergies, phobias, boundary illnesses, multiple sclerosis, and memory disturbances (see above, "Depression," and below, "Keeping the World At Bay: Allergies and Phobias," Multiple Sclerosis: Some Impressions," "The Walking Wounded: A Way of Life" and "Memories of Abuse: A Call For A Balanced Perspective"). This is primarily because we have had occasion over the years to write about these subjects with the feedback of clients and friends. The principles we outline would also apply to more extended discussions on cancer, diabetes, and arthritis. Perhaps a future book will contain writings on these subjects. At this time, we are at work on papers relating to cancer and arthritis. They are not in a state of readiness as this book goes to print; hence, we plan to publish these works elsewhere.

Using Symptoms for Location

As we have discussed (see above, "Location"), one of our human tasks is to locate ourselves, and make a world for ourselves. In the midst of profound insecurity and anxiety (see above, "Anxiety: Friend Or Foe?"), humans struggle to find some dependable security. Many people find predictability in suffering. Although they experience discomfort in illness processes, they also come to know these very well, and often are reluctant to give up their symptoms for fear of the emptiness that rises when they depart from what they know. Suffering is not pleasant; but, it can be predictable and familiar. Thus, illnesses and various symptoms and different ways of suffering can provide a way for individuals to locate themselves.

Illness and Health in Relationships

People manifest their fixations in relationships, often defending themselves with each other from fear or insecurity. In this holding back, they tighten in their energy; this can ultimately manifest as illness.

It would seem logical that people would do better without other people. When individuals have had a history of enduring violence or boundary violation, they are often reluctant to come close to others. They believe their hesitancy keeps them safe (as at one time it probably did). They develop patterns of withdrawal or defensiveness in order to protect themselves from violation. Yet, in this walled approach, they tighten in themselves, and set the stage for illness to take root.

We sometimes give a talk humorously entitled "Relationships Make Me Sick." The main thesis is that illnesses arise from the fixated stances acquired in early relationships. These attitudes of tightness persist in later relationships; they give rise to distress on the various levels of being, and can ultimately manifest as full-blown illness states. The holding back in the relationship has produced the illness. We go on to say that an intimate relationship can be a garden where people can discover themselves, their loving, their meaning and their health and vitality; but this takes the courage to face difficult issues.

So, relationships are where people become stuck. Yet in relationships, people can also become free. When they are willing to engage in an ongoing relationship of intimacy and revelation, they can face the fear of coming close to someone else, and can thus open their capacity for engagement with their partners, with themselves, and with life. The relationship becomes a place of healing.

Dialogical Healing

Our work together over almost three decades has focussed on the relationships area. We are more and more convinced that illnesses are most often an expression of some separation. Healing occurs when the apparent separation is rejoined. Much of human ailments reside in the domain of flawed relationships, with objectification and isolation being key factors in maintaining distance. People can heal from this by becoming vulnerable with each other, opening and revealing their authentic nature, becoming inclusive of the world of each other. Through dialogue, people can come to appreciate, know and love each other and themselves. To us, *all healing occurs in dialogue*.

Learning to Dialogue for Health

In our work, people frequently come to our programs for help. They often approach the leaders in the traditional framework of seeking healing from a professional. If the leaders were to succumb to this invitation, people could remain tied to them, and fail to make use of the group process. In the group activities, people are invited to reveal their inner thoughts and feelings, becoming vulnerable with each other. As they do this over the days of a program, they establish intimate relationships with other members of the group, and come to feel more at home with themselves. They practice open communication, and acquire skills that they can use to open with others when they choose; the group is like a learning laboratory where they develop skills of intimacy. Having learned and practised these skills, graduates can take these abilities to their significant life relationships (with family, spouses, lovers, and business associates), in order to develop and sustain ongoing intimacy. In this atmosphere, they learn to open themselves, to release the blockages in interpersonal energies. With this unblocking comes release of life flow; in this way, people are healed in the intimate relationships they develop.

Learning From Our Illnesses

In the healthy open state, the person can grow and mature, to reach the full depth and expanse of self-expression and individuation. This does not mean avoiding illness; rather, it means embracing whatever illnesses we have:

> *Medicine can cure the body. But soul, poetry, is capable of living in, longing for, choosing illness. Only the most fanatic researcher upon cancer could share with the poet the concept that cancer is a flower, an adventure, an intrigue with life.* —Robert Duncan [6]

Notes

1. Rudolf Virchow quoted in K. Menninger, M. Mayman and P. Pruyser, *The Vital Balance* (New York: Viking Press, 1963), p. 41.

2. D. Connelly, *Traditional Acupuncture: The Law of the Five Elements* (Columbia, MD: Center for Traditional Acupuncture, 1979).

3. V.E. Frankl, *Man's Search For Meaning* (New York: Simon and Schuster, 1962), p. 97.

4. Ibid., p. 76.

5. B.R. Wong and J. McKeen, *In And Out Of Our Own Way*, (Gabriola Island, B.C.: PD Publishing, 1995), pp.34-35.

6. Robert Duncan, in *The New American Poetry* edited by D.M.Allen (New York: Grove Press, 1960), p. 403.

Empathy, Resonance and Energy

When two people understand each other in their inmost hearts, their
words are sweet and strong, like the fragrance of orchids.
                                                    —Confucius [1]

Empathy, Inclusion and Resonance

According to Webster's Dictionary, *empathy* is "the imaginative projection
of one's own consciousness into another being."[2] *Inclusion* is the deepest
expression of empathy, involving very sensitive interactions in an I-Thou
dialogue (see above, "Objectification"). *Resonance* is a phenomenon of
energy. One tuning fork responds to the vibrations of another tuning fork
of the same frequency by beginning to vibrate itself; they vibrate together
in resonance. Similarly, when two people are close and identify with each
other, this vibrational activity of resonance occurs between them. Empathy
and inclusion are psychological expressions of that resonance.

Metabolic Energy and Universal Energy

There are two types of energy: *metabolic energy* and *universal energy*.
Metabolic energy is the byproduct of digestion and assimilation of food; it
is a physical energy, which is limited and can be depleted. On the other
hand, there is no limitation to universal energy; it is boundless, and ever
present.

Energy Transfer: A Common Misconception

A common notion is that empathy is one individual's capacity to actually
feel another person's feeling, much as understanding is one's ability to know
another's ideas. Frequently, reference is made to an ability to feel another
person's "vibes" (vibrations), suggesting some form of *energy transfer*; for

example, people think they can feel someone else's anger or sadness by taking in the vibration. Many believe that one person can affect the lives of others through energy vibrations; thus, people are seen to have responsibility for the emotional lives of those around them. A common belief is that some people's energy is "toxic" and should be avoided, and the energy of others is "nutritive."

The human body creates metabolic energy through the process of digesting and assimilating food. That energy is the fuel for people's experiences, including their emotions. Most assume that this energy is able to influence and control others; the greater the energy, the more powerful the person, behaviour, or feeling. People generally believe this energy can be transmitted to others, to heal or harm them. Furthermore, sensitive people seem to "pick up" this energy, to absorb it, to feel what others feels. Such a notion supports the concept of field dependence. It is as though we are radio receivers in the midst of a huge number of transmitted energy vibrations, vulnerable to their influences.

We propose that the notion of energy transfer involves a number of misconceptions, and that no energy can ever be transferred.

Caretaking and Burnout

Having lost the sense of connection with themselves and with others, most people have opted for a political rather than personal mode of relating; thus, they take care of each other's welfare and feelings. In energy terms, they depend upon their metabolic energy, since they have lost touch with the universal energy. [3]They try to use their metabolic energy in order to influence people and things around them, to ensure their own safety. Life takes on all the attributes of obligations and roles, made possible only by blocking the experience of the cosmic energy flow, through objectification and defensiveness. Of course, this is an appealing option because it provides excitement and a sense of meaning in life.

This notion of separation sets up a motif where people seem to be able to help each other and be helped. Indeed, social agencies have been developed in order to take care of other people; this defines some as clients or patients, and others as caregivers. In this view, people are seen to be victims of each other and of circumstances, rather than the creators of their own experience. This approach has its place; however, if it is the only one, it is very limiting to the growth and development of autonomous individuals. When people hold these irresponsible field dependent attitudes, their personal development is severely limited. This underlies the structure of caretaking; when people believe they can transmit and receive energy, they then experience energy loss or deficiency. This thought form is reflected in our health care systems, and in many of the essential concepts of therapy and healing.

An alternate view is that people do not lose energy; they merely invest the energy in fixations and blockages. If people can learn to let go of fixations, they can re-mobilize their own reserves of energy, and then are not dependent upon anyone else to help or heal them.

Universal Energy

Beyond the limitations of the notions of metabolic energy, there is one universal energy that flows through all forms and beings.[4] At human conception, that unity energy is particularized into the pattern of that individual, and enlivens that being during the entire life span. The body's metabolic processes are the means of utilizing that energy in each person; the energy is not created, it is *organized*. Fundamentally, the energy does not belong to the body; it belongs to the universe. We all swim in the same energy pool; thus, people always remain connected with one another at a deep energy level. The uniqueness of people is determined by genetically inherited traits that structure their energy patterns, plus all of their energy blocks and resistances (Reich's "character armour"[5]) that they develop through experiences within their families, and in society. If one could eliminate all of these energy blocks and resistances (a goal that some spiritual practices and religions propose), the individual would disappear in a peak transpersonal experience of oneness, merging with the basic unity of the cosmos.

In this concept of universal energy, separation is seen as an illusion based on the defences of the ego. It is this illusory ego that seems to create, transmit, and receive energy vibrations; it appears to have the power to influence and affect other people, to be able to "know," across a gap, what is happening in the world of another person. The gap is crossed through empathy and understanding, a process that would seem to require some energy transfer. If energy could be transferred like this, such activity would tend to result in an energy loss or drain; this is often reported by counsellors, who "burn out." We propose that they only burn out because of their attitudes of separation and obligation and dependency. Burnout is a by-product of a limited view of life and energy.

Resonance

Suppose that there is no energy transfer, but rather, that energy is in constant flow among all things and all people, blocked only by individual or group resistances, which have mostly been developed out of hurt or fear.

When a person hurts, other people, who are always connected at a deep level, will feel their own hurt *in resonance* with the suffering individual. In similar fashion, when people understand someone else, they have a felt experience of understanding themselves as they resonate *in relationship* to the other. This would be "recognition" (from the Latin root *re + cognoscere:* to know again, to be reminded of something about the self connected to the other[6]). In recognition, one person is stimulated to resonate and release static blocks to energy flow. If a person is free of the power motivation to take care of others, or to push others to change, or to escape the influence of others, that individual does not lose energy; instead, energy is set into motion within the individual as a resonance, which is experienced as a sense of aliveness, fullness, and movement. Instead of experiencing "burn-out," persons in resonance would feel more energetic and would know themselves all the more. Because the energy is not their own, but rather is the expression of the infinite cosmic energy, it is always available. Energy is never lost, only restrained or liberated.

What Is Energy?

There are numerous energy approaches to health and healing. Shiatsu, rolfing, acupuncture, polarity therapy, Reichian body work, acupressure, and various forms of massage all utilize the concept of an underlying energy that can be released. Whether this energy is called qi, or prana, or vital force, or simply energy, the assumptions about it are similar. A common misconception is that energy is physical stuff, with physical properties; this is the process of "reifying" the energy (literally making a "thing" of energy). The following assumptions are useful in moving beyond the restrictions of this mechanistic, physical concept of energy. They are not necessarily true; rather, they are ways to think about energy in order to introduce new perspectives.

- *Energy is a verb, not a noun.* There is no such thing as energy; there is only *activity* that is described in terms of energy. So, when we speak of "life energy," this term describes activity, not a measurable physical entity. A person does not possess energy "stuff" that is bound up and needs release; rather, the individual expresses more personal potential by active engagement with the world.

- *Energy concepts describe invisible events.* The individual is involved in an active, dynamic *process*. In the Chinese articulation, energy is seen as like the wind, which is invisible but has visible effects, such as the waves on top of a pond stirred by a breeze. The concept of energy is merely a useful way of describing the deeper, hidden patterns that are manifest in the individual personality.[7]

- *Energy is relationship in action.* The energy of the body exists in the relationship of the body structure to itself.[8] If the structures are bound together, the energy is *fixated*; if the structures have a more fluid relationship, the energy is less bound and hence more abundant in its effects. A variety of different energy conditions are possible at different times in an individual's life; the ancient Chinese concept of the five elements (the "five stages of change") codifies the categories within which the myriad energy states tend to organize. When someone is radiantly alive, we speak of that person as possessing an abundance of *free* life energy; conversely, an individual is said to be *blocked* in expression of energy in the states of illness or depression. Death is an absence of energy, a cessation of the life process. If an individual is radiantly alive, this does not mean that the person has an abundance of some entity; if the person is depressed, it does not mean that some *thing* is lacking—rather, the energy is bound up in fixated patterns. Furthermore, there is no good energy and bad energy; there are merely *different conditions* in which the individual's life process participates. It is not good to have high energy and not bad to have low energy; "high energy" merely describes situations wherein the individual has much freedom of possibility and responsiveness, and "low energy" states involve retraction, and less differentiation of expression.

- *Energy is a process of change.* Life energy is a process in a continual flux. There are shifting alternatives of rest and movement, unfolding and folding, expansion and contraction, evolution and involution. All that remains constant is the process of change itself; even nonchange is seen as a temporary state in the process of change.[9] This is the "forever flowing constancy" of Taoist philosophy.

- *Energy is an holistic concept.* The concept of energy can be used to engender an holistic approach. The complaint of many people seeking attention for symptoms is that a mechanistic approach, which sees their symptoms as physically based, tends to ignore other dimensions of their being. Utilizing concepts of energy to express the relationship between the various dimensions of the person can overcome the tendency to reduce the individual to an aggregate of symptoms. Von Bertalanffy puts it this way:

  We may state as a characteristic of modern science that [the] scheme of isolable units acting in one-way causality has proved to be insufficient. Hence, the appearances in all fields of science of notions like wholeness, holistic, organismic, gestalt, etc., which all signify that in the last resort, we must think in terms of systems of elements in mutual interaction.[10]

- *Energy is unifying and integrating.* Energy can be seen to be the process of *integration* that unifies all dimensions of the individual—body, mind, spirit, emotions, and environment—into a whole person located in the cosmos. The "energy" is the relationship that exists between the various dimensions. Using the concept of energy is useful to articulate the correspondence of one dimension with the others.

- *The energy body matrix might not exist.* From the viewpoint of traditional Chinese acupuncture theory, there is an energy body that underlies the other dimensions of being, radiating and giving rise to them. This *energy body matrix* is visualized as a circuitry of channels called *meridians*. Much scientific investigation has been devoted to the question of whether these meridians exist. Although the energy theory can explain some effects that have been experienced, no anatomical channels have been found, and no physical energy stuff has been isolated. But it does not really matter whether the energy exists and flows through meridians or not: this is merely a belief system, useful for organizing our perspective on reality. It is neither true nor false; it is merely a system of concepts. One does not have to prove that the energy exists in order to utilize the concept, any more than one has to accept that an actor on a stage is in fact the character represented in order to be moved by what is said. The process of utilizing any new belief system involves the willing suspension of disbelief—ceasing to resist long enough to see how the world looks when one assumes such a perspective.

- *Energy concepts go beyond the merely physical.* The practical utility of the energy concept is that it provides a framework by which one can view another individual as a whole person, and can consider the life process as it manifests in a number of perspectives. So, when a person sits in front of you, you can imagine this to be an energy event, which is indeed that individual's personality manifestation at a given point in time. When a person is stuck or limited, the aim is not to unblock or release energy: it is for an individual to find more possibilities for a rewarding, full life. By appreciating the interrelationships of that person within interpersonal and intrapersonal realms, we can come to recognize the presence of the other. Finally, what one can do in interaction with a client or friend is to appreciate the phenomenon of dialogue, where two energies meet. In this meeting, both individuals are challenged to become more present to themselves and each other; what occurs is the unfolding and expression of the potentials of each individual. Such a dialogue occurs on all dimensions—physical, emotional, intellectual, and spiritual. In integrative approaches to healing, there are these energy meetings at all the levels; thus, when one touches another person physically, there are many other nonphysical interactions. By utilizing nonconstrictive energy concepts, we make it possible to move beyond the limitations of the purely physical.

- *What is energy?* On the one hand, energy is nothing but a series of concepts useful in describing phenomena. On the other, it is the miracle of life that emerges as one human soul is revealed to another; it underlies the ineffable, mysterious events that occur when two people meet and touch in intimate dialogue.

Notes

1. Attributed to Confucius, *Source Unknown*.

2. *Webster's Collegiate Dictionary* (Springfield, MA: G. and C. Merriam, 1947), p. 326.

3. J. McKeen and B.R. Wong, *The Relationship Garden* (Gabriola Island, B.C.: PD Publishing, 1996), p. 13.

4. Ibid., p. 11.

5. W. Reich, *Selected Writings* (New York: Farrar, Straus and Giroux, 1973), p. 53.

6. J.C. Traupman, *The New College Latin and English Dictionary* (New York: Bantam Books, 1966), p. 261.

7. R.Wilhelm and C.F. Baynes, *The I Ching, or Book Of Changes* (Princeton: Princeton University Press, 1967), p. 235.

8. R. Feitis, ed., *Ida Rolf Talks About Rolfing and Physical Reality* (New York: Harper and Row, 1978).

9. R.Wilhelm and C.F. Baynes, *The I Ching, or Book Of Changes* (Princeton: Princeton University Press, 1967), pp. 280-81.

10. L. Von Bertalanffy, *General Systems Theory* (New York: Macmillan, 1984), p. 45.

Western & Eastern Medicine: Collision or Cooperation?

Introduction

A medical model is a product of the culture in which it develops. The basic assumptions of a society, which generally are not questioned, form the foundation of the medicine that is practised within that society. From the very beginning, eastern and western medicine have developed from utterly different assumptions. To clarify the differences between these two medical forms, we need to understand the roots of eastern and western cultures. Here, the term "western medicine" refers primarily to allopathic medicine as practised in the United States and Canada; "eastern medicine" for the most part refers to traditional Chinese medicine, as this is the eastern form with which the authors are most familiar.

Western Analytical Science

Western thought has culminated in the scientific method. Analysis and logic are the underpinnings of western culture. Western language is one of *separation* and *distinctions*. The underlying assumption is one of separateness, each individual acting on a world and being acted on by it. The prototype of this way of thinking is Newtonian mechanical physics, which investigates the laws that govern the behaviour of discrete particles in space and time. This view assumes a causal order in the universe, where one event in space and time precedes and affects events that follow it.

Eastern Unity Viewpoint

Eastern thought has developed in a different milieu. From its beginnings, Chinese culture has assumed a *unity* underlying apparent diversity.

Participation and *intuition* are the mainstays of operation. The language forms do not make distinctions in the same manner as those in the west. For example, the Chinese language is made up of ideograms—pictures that represent reality. There is less emphasis on things that are separated in space and time, and more emphasis on *process* and *interrelationship*. In addition to causal order, other dimensions of operation are assumed, where events take place in space and time operating with an "acausal connectedness" (synchronicity)[1].

A Call For Integration

In the past several centuries, some advanced thinkers in the east and the west have moved toward integration of these two ways of thinking. Although the assumptions of the two world views are very different, we now have an opportunity to create an amalgam of them. Specifically, in reference to eastern and western medicine, it is possible to achieve a functional relationship between these two vastly different approaches, by understanding the attributes of each system.

Differences in the Two Approaches

The western world has largely misunderstood oriental medical perspectives. With the opening of exchange between Asia and the west, we now have an opportunity to clarify our information and to forge a relationship between two very different perspectives on health, illness, and healing. Traditional western medicine assumes a separation of human beings into *parts*; this dualism extends to a distinction between mind and body, and emotions and spirit. The traditional oriental approach, however, emphasizes the relationship between *interpenetrating* dimensions (body/mind/spirit/emotions/environment); thus, eastern medicine is *holistic* in its view.

Whereas traditional western medicine has grown up within the *scientific analytical* heritage, eastern medicine has from the beginning used a much more *phenomenological* approach. In the west it is important to stand back, observe, and then diagnose and act on the patient as an outside agent. In the eastern approach, the practitioner blends with the patient and comes to appreciate the world through the patient's eyes; the empathetic resonance that comes from this close meeting is analogous to diagnosis, and treatment emerges in the dynamic interplay of the personalities of the practitioner and client.

Traditional Chinese Medicine vs "TCM"

The reader should note that "traditional" Chinese medicine in this book refers to an ancient system that arose some three thousand years ago in feudal China; the concepts have evolved in a largely Confucian and taoist frame of reference, down through the ages. In the establishment of communism in 1949, these ideas were dismissed, along with the cultural associations that accompanied them; this form of medicine became politically incorrect. Much of the ancient traditions have been purged, and lost in China; they survive in schools of acupuncture that have existed in Europe over the past two centuries, originally developed from the ideas transplanted to Europe by Christian missionaries returning from China.

Eastern medicine is taught in professional schools in China today as "TCM," meaning "traditional Chinese medicine." Note that this is not the "tradition" of the ancient taoist/Confucian approaches. Instead, it seems to be a more mechanistic approach, the product of an attempt to locate past wisdom within the modern sociopolitical context. Many of the ideas of ancient Chinese medicine have been rejected by the modern Chinese in a similar fashion to the way they have been dismissed by western scientists. A strange irony!

Language and Reality

Language is made up of assumptions that construct reality. There is a tendency to believe that what one sees is "true" rather than the product of a way of thinking, a perspective. For example, in the west there is an inclination to think that the only reality is one that can be described in our western terminology. As the language of the west lends itself to a subject-object dichotomy, our "reality" is one of separate objects. In the Chinese culture, a pictorial series of ideographs make up a fluid relational language in which the whole is emphasized. A concept of energy that underlies physical reality is a natural consequence of such a language.

Translations of relational Chinese ideas into reifying western language have often involved misinterpretations of the oriental concepts. Sometimes these concepts are rejected as "antiquated" or simplistic, because they are not appreciated in light of the culture from which they were derived. Many of the oriental theories are very sophisticated, with profound application. An example involves the "five stages of change," a cornerstone theory of eastern medicine that is generally mistranslated as the "five elements" and rejected as outmoded. This theory can facilitate a subtle understanding of change and development of personality (analogous to Piaget's concepts in western psychology[2]). The ideas involved in Chinese medicine have a long history of development; indeed, the concepts are still unfolding in the light of modern research. It is poor logic to dismiss an entire medical system because the deep historical roots of its conceptual matrix differ from the sources of one's own particular framework.

Comparing The Two Systems

One can find merits and shortfalls in both eastern and western approaches to medicine. Western medicine falls short in appreciation of the "world" of the patient. The natural healing approach of eastern medicine is less decisive in its ability to intervene (for example, in emergencies), and can be less effective in acute situations. Whereas the traditional western approach has emphasized treatment of illness, the traditional Chinese approach has stressed health and way of life rather than the disease process itself. Moreover, the underlying theme in western preventive medicine is *blame* for the results of life stances and activities; the eastern approach is more compatible with *consequences* for actions. The western system is a moral one, rooted in causal thinking; the eastern approach is amoral, developed out of associative thinking.

Traditional oriental medicine is interested in curing disease before it manifests. Eastern medicine assumes that disease is a manifestation of blocks in the energy matrix; these blocks can give rise to disease within any of the various dimensions of being (physical, emotional, mental, spiritual, environmental). The aim in oriental medicine is to understand and reharmonize the life-style pattern of the individual, before the disordered pattern has a chance to get a deep hold and manifest as disease. Oriental medicine is anticipatory and emphasizes life-style.

Traditional western medicine has developed into a magnificent system of cures. Once a disease has manifested, the western approach has elegant and far-reaching ways of dealing with it. A common assumption is that diseases are "things," entities, which develop within the mind, *or* the body, *or* the emotions, *or* the spirit. Intervention occurs after the disease has manifested. There is a great difference in Chinese medical science (which is a phenomenological, inductive approach) and western medical science (which is analytic and deductive). Thus, it is difficult for western science, which has investigated "things," to comprehend a science that has studied "dynamisms." The methodologies and assumptions underlying the two approaches are different; however, they are quite complementary when well understood and practised. Whereas western science has largely been quantitative, Chinese science has emphasized qualitative analysis. Western science has set out to be completely objective; Chinese science includes the subjective experience of the human participant-observer.[3] At this stage in history, Chinese science is incorporating the western scientific approach; western science now has an opportunity to learn much from the rich legacy of traditional Chinese science.[4]

Misunderstanding the Asian System

Acupuncture has been seen in the west as the main component of oriental medicine, and has been misunderstood as merely a tool for analgesia. Most of acupuncture is not for pain relief; this is a recent and somewhat incidental use of a broad-based medical perspective. Until now, western medicine has tried to incorporate acupuncture into itself as a tool, rather than seeing it as a function of a highly integrated medical system that goes far beyond mere relief of symptoms. Acupuncture is not itself a total system of medicine. Rather, it is an important approach in traditional Chinese medicine (along with moxibustion, herbalism, diet, massage, and life-style counselling). To consider oriental medicine as only acupuncture would be as inappropriate as to say that the prescribing of antibiotics is the entirety of western medicine.

Modern western medicine relies upon technological tools to facilitate diagnosis and treatment; traditional oriental medicine emphasizes the experiential interaction of practitioner and client without the use of elaborate ancillary tools. Because the Chinese approach emphasizes pulse diagnosis and involves little use of machinery and technology, it can be seen as imprecise. However, pulse diagnosis is an exhaustive correlation of numerous qualities and parameters that together provide a deep clinical picture of the individual. As well, detailed history-taking and physical examination are important tools of classical Chinese diagnosis.

Life Style Counselling

Western medicine boasts a long line of medical practitioners who were well versed in life-style counselling and in appreciating the whole patient. Dr. William Osler, the father of Canadian medicine, had much to say about the art of medicine ; incidentally, he used acupuncture as part of his medical approach.[5] Western medicine has in recent years been involved in technological development, and the teaching of the art of medicine has been de-emphasized. By appreciating eastern medicine, which stresses the art, western medicine can learn about its own roots.

Responsibility, Not Blame

Life-style counselling is sometimes misinterpreted by western thinkers as a system of blame. There is considerable difference between "I am responsible for my illness process" (I am the one who is involved in this process) and "I am to blame for my illness" (I caused my illness). The term "preventive medicine" implies a moralistic perspective, seeing disease as a bad thing to be rooted out. From a meta-perspective, illness and health can be seen in dynamic interplay; then people can achieve an holistic appreciation of the causes and consequences of illnesses and health. An integrated practitioner would not harangue patients about their life-style, but would instead educate about the *consequences* of life-style choices.

A Broader View

It is worth stating that practitioners should study their own personal health/illness and vitalizing/constraining orientations. A limitation of the western approach is that physicians readily assume they are studying others. Practitioners can learn much from their own life, including their health and illness experiences. Integrated practitioners *resonate* with others through the medium of their own energy body matrix, while maintaining a functional level of objectivity.

The concept of disease should be deeply understood. From the perspective of *clinical philosophy*, disease is merely one consequence of a nonvital life style; it is neither good or bad, but simply an expression of life-energy patterning.[6] We believe that a practitioner should be able to recognize the subtle signs of the presence or absence of life and wellness. As well, one could be equally versed in traditional western and eastern approaches in diagnosis and treatment of illness conditions, and thus take a synthetic approach to counselling for life and wellness enhancement.

Integrating Both Approaches

One could say the western approach is too hard and distancing; on the other hand, one could criticize eastern perspectives as too soft and lacking in objectivity. We propose that a mature medical perspective involves a synthesis of these two approaches. A practitioner should be able to move fluidly from one point of view to the other. In a sense, it should be possible to put on eastern medical glasses that permit a subjective, close-up view of the client's condition. It should then be possible to adopt the more objective viewpoint, analyzing and acting from a distance. Optimal learning would arise out of a framework of thesis-antithesis-synthesis.

Traditional Chinese medicine is not an enemy of western medical science; neither is it a quaint, outmoded approach to be discarded. Each system of thought has much to learn from the other. It would be a tragic shortcoming to lose the potential benefits of mutual understanding by maintaining a myopic, prejudiced attitude. We propose that the most constructive vantage point is to see Chinese science (with acupuncture being a case in point) as a system of thought with its own parameters, modes of operation, and consequences, and to see western science as a different system of thought. If one were to achieve this eminently mature intellectual perspective, it would be possible to construct a meta-science that would include understanding from both seemingly contradictory systems. This does call for a broad vision; it involves seeing the thought structures from an evolutionary perspective, through the lens of general systems theory. If, after all, what we are concerned with is the health and well-being of humanity, then we are called upon to overcome our limited viewpoints and to achieve the most beneficial perspective for the sake of the individuals seeking medical attention, and for the advancement of science.

Notes

1. C.G. Jung in R. Wilhelm and C. /Baynes, trans., *The I Ching Or Book Of Changes* (Princeton: Princeton University Press, 1967), p. xxiv.

2. J. Piaget, *The Principles of Genetic Epistemology.* translated by Wolfe Mays (New York: Basic Books, 1972).

3. Sobel, D. (Ed.). *Ways of Health: Holistic Approaches to Ancient and Contemporary Medicine* (New York: Harcourt Brace Jovanovich, 1979).

4. T. Kaptchuk, *The Web That Has No Weaver: Understanding Chinese Medicine* (New York: Congdon and Weed, 1983).

5. W. Osler, *Aequanimitas* (New York: McGraw-Hill, 1906).

6. P. Koestenbaum, *The New Image of the Person: The Theory and Practice of Clinical Philosophy* (Westport, CT: Greenwood Press, 1978), pp. 463-65.

Transference

The transference object always looms larger than life size because it represents all of life and hence all of one's fate. —Ernest Becker [1]

Early Anxiety

Especially at birth and during the earliest years, each individual is extremely vulnerable to the vicissitudes of life, requiring food, warmth, liquids, and physical stimulation. Many have speculated that at some level, children feel a sense of terror at the possibility of being abandoned to face the elements alone. Living in dread over this possibility, children are totally dependent on their caretakers; to the little people, their parents seem to be powerful and extremely important, the arbiters of the child's fate. Parents can appear powerful and god-like, much bigger and wiser than the child, who in comparison is small and helpless. Youngsters quickly learn that they should do everything possible to please or control the guardians of their existence.

As object relations theorists have proposed, people need to separate from the parents. Such separation can be done in a variety of ways. The most common way is through denying one's dependence upon parents, in order to become independent; this process of *individualization* often involves rebellion and willfulness. Less commonly, the separation may proceed along a path of *individuation*; for these people, their dependency needs are acknowledged rather than denied, but also are not seen to be the chief determining factors in the person's behaviour. In individuation, separation occurs more organically as individuals develop mastery of their own capabilities; in this case, the desire to separate is determined from within the person, not from outside. Decisions are responsive to current situations, rather than in rebellion or compliance. An anonymous pundit once put it this way:

Ultimately, you need to decide to wear a raincoat in the rain—even though your mother told you to do so!

234

Projection and Transference

As children grow in competence, developing increasing self-reliance, they become less dependent on their parents for survival. However, the early fears of abandonment do not die easily. Most people, even those who are seen as the most competent in our society, still carry within them much of their early dread of being left alone, with an underlying fear that they will be unable to survive without (parental) support. This dynamic of seeing oneself as small and helpless, and others as more powerful, shapes many people's psychological development, and determines the nature and quality of their future relationships.

As children grow and come into contact with other people, they assume that the new people have power and wisdom similar to their parents. In other words, the children *project* onto these other people the same qualities and capabilities that they have experienced with their parents. This process of *transference* is an attempt by children to keep their environment stable, controllable, and above all safe. Through this process of transference, young people create the psychological and emotional environment in which they will live and develop. If people's earliest years are filled with experiences of rejecting and hostile parents, they tend to expect this from all future authority figures (as well as future intimate partners, to the extent that they are seen as being parental). If the early parent-child transactions were primarily loving, that would be the character of the expectation placed upon future relationships.

Popularization of the Term "Transference"

The word "transference" was originally a psychoanalytic term that was used to describe projection in a therapeutic relationship; now, the word has come into common usage to describe phenomena of projection in nontherapeutic everyday relationships too. People tend to transfer their attitudes and experiences developed in their relationship to their early protectors to people who appear later in their life. It seems as if people are always working out their issues with their parents in every relationship that follows:

> The transference object becomes the focus of the problem of one's freedom
> because one is compulsively dependent on it; it sums up all other natural
> dependencies and emotions. —Ernest Becker [2]

Transference in Relationships

In interpersonal relationships, this propensity toward projection ("ghosting" or "placing hats" upon others) makes it difficult to ever get to know others for who they really are; others are always seen through the screen of transference. Generally, this screen is very important in establishing relationships; it determines the people to whom we will be attracted or repelled. These attractions and repulsions determine the nature and quality of interpersonal relationships. Transference is a strong motivating influence in the selection of partners and friends: people choose those upon whom they can most easily project their desires and needs.

Therapeutic relationships are only special kinds of interpersonal relationships, in which the activity is directed toward helping the client. The nature of that help depends upon the therapist's orientation; it ranges from attempting to "cure" to attempting to "educate" to merely trying to "console." Whatever the goal, most therapies make use of the client's natural tendency toward transference. For some therapists, that transference is used to control the client's behaviour, as a parent would a child. Others object to using transference in that way, seeing it as a means of fostering dependency upon the therapist and therapy. In any relationship, it is important to understand how the transference will be used.

Transference can be used to foster either individualization or individuation in any kind of relationship. Individuated persons will ultimately have little need of transference, because they will be more self-determining, less fearful of being alone, and more confident in their own competence. Through recognition and acknowledgment of the transference, both parties involved will have the information they need to choose their feelings and behaviour. Instead of being driven by unconscious forces, individuals can take charge of their own lives.

In any encounter between people, the transference phenomenon should be elucidated. If it is not recognized and acknowledged, people have a tendency to become stuck in a way that reflects past experiences (e.g. defensive, rebellious, compliant, or regressive attitudes) rather than making new and healthier individuated choices. When people move their transference toward resolution, it usually proceeds in the following, somewhat predictable, stages.[3]

The Stages of Transference and Countertransference

The magic stage is related to the "bonding stage" of the object relations developmental continuum. Individuals in the magic stage of transference see others as able to provide the kind of care that they believed they had, or dreamed of having, as a child. During this period, people expect a cure from therapists (or teachers, or lovers) who are seen to be all-knowing and wise.

The leaning stage is related to the mirroring stage in object relations development; parents reflect back to their children the latter's revealed feelings, along with parental reactions to their children's feelings and actions. In therapy this is a period of reflective interpretation, with the therapist attempting to see through the armour or facade of the client in order to provide the reflection of a direct mirror. In Horney's perspective (of Ideal, Real, and Authentic Selves), the process of creating self-hatred is uncovered.[4] In psychoanalytic terms, the parental projections are explored. In humanistic psychological terms, therapists reveal their countertransference (which is the analytic term that describes the projections that the therapist makes on the client) and personal reactions, in order to establish a more realistic interpersonal relationship in the present; healthy narcissism and self-compassion are reinforced, and recognition of the transference process and self-responsibility is encouraged.

The self-reliant stage is related to the "rapprochement stage" of object relations development, when the child is prepared to accept a separation from the parents, recognizing and accepting in them their differences, their good qualities as well as their faults. In therapy, it is a time of realistic assessment and acceptance of the differences between the client and the therapist. Both parties can recognize each other as separate persons capable of being intimate without losing personal boundaries.

Negative transference can occur in any of the above stages. In this process, clients are unable to integrate the so-called "good" and "bad" parts of themselves or their therapist; they often interpret that their therapist is not meeting their *perceived* needs, similar to what they have likely believed about their own parents. The therapist is polarized into being all-good or all-bad; the client may terminate therapy with unresolved feelings. Hopefully, the therapist will have the opportunity to help the client recognize this process and thus achieve some useful insight into what is often a characteristic manipulative or self-defeating behaviour.

Separate and Alone

Janet Malcolm, writing about psychoanalysis, has maintained that Freud's most original and radical discovery was how we all invent each other according to early blueprints.[5] Transference suggests that personal relations, the most precious and inviolate of entities, are actually messy jangles of misapprehensions, at best an uneasy truce between powerful solitary fantasy systems. Even (or especially) romantic love is seen to be a fundamentally solitary experience, profoundly impersonal. The concept of transference at once destroys faith in personal relations and explains why they are tragic; we cannot know each other through the lenses of our projections. We must grope for each other through a dense thicket of absent others. We cannot see each other plainly. A horrible kind of predestination hovers over each new attachment we form.

> *"Only connect," E.M. Forster proposed. "Only we can't," the psychoanalyst knows.*[6]

Notes

1. Ernest Becker, *The Denial of Death* (New York: The Free Press, 1973), p. 146.

2. Ibid., p. 146.

3. J.L. Rosenberg, M.L. Rand and D. Asay, *Body, Self & Soul: Sustaining Integration* (Atlanta: Humanics Ltd., 1985), pp. 218-25.

4. K. Horney, *Neurosis and Human Growth* (New York: W.W. Norton and Co., 1950).

5. J. Malcolm, *Psychoanalysis: The Impossible Profession* (New York: Vintage Books, 1982), p. 6.

6. Ibid., p. 6.

Is Change Possible?

To be what we are, and to become what we are capable of becoming, is the only end of life. —Robert Louis Stevenson [1]

Introduction

Can a leopard change its spots, or a tiger lose its stripes? The advent of the human potential movement ushered in an era of hope for the overcoming of human shortcomings and woes. Since the proliferation of growth programs that began in the 1960's, there has been an unspoken assumption that change is possible and that the potentialities of the human being are virtually limitless. The underlying theme seems to be that one does not have to tolerate personal or situational limitations: life is what you make of it, and you are totally responsible for everything that happens to you. If you don't like your life the way it is, you simply need to "get off your position" and create a new life more to your taste. In short, you are in the driver's seat, and the possibilities are limited only by your aspirations, your desire for change, and your willingness to "go for it."

The Morality of Idealism

The recipe for this way of living includes a liberal dose of *moralism*. Everything is seen in terms of right and wrong, or worse and better, or greater and lesser. In short, it's not okay today/here/now/with me; however, it *could be okay* tomorrow/there/then/with a better me. Life today is not good; tomorrow will be better. I am not very realized today; I hope I will become something greater in the future.

This perspective has led people to a great deal of idealistic goal setting and personal ambition to change themselves or their circumstances. How often have you said such things as "I need to change my life (work, partner)" or "When I finally accomplish this, then I'll be happier" or "When I finally achieve this, then everything will be great." The basic theme is that *things are not okay as they are* and that there is a better day coming in the future, after the necessary changes are made to create a richer life. Often, a deep-seated depression accompanies this attitude, when people assume that things are not okay as they are. Along with the depression comes an ambitious drive to change oneself, one's life, or one's situation, in order to approach the desired changed condition. Many believe that with enough effort and attention, they can even restructure their personality, eradicating bothersome traits and giving birth to brand new ones. Generally, this thrust to change is accompanied by guilt and despair, when aspirations are not realized.

Transcendence

Another interpretation of change involves an attitude that one can *transcend* (literally rise above one's circumstances and deal with it all from another plane). If life is bothersome, just ignore the troubling aspects and move beyond them. For those who adopt this frame of reference, there often is a floating feeling of blissful detachment. However, this approach operates against living participation, and people who adopt it are largely detached from the world and other humans. Hence, in transcending, people leave life without having fully entered it.

Devaluing the Self

The attempt to change oneself through idealism and striving into something better is generally accompanied by a continual self-devaluation. In all the years that we have worked with people, we have always found this attitude to be counterproductive to personal development. The more people try to get away from their situation, the more stuck and fixated they become. The mechanistic "change me" perspective and the idealism and hope of a better tomorrow operate against full participation in a life in the present. The goals of idealism kill present circumstances and interfere with the organic development of events. Craving for improvement interferes with the expansion of the present into a vigorous future. People can become fixated in the attempt to escape from where they actually are. In trying to affirm an image, a simulacrum of how things could be, they fail to exist fully. Pursuing the illusion of change moves towards nonbeing.

We propose an alternative: to courageously resist the dissatisfaction of the achievement ethic, and *affirm the substance of our lives* in the present, thus contributing to the unfolding of *beingness*. Rather than focussing on an unreal image, we emphasize facing the facts of the living present, accepting one's actual condition, and moving from here.

The Radical Hypothesis

Our hypothesis is this: *change is not possible*. It is pointless to try to change our given biological structure or our basic personality. If you were born a woman, then a woman you will be. You cannot eradicate your life history by forcing yourself to ignore it. Everybody is dealt a hand in life; most people are afraid to play their hand or get mired in resentments over not receiving better cards. Wouldn't it be better to play it out as best we can, even with insufficient advice and information along the way?

We have found that this attitude frightens many. There is a certain security in getting ready for the future, which will be better. If one drops the idea of there being future possibilities at all, and directly focuses on life as it is, a rush of fear floods in. Is this all there is? Is there no salvation from my lot? At least when I am sick, or in need of change, then I believe that I know who I am; I know what to expect of myself and others, and I have a certain sense of security in this. If I don't have this definition of myself as a patient, or as someone needing change, then who am I?

It seems likely that the structure of the personality is largely set from the early days of life. One inherits traits, and these are affected by experiences in early childhood. By the time the individual is only months old, the basic personality pattern has been determined in quite a profound way. This *deep structure*, which is an amalgam of inherited tendencies, early experiences, and learning, will persist for the lifetime of the individual. The deep structure is not a thing, and it is not anatomically located; rather, it is formed of the interrelationships of deeply ingrained tendencies of activity in the personality. We assume that all so-called "therapies of change," which aim to alter the basic matrix of the personality, are doomed to fail.

When people come to one of our programs with a certain "problem" they want "fixed" (that is, they want therapy), their initial work is to come to terms with their somewhat unrealistic ambition to get rid of this problem. If the identified problem is depression, they want to get rid of "it"; if they are allergic, they want a cure. If they have a tendency towards addiction (tobacco, alcohol, drugs, people), they want to have this addiction removed by some kind of psychological surgery. We recommend that they stop trying to get over the "problem," and instead sink into it and get to know it. What people call allergies are often elaborate expressions of a deep fear of intimacy. Dependencies often mask an underlying issue of faith and commitment. "Depression" is often an umbrella term for mood tones that are socially unusual, yet very life extending.

In short, *there does not need to be any problem at all!* People are not diseases to be cured. Each is a unique human being, with a personal history, distinct tendencies, and idiosyncratic ways of experiencing life. If people relinquish their ambitious (and fruitless) desire to approach the "normal," they can more readily come to grips with who they are. Instead of therapies of change, we propose an *educational uncovering* and *revelation*, wherein each individual can become more aware. The key is to stop trying to get away from oneself and settle more deeply into one's own experience. Then something wondrous can occur.

Transformation

Although it is not possible to change one's history or deep structure, it is possible to transform the *expression* of the deep structure. The basic tendencies remain; how they are expressed can be modified. This transformation is quite different from a transcendence that springs from denial, where one tries to rise above oneself. In transformation, the basic deep structure is accepted, acknowledged, and studied. Ever-deepening self-knowledge arises from such an investigation of one's tendencies. In the absence of a struggle to change these patterns, one can become more and more aware of them, and even learn to anticipate them before they manifest themselves. Hence, it is possible to achieve a relative ease and freedom with oneself. The patterns are the basic plot of the play that one is living; if people know the lines and scenes, they can more fluidly perform their part. Just like the pianist who is free to alter the expression and tones of a piece that is thoroughly practised and known, individuals have the opportunity to shift the emphasis between their various patterns (the "melodies") once they are evident.

Thus, transformation does not involve change of the deep structures; rather, it means *shifts in perspectives* on these patterns. The deep structures themselves remain the same; yet the expression is exquisitely varied and ever new. For example, the fascination with knives that many young children have (deep structure) can be transformed into the grace and craft of the skilled surgeon. Or the interest in incision and sharp cutting objects (deep structure) could also be transformed into the keen mental attitude of the discerning academic. The careful protection of the self from invasion by a foreign substance that typifies the allergic personality could well be used to design foolproof security systems. In short, there are creative outlets and uses for any personality pattern.

Foreground and background can shift. Take, for example, an individual who is outwardly defensive and difficult to approach, and inwardly very gentle and caring. This person could, with awareness, shift the emphasis of these two basic deep structures. The result could be a warm personality with strong self-definition.

Transcend and Include

In his groundbreaking book *A Brief History of Everything*, Ken Wilber outlined a concept of "transcend and include" which is compatible with our notion of transformation. To Wilber, the basic structures do not change; however, their relevance and potency alter as the individual evolves. What is important to a child is often quite insignificant to the same person as an adult; nevertheless, the basic personality structure is the same, *with a different emphasis*. Wilber proposes that people should not try to rise above anything; as they proceed into the next developmental phase, they pass beyond the limiting constraints of fixed attitudes about their patterns, while retaining the essential features of the patterns themselves. Wilber says, "evolution is a process of transcend and include, transcend and include."[2]

We would say the same; our words would be "evolution is a process of continuous transformation." We wrote about this issue in *The Relationship Garden*. People can work through the issues that arise in dialogue, and grow "through progressively and repeatedly accepting these issues."[3] People do not need to rise above their circumstance, as some religious practices would maintain; they can accept their patterns of existence repeatedly, gaining deeper integration within themselves.[4]

The Landscape of the Self

When people adopt the attitude that they do not have to get rid of parts of themselves, and instead can accept all aspects of their life patterns, they can see existence as a landscape with different terrains and climates. No parts of the landscape need to be corrected or discarded. Indeed, their existence cannot be changed. But individuals do have the choice as to how much time they spend in the different parts of their landscapes, and how significant these parts are to them. In our book *In And Out Of Our Own Way*, we further discuss the notion of the landscape of our lives:

> We all have our mountains of exhilaration, surrounded by our cliffs of danger and hardships. [5]

Conclusion

In our view, change of the basic personality is not possible. Often, seeking for change is a way of anesthetizing the anxiety of nonbeing that accompanies life. To accept one's deep structures and tendencies often involves embracing this anxiety. To devote oneself to knowing one's basic patterns (and accepting the accompanying anxiety) rather than trying to eradicate them, will allow for more self-acceptance, more self-responsibility, a greater inner strength, and a heightened self-esteem.

Transformation is the ever-unfolding expression of deep knowledge of the self. The more thoroughly people know their patterns and tendencies, the more varied, creative, and spontaneous they can be. What others claim to be "change," we identify as transformation. In transforming, nothing new has been added. Individuals can only become more fully alive, more aware, more creative, more in touch with their place in relationship to others and to the universe as a whole. In short, all that they can become is more of themselves.

To Dare

To laugh is to risk appearing the fool.
To weep is to risk appearing sentimental.
To reach for another is to risk involvement.
To expose your ideas, your dreams,
before a crowd is to risk their loss.
To love is to risk not being loved in return.
To live is to risk dying.
To believe is to risk despair.
To try is to risk failure.
But risks must be taken, because the greatest hazard
in life is to risk nothing.
The people who risk nothing, do nothing,
have nothing, are nothing.
They may avoid suffering and sorrow,
but they cannot learn, feel, change,
grow, love, live.
Chained by their attitudes,
they are slaves;
They have forfeited their freedom.
Only a person who risks is free.

—Author unknown

Notes

1. R.L. Stevenson, in *Bartlett's Familiar Quotations,* 15th ed., edited by J. Bartlett (Boston: Little, Brown and Co., 1980), p. 668.

2. Ken Wilber, *A Brief History of Everything* (Boston: Shambhala, 1996), p. 30.

3. J. McKeen and B.R. Wong , *The Relationship Garden* (Gabriola Island, B.C.: PD Publishing, 1996), p. 71.

4. Ibid., pp. 172, 173.

5. B.R. Wong and J. McKeen, *In and Out Of Our Own Way* (Gabriola Island, B.C.: PD Publishing, 1995), pp. 151, 152.

The Helping Relationship

Since man is endlessly emergent, in continuous flux, changing as his world changes, what is psychoanalytically "true" now was not true fifty years ago and will not be true fifty years hence. Psychoanalysis is a child of its time.
—Edgar Levenson [1]

In the twentieth century, the helping professions (including medicine, psychology, and the other social sciences) have been affected by a series of social events that can be divided into three broad periods: the *Mechanistic Era*, the *Communications Era*, and the *Structuralist Era*. These eras have had a marked influence on the values and practices in the helping fields. [2]

The Mechanistic Era

Most of the advances of the early twentieth century came about because of an adherence to scientific thought and discipline; the human organism was seen as a miracle of mechanical perfection whose working parts could be isolated, studied, fixed, and even replaced when damaged or lost. In general medicine, most attention has been given to the efficient working of the various parts rather than to the whole person. Contained within this model is a belief in *authorities*, who are believed to know what is right or good for the majority. This hierarchical attitude has dominated the physician-patient relationship, spawning within patients a sense of helplessness about themselves while fostering a feeling of awe and dependence upon the physician-healer.

From the beginning of this century, psychiatry, though less scientific in nature, developed these same characteristics because of its alliance with the medical model. Freud and his professional descendants were steeped in the mechanistic medical model; hence, modern psychology contains within it a "psychohydraulic" notion about the psyche being like a machine. In this perspective, much attention has been given to those who seem to have poor working parts, or whose functioning and performance has become inefficient, or somehow deviant from the norm.

The Communications Era

Toward the end of the Second World War, a broad new understanding of communications developed; this was prompted by the rapid advances in electronic technology, many of which had been developed for the purposes of war. The onset of the communications era was rapid and dramatic, reaching its peak in the 1960's, when its offspring were old enough to exert power and influence over the direction of society's systems. Amidst the social and political disorder of the times were some new visions of people and their place. Problems of all sorts were seen to be issues of communication and information transfer. Professionals in the behavioral sciences developed a great interest in trying to enhance communication between people; this gave rise to theories of social psychology and studies in communications. This was the generation of immediate gratification, with "here and now" interest in the present, a rapid identification with groups (minority, majority, special interest, and so on) and a valuing of change, often merely for the sake of change itself. The prevailing fear of the individual was *fear of isolation*; people had to "belong." These factors had an influence on the helping professions of the day. In Edgar Levenson's words:

> *Psychoanalytic theories, in sum, are not competing versions of timeless, immutable truth. They are time-bound perceptions of human change.*[3]

Amidst this interest in communication, humanistic psychology rose to the fore, championed by growth centres such as Esalen Institute in California, and popularized by the media. Humanistic practitioners, dissatisfied with traditional psychotherapy—which appeared to be lengthy, time consuming, of limited availability to the public, and apparently relatively unsuccessful—developed a wide spectrum of methods, some new, many ancient. Thus, a whole new array of techniques and vocabulary was developed outside the auspices of traditional psychology and medicine; these included gestalt therapy, rolfing, encounter groups, T-groups, psychodrama, art and drama therapy, dance and movement therapy, meditation, Reichian breathing, primal therapy, and transactional analysis. Many of these techniques have now been assimilated into institutional programs and educational centres. However, professional bodies representing traditional schools of thought and practice (such as universities, and medical and psychological organizations) were often very resistant to the approaches of what was derisively described as the "culture of narcissism."[45]

The Structuralist Era

In the last two decades of the twentieth century, the sociocultural landscape once again had a major shift. Led by environmentalists who had become aware of the destructive inclinations of the human animal (which was threatening itself, other species and the environment), a whole new wave of awareness swept the western world. A natural philosophy of *interdependence* began to be voiced by sociologists and anthropologists, who saw an order in the universe based upon *interrelated systems*. This structuralist philosophy (studying the predilection towards "structuring" into certain patterns) gradually began to pervade all walks of life. The health practitioners who embraced this philosophy became interested in the *patterns* of individual behaviour (life-style); their effort was to clarify these patterns for people, so that individuals could have more awareness of their *responsibility* in life itself. Their focus was different—consequences of behaviour, freedom of choice with sensitivity to others, and valuing of individuality and idiosyncrasies became more important than communication.

Now, people began to experience *fear of loss of themselves*, of their identity, their uniqueness. Remarkably, in the 1960's, people were afraid to be isolated, and wanted to be closer; now, in the 1990's, people were afraid of intimacy, and recoiled from contact! As the landscape shifted, the traditional helping professions showed little interest (other than active resistance) in these changes. Similar to their attitude about the communications techniques of the previous era, the traditional schools dismissed the changes in the structuralist period, and persevered in the mechanistic foundations of science. Because of the important implications these developments have for the helping professions, politically as well as therapeutically, these new perspectives are dangerous to ignore.

Every Illness Tells A Story

To the traditionalist, illness is a mechanical malfunctioning requiring mechanical alteration (drugs, diet, or surgery) to correct it. From this mechanistic view, illness is accidental, a result of helplessness or aging, a failure of will, or the result of a victimization by external circumstances. From the perspective of the communications approach, illness represents an attempt to communicate. People presenting with symptoms are attempting to "say" something about their experience of the world that they seem unable to express in any other way. Thus, there is contained within any illness, psychological or physical, a story from that person's life.

Often clients are unaware of the messages they are trying to convey through their illnesses; indeed, it is generally this lack of understanding of what they are trying to communicate that results in the production of symptoms. Illness exists in face of a *failure to communicate* in any other way. A dramatic example of this is blindness in conversion hysteria, wherein the person expresses an unwillingness to see or face something. A more mundane example is the angry eruptions in psoriasis, which manifest because of a person's inability to express anger more directly. Implicit in this concept is the notion that if people could find other ways to communicate, they would not have to be sick. People who are manifesting illness often experience being isolated and believe that they are not understood; indeed, they likely are not understanding themselves.

The Communications Approach

A practitioner functioning in the communications mode will be attentive not just to the *content* of the client's story, but also to the *quality* of the presentation, alert for clues that help to fill in the full meanings that the person is trying to convey, often unconsciously. The practitioner acts as a good listener, attempting to understand and to help the client to come to that understanding. When this is effective, the client experiences being understood, and hence no longer isolated. A therapeutic session in this mode functions in much the same way as a confessional; the person overcomes the barriers that create isolation by contacting another human being, in this case the practitioner, and revealing themselves. When the failure to communicate is overcome, the illness is no longer necessary. The difficulty with the communication approach is that, although the symptoms are often alleviated, lasting change often does not occur. Clients who experience being understood and thus less isolated in contact with the listening professional, often return after the appointment to the same life-style, and continue to live in the way that created the illness pattern in the first place (for example, alcoholism). We believe that no lasting change can occur without individuals becoming *aware* of the *contextual patterns* in which they live.

The Structuralist Approach

The interpersonal field offers only an expansion of awareness, an enrichment of pattern, not the satisfying linear explanations of intrapsychic drive theory.
—Edgar Levenson [6]

In the structuralist approach, clients are seen to be full, active agents in their own lives. Individuals are not victims of outside forces; rather, when there is illness, people are living in a way that participates in illness. Illness persists because of the *lack of awareness* of the patterns that produce it. When clients become aware of these patterns, they alter or avoid them. This *self-responsibility*, which includes being responsible for the illness patterns, is different from blame. People are responsible for having a cold, or a broken arm, insofar as they are the ones experiencing this phenomenon; in this way, the individual *participates* in the illness process. However, the person with the illness is *not to blame*—no one is. This is not a moral situation. Rather, from the structuralist viewpoint, what is significant is the *awareness* of *process*, and coming to appreciate one's relationship to that process. With adequate awareness, the relationship to the illness process can change.

Practitioners functioning in the structuralist framework adopt a phenomenological approach. Their aim is, as fully as possible, to come to see and appreciate the world through the client's eyes. Thus, they value empathy and inclusion (see above, "Empathy, Resonance and Energy"). These practitioners will not try to manipulate their clients' lives from arm's length (mechanistic approach) or passively listen and understand (communication mode); instead, they become *involved* in their clients' experiences, mutually sharing thoughts, interpretations, and feelings as a way of facilitating clients' awareness of themselves in relationship to their practitioners, and ultimately to their families, society, and the entire world. This challenges practitioners to bring themselves as persons to the encounter. Edgar Levenson has written extensively about this:

> The interpersonal therapist must grapple with the **real** matrix of events and personalities in which every therapy is embedded. It is not a question of what the patient has projected "onto" or "into" the therapist, but of really **who** the therapist is and **what** he brings to the therapy encounter.[7]

The client is also challenged, to take the material from the helping encounter into regular life:

> All that therapy can do is enrich the patient's knowledge of himself, his mate, and their interaction. The decision, though, usually remains a decision, and painful choices must be made.[8]

The function of the helping relationship is to provide a broader viewpoint for the client; the rest is up to the client.

> The larger and wider the patient's perspective, the better equipped he is to live in the real world.[9]

We agree with Levenson that the client's work is to develop a life of dialogue and intimacy. His summation:

> I would prefer that patients leave therapy committed to the lifetime pursuit of dialogue, with the recognition that "intimacy" may be more the epiphany of hard work at living than the directed goal.[10]

Notes

1. Edgar Levenson, *The Fallacy of Understanding* (New York: Basic Books, 1972), p. 19.

2. Ibid., p. 58.

3. Ibid., p. 19.

4. Christopher Lasch, quoted by J.F. Stacks, "Aftershocks of the 'Me' Decade," *Time*, August 3, 1981.

5. Christopher Lasch, *The Culture of Narcissism* (New York: Warner Books, 1979).

6. Edgar Levenson, *The Ambiguity of Change* (New York: Basic Books, 1983), p. 31.

7. Ibid., p. 21.

8. Ibid., p. 118.

9. Ibid., p. 164.

10. Ibid., p. 106.

Therapy and Education

When people encounter a particular problem in life, they are faced with the question as to what kind of help they need, therapy or education?

Therapy

Webster's Dictionary defines "therapy" as "the treatment of disability or disease, as by some remedial or curative process"; the word itself is derived from the Greek word "therapeia," which refers to service rendered to the *sick*.[1] Therapy assumes that problems result from illness, which occurs with some breakdown of the person, or some weakness in their body or mind that made them vulnerable to invasion or ill effects from without. People are seen as largely helpless in face of the forces of trauma, bacteria, other people, institutions, and social systems. The assumptions underlying the therapeutic attitude are mechanistic, and involve the notion of victimization.

Scientific principles dominate western thought, and increasingly permeate attitudes around the rest of the globe. The common scientific viewpoint assumes that people are like machines, made up of interacting parts; these parts mostly function in an orderly, predictable, and comprehensible fashion in order to ensure organismic survival. In this paradigm, something or somebody is malfunctioning when a part no longer performs its customary duties, interfering with the predictable and assigned function of the total organism. If a part fails, the machine declines in efficiency or stops altogether; that broken or "sick" part must be found and repaired, or replaced. No matter whether the defective item is an automobile, a washing machine, an alcoholic, a criminal, a cancer patient, or a schizophrenic—the attitude is the same.

Therapy Involves Victims and Blame

In the mechanistic model, a machine (or organism, since they are the same) requires adequate care to ensure proper operation. The breaking-in period of a new automobile assures later good functioning; this is not much different than the prevailing cautions about child raising. When people "break down" in later life, the main question seems to focus on their early childhood, the "breaking-in" period—what went wrong *then*? When people are breaking down, something *wrong* must have been done to them at some time in their life. Here we see a subtle but definite attitude of victimhood in which blame can be ascribed to parents, priests, teachers, germs, institutions, societies or anybody that is thought to have power. The victims of such experiences are deemed to be in need of therapy, to return them to happy and efficient functioning; then they will be capable of maintaining their places and functions in the orderly scheme of society.

Psychotherapy and Blame

In such therapy, the recipient (client) assumes a position of relative helplessness. The therapist knows best, and in many instances is credited not only with superior knowledge but also with magical powers. Client and therapist are joined in the task of uncovering the perpetrator(s) of the "illness" (the malfunction). Once the villain is determined (through *insight* in psychotherapy), proper action depends on the culture and the times.

Currently, it is fashionable to finger the culprits and publicly humiliate them, as has repeatedly been done throughout history. The French did it with the guillotine during their revolution; the Chinese did it during their Cultural Revolution; witches were treated this way in Europe; in the United States, suspected communists were assailed. Christians have had it both ways, originally being persecuted by the Romans, only to turn around and do the same to others later. Christian purges were exacted savagely during the Crusades; the persecution has been done in more civilized fashion recently by the Moral Majority, in their campaigns against anything with which they disagree. In addition, Christians have done the same to themselves (as evidenced in the evangelistic movement's persecutions of their own ministers). Now, the race is on to point the finger at sex abusers, perpetrators of family violence, sexual harassers, and all violators of power in the workplace. Certainly, it seems highly desirable to identify and to change these situations. But can it not be done without emphasizing the helplessness of the so-called victim?

Social Cures

As with therapy, many of society's "cures" for unhealthy behaviour and situations reinforce the helplessness of the victim. Welfare assistance programs, soup kitchens, and many government bureaucracies contribute to this helplessness. Although such programs are established to fill real needs, the tendency of people is to begin to expect such aid as a right, an entitlement (see above, "Entitlement"). Use of these services when they are not really needed tends to promote a greater sense of helplessness. Canada's once nearly ideal health delivery system is in danger of erosion by such an attitude among its users. The legal system is becoming a large industry of people demanding redress for victimization by others. Similarly, unions, professional organizations, and special-interest groups are all gaining more control over people's lives, in their constant efforts to ensure that individual rights are being preserved. As these forces become more powerful, people become more helpless, more dependent on them, more ready to complain, to whine, to demand. The sense of personal responsibility, the experience of being in charge of their own lives, of being the directors of their own affairs, is gradually slipping from their hands.

The Limitations of Therapy

Working with people over a combined eighty years of practice and teaching has led us to believe that those who need the most help, physically or emotionally, are those who have given in to the seduction of believing that they are the victims of external circumstances. Because of a belief that people are helpless agents in the scheme of their own lives, many have an inherent trust in therapy. Somebody out there did them wrong; somebody out there knows how to set it right. In this way of thinking, the therapist knows best. And yet, therapy as it is practised is based on very inexact approaches that have rarely been able to meet even the most basic requirements of the scientific method, while continuing to make extravagant claims of understanding and knowing. This is not to say that many people have not been helped by therapy; but we should not forget that equal numbers have been helped by healers of all persuasions, many of whom would be offended to be included in a scientific framework.

The Structuralist View

Consider for a moment the suggestions made by the proponents of a structuralist philosophy (see above, "The Helping Relationship"). In this perspective, human beings are more than the sum total of their parts; further, in all situations, the whole is present in all of the parts. All human behaviour is an expression of the individual and the universe; in this way, people are never abnormal, but are merely *idiosyncratic* (unique). At all levels of being, people are always expressing their own idiosyncratic patterns; these patterns can be seen and interpreted in the body, the spirit, the mind, the emotions, and the environment. Any holding or fixation of energy at any of these levels is exhibited as a resistance or block at the other levels too. Similarly, each individual and all things on earth express the energy pattern of the earth, which expresses the energy pattern of the total unity of the universe. The various levels are actually a *continuum*, from the central core of all things to the superficial expression of each person. The continuum can be divided into a "deep" (universal) structure, which humans share with all things, "sociocultural" (human) structures, which include familial, national, and cultural patterns, and "idiosyncratic" (superficial) structures, which are unique to the individual.[2]

Conventional Education

Most education at home and school teaches the values and methods of the sociocultural structures, and tends to ignore or devalue the deep and idiosyncratic structures. In this way, the individual learns to erect walls and play roles as the Ideal Self. The abandonment of the Authentic Self gives rise to self-hatred (see above, "The Ideal Self: Striving For Perfection"). Proponents of this type of educational model view the individual as a clean slate, upon which the educational system will write what is important for that person's adaptation into society. This is not really education; it is a form of indoctrination.

Structuralist Education

The root of the word "education" is from the Latin, meaning to "lead out from" (*e*, out and *duco*, to lead).[3] Thus, in its original meaning, education involves drawing out from the student what is already there as potential. The structuralist view assumes the individual to have *pre-existing patterns* at all levels of being. In this holistic model, structuralist education provides the stimulus to *awaken inherent potentials* within individuals, helping people to discover these personal truths within themselves. This is the nature of "heuristic education," where rote learning is replaced by situations in which people can discover for themselves. In this holistic approach, people are seen to be complete within themselves; initially they are inexperienced and unexpressed, more potential than actualized. The task of education is to facilitate people's discovery of themselves, their own nature, and their place in the world. The mirroring and stimulation of interpersonal relationships are tools for people to grow to fruition.

To educators of this persuasion, the challenge is to create situations in which people are able to discover their own possibilities. This holistic educational model also applies to practitioners of the healing arts: clients are not illnesses that need to be cured, but rather they are beings that need to discover themselves in an educational process. Traditional therapy and conventional education often undermine self-development; structuralist education aims to bring forth the realized person, full of promise and challenge and bounty. Teachers and health practitioners can be midwives, helping people to give birth to themselves, to actualize the potentials that their deep structure holds as a promise. The method is in intimate dialogue person-to-person, rather than in the power dynamics of indoctrination and "fixing." A noble endeavour!

Edgar Levenson's words apply to both education and helping:

> It should offer, not cure, peace of mind, idealized relationships, but awareness, the exhilaration of reality, of the sense of struggle, and the opportunity of being flooded with the variety, richness and unending flux of human experience.[4]

Notes

1. *The Living Webster Encyclopedic Dictionary of the English Language* (Chicago: English Language Institute of America, 1971), p. 1019.

2. Edgar Levenson, *The Fallacy of Understanding* (New York: Basic Books, 1972), p. 40.

3. *The Living Webster Encyclopedic Dictionary of the English Language* (Chicago: English Language Institute of America, 1971), p. 313.

4. Edgar Levenson, *The Fallacy of Understanding* (New York: Basic Books, 1972), p. 223.

Allergies and Phobias:
Keeping the World At Bay

Two Stories

To a casual observer Jane's life is highly successful. She is attractive, well educated, and has a good, well-paying job. But her outward appearance of success masks an inner turmoil that runs deep and disrupts the entire fabric of her life. Jane has been going from doctor to doctor for the past several years, trying to find someone who can explain the extreme, yet vague, symptoms that she experiences. And although many professionals have provided treatments, suggestions, and attention, she still suffers from myriad complaints with little relief. She is puzzled, frustrated, and frightened by what seems to be happening to her. Her inner life is a private hell. Whereas she used to have extraordinary vitality, she has been finding increasing difficulty getting through her work days. She sleeps a fitful thirteen-hour night; she feels tired all the time and does not have enough energy for her other interests or for keeping up socially. Her friends are beginning to stop calling; more and more, she is by herself at home in bed. Her life dreams are fading as she struggles to get through just one more day. She has been told that her headaches, listlessness, and nasal symptoms add up to an allergy syndrome. She feels a little better on a special allergic diet that has been prescribed; yet, she is beginning to fear that she is never going to get well or regain her previous happy, carefree life.

Audrey, who has been experiencing similar fatigue symptoms in a city far away from Jane, seems to be in a different situation. Because of her intense fears of leaving her home, she has been told that she is "agoraphobic." She scarcely ever leaves her apartment; family and friends must come to visit her. Although she conducts her successful business from her home, she is coming to recognize that her life is closing in on her; yet, the thought of going out for an evening is so fearful to her that she simply refuses to date. The extreme anxiety she has been feeling for the past several years has been significantly reduced by her limiting her activities and by the large doses of tranquilizers and antidepressants that she takes daily; yet, with her diminished anxiety, she feels dulled. This attractive young woman is becoming more and more socially paralysed as her condition takes deeper hold.

The Scope and Nature of the Problem

There are many people living similarly restricted lives. On the surface, they appear to be fine; but inside, they experience a desperate dread that something is not right. A growing number of young people are suffering from apparently different syndromes that have remarkably common underlying themes. Sometimes the diagnosis is "phobia"; at other times the label is "allergy," or, lately, the popular "total allergy syndrome." In these different conditions, there are unmistakable common threads that run through the separate stories. What accounts for the similarities in such an array of troubles?

As we came to know a number of these people over many years, we recognized that all of them are dealing with fundamental issues of *boundary distinction*. They are ill because they have not learned to define themselves in some fundamental ways.

Physiology of Boundaries (The Immune System)

The immune system is a biological complex that functions to protect the integrity of the physical organism; with its various antibodies, it is like an army that defends from outside invasion. The immune system maintains the boundary of the physical being, distinguishing and keeping out what is "not me" and holding in place what is "me." When a person's immune system malfunctions, disease states ensue. Allergy involves a hyperreactivity to certain outside conditions (e.g., hay fever, drug hypersensitivity, food allergies); the defence is excessive. When the immune system is underactive, as in extremely debilitated states or in illnesses such as AIDS, the person is physically vulnerable to assault from what might ordinarily be harmless circumstances. For example, a person with a lowered immune defence system is more susceptible to infections and is less able to fight them effectively.

The Process of Separation/Individuation

In object relations theory, the infant "hatches" from the mother-infant "symbiotic dual unity" during the process of ego development. The developmental project for children is to become a separate human being by acquiring a sense of themselves that is distinct from the mother (and by extension, distinct from the environment). This project is well under way by two years of age, when the child is first learning to move away from the parent while still craving the protective milieu of parental love and acceptance. Thus, youngsters are in a process of *separation* (learning to be psychologically and physically separate from the mother) and *individuation* (developing a unique sense of themselves in an individual life experience).[1]

For many children, this process is not smooth; the child either hastily and prematurely splits from the parent instead of developing a separation, or does not separate, remaining symbiotically and dependently bound to the psyche of the parent. In a sense, the child either develops brittle and artificial boundary distinctions (walls) or remains somewhat fused with the parent. The former is analogous to hyperactivity of the immune system; the latter is analogous to inadequate immunity to the outside world. In later relationships, these early defensive patterns of splitting without relating, or fusing without distinction, are likely to be reproduced. These processes probably underlie much of what are dubbed "allergies" and "phobias."

Chinese Medicine Perspective (The Earth Element)

In the framework of the five stages of change in traditional Chinese medicine, the issues of the earth phase are those of incarnation. In other words, the human body is the medium through which the other dimensions of being are expressed and made manifest. The definition of the individual takes shape and form through the mediation of the earth energies. The earth issues have to do with relationships, the physical being, separation/union, the mother/child interaction, and nurturing. Individuals with difficulties in the earth aspects of the energy body matrix will exhibit symptoms in the body, in relationships, and in self-definition. Thus, from a Chinese medical viewpoint, people with allergies and phobias have some disturbance in the earth phase of their energy body.

The Story Underlying Allergies and Phobias

In the lives of the individuals cited above, and the countless others like them, the dominant theme seems to be a problem with boundary distinctions. These individuals are highly intelligent and generally are very creative people. Hence, they are unwilling to follow a standard life path. However, these people are generally very frightened of the passions that surge through them; they fear their erotic impulses, are anxious about their high level of energy, and are afraid of the unusual thoughts that pass through their minds. These creative individuals are unwilling to live a commonplace existence; yet they are cast into an existential maelstrom of anxiety and uncertainty without sufficiently developed boundaries that would help them to determine where they belong and what they wish to do in the universe. They resist succumbing to the safety of the standard cultural patterns (get a job, get married, and raise children); yet they are reluctant to risk a full-blown creative life. They are caught in the hinterland between the commonplace and the unique. They wall themselves off from the regular world with an illness process; in a sense, they become "allergic" to the commonplace, or develop "phobias" that protect them from conventionality.

Within themselves, they often experience deep despair, as they do not fully engage with their life; this despair is commonly supplanted by symptom complexes. The bulk of their creative energy is dedicated to producing an illness metaphor in which they can justifiably live. Instead of devoting themselves to artful living, they become increasingly enslaved by the illness system that they create and maintain. In a way, their illness provides social justification for their unusualness, without the risks of full-blown creativity. The uncertainty of the creative impulse is reduced to the predictability of an illness condition ("I couldn't possibly go there" or "I can't handle that.")

These people are generally under forty, intelligent and attractive beyond the usual. All of them experience varying degrees of anxiety, fatigue, lessened energy, disturbance of sleep patterns (for example, sleeping up to thirteen or fourteen hours per day without being refreshed), bodily tensions, and symptoms related to eyes, ears, nose, and throat. They are increasingly socially isolated. Although this is often rationalized ("I'm allergic, so I can't go there . . . eat that . . . do this"; "I simply have to get twelve hours of sleep"; "I'm afraid to go out at night—it's a phobia"), there is an underlying *fear of intimacy*. Their relationships are dependent; they will not risk the uncertainty that would accompany the vulnerable exposure of themselves in intimacy and interdependency.

In summary, they have been afraid to face the passion and the creativity that course through them. They generally are afraid of vulnerability and have a *high need for control*. They experience themselves as victims of life, and adopt a stance in which "life does it to me." They tend to recognize that those who follow cultural convention are enslaved and dead. However, they themselves become trapped in their victim stance, which keeps them imprisoned in the cage of the illnesses they have created.

Statements From Allergy and Phobia Sufferers

In the words of one such person, who took more responsibility for his condition:

> I created total allergy syndrome. I experience a great fear in becoming vulnerable and have throughout my life often denied intimacy because of that fear.

> I also experience life very intensely: my emotional range consisted of jagged peaks of joy, even ecstasy, and very deep sadness and pain. The instability that I experienced from this caused much despair in my life, and I sought ways of becoming stable.

> I see total allergy syndrome as an extension of this disconnectedness from my essential self and as a reaction to the denial of my natural life.

> I am terrified of being who I am. I see myself as a little boy overawed by life and fearful of the pain and sadness that I find in life.

Another young person relates:

> My illness is the result of a lack of self-expression.

Another:

> Basically, I am finding that there is something emotional or psychological [that is, ingrained attitudes, behaviours, and suppressed feelings, needs, and desires] behind every physical allergic reaction. Awareness of the underlying factors improves the symptoms and allows me to take charge and control them much of the time.

And another:

> The challenges in my life were masked in attacking the same mundane exercises day in and day out year after year after year.

> I created the fears and these fears help me to survive situations I otherwise would not look at.

> I haven't the means to know what would constitute "value" [in my life]. . . I now know that I have to find my own definition of worth and make a strong and fully conscious decision to live it.

> This place of desolation is a large part of my pattern; it comes up over and over again starting very early in my childhood memories.

> What I've realized here is that my stubborn resistance to my own mortality only serves to further fuel my feelings of fear and anxiety. I also feel that I isolate myself from others at these times and become very lonely.

The Way Out of the Trap

We have worked with numerous people over the past thirty years who have made significant improvement in these conditions. They have struggled to *take more responsibility* for themselves and their life circumstances (including their symptoms). As they came to see that anxiety is just the life energy coursing through them, they learned to embrace increasing amounts of anxiety. As their tolerance for anxiety increased, they were able to face one of their largest fears: of being close to another human being. As they took increasing responsibility for their process, they began to understand the secret codes of the illness metaphor; they came to see the symptoms as messages from their inner being, calling for reunion with themselves. In a way, the illness, which previously was an enemy, became a friend. At bottom, they were afraid of nonexistence. They were afraid to stand on

their own and face another person. They were either isolated, or refrained from intimate contact by maintaining dependent relationships.
The following words speak for themselves:

I've learned that anxiety can be energy running through me.

I no longer fit into a mould of what I think I should be. I just am, marching to a different beat.

Everything I hold or lock in makes me sick. I need and want to be around people I can let go with.

I believe that I am well, whole, integrating . . . that I have learned and know all I need to be well and express myself in the world. What I need and want to do now is develop the self-love and confidence to trust it and do it.

I also realize that I must surrender myself to the pain, to the sadness, in order to experience the joy and intimacy that life will provide.

I seek now the courage within myself to surrender and to live.

Acceptance of the Illness Process

The courage that we have witnessed in people facing these difficult issues has been inspirational. As they have taken responsibility for their illness process, they have opened to their own life and creativity again. Instead of fighting illness, they learned to acknowledge it, accept it, and work with it. One individual put it this way:

I see my allergies and symptoms as friends/guides to keep me in tune with myself and on my path of health and growth. It is an ongoing process. This is a beginning, not an end.

Notes

1. N. Wong, "Borderline and Narcissistic Disorders: A Selective Overview," *Bulletin of the Menninger Clinic*, 44(2), 1980, pp. 101-126.

Multiple Sclerosis:
Some Impressions

This is a lengthy chapter concerning a specific ailment. We are devoting this much attention to this subject, since it illustrates many principles that one can apply in studying any disease process. Although we are focussing on Multiple Sclerosis, much can be learned that applies to cancer, cardiovascular disease, arthritis, and numerous other difficult medical conditions.

The Disease Description

Multiple sclerosis (disseminated sclerosis, MS) is a chronic disorder of the nervous system, typically affecting young and middle aged adults. The most common major disorder of the nervous system in the western world, it is said to affect about 1 in 2000 people in the UK. Women are affected 50% more frequently than men. Although the cause is uncertain, there are suggestions about inherited susceptibility. Some speculate the disease might be related to auto-immune damage, triggered by a slow virus or other infection. The disease is much more common in temperate regions than in the tropics. Immigrants from the tropics to temperate areas acquire the higher rate of MS when they settle in more temperate regions; thus, the disease seems more related to geography than to genetics. The myelin sheaths surrounding the nerves in the brain and spinal cord become damaged, leaving fibrous scarring in hardened (sclerosed) patches; the damage can be widely scattered through the nervous system.[1]

There is a wide variety of clinical nervous system signs and symptoms, which are well documented in the medical literature. The disease is prone to relapses and remissions. In the early stages common symptoms include limb weakness and heaviness, blurred or double vision in one or both eyes, tingling and numbness in a limb or in the trunk, vertigo, and unsteadiness or poor balance in walking. The bladder can be affected, causing frequency, urgency or difficulty passing water. The first attack often clears up completely within a few months; often there is a recurrence within two years. Some people continue to recover after relapses; others enter a progressive stage, with weakness and deterioration continuing. As well as increasing motor disability, there may be urinary retention or incontinence, slurred speech, and mental changes with emotional lability, depression or euphoria. There is no definitive curative treatment that is known to western science. In acute flare-ups, corticosteroids are often prescribed; this helps the immediate episode, but does not seem to alter the long-term outlook.[2]

Our Observations

Over the past twenty years, we have seen dozens of people with the diagnosis of MS who have attended experiential programs. During this time, we have built up some impressions about this disease process, and the people who suffer with it, and we have come to identify a personality profile for the people with MS. In general, they have a high need for *control* in their lives. They tend to be much above average in *intelligence*. Often, they are *goal oriented self-hating achievers*. Lurking under an apparent independence often is a profoundly held *victim stance*; these people are often ferociously *independent* to compensate for their interpretation of being controlled by others in their lives. People with MS often *procrastinate*; they have a difficult time translating thought into action. They are good talkers, and make lots of plans; however, they literally become paralysed when faced with the challenge of putting their dreams into action. Although some of them have been athletic in earlier times, they commonly experience a progressive *weakness*, often accompanied by muscle *tightness* and *shaking*.

Through the years, we have asked all the clients we have seen with MS to provide a summary of their perspectives on their illness process; indeed, we have made similar requests to people with other illness profiles too. Whereas people with allergies and phobias and chronic fatigue syndrome were very eager to deliver summaries of their personal learnings about illness patterns, the people with MS were distinctly reluctant to respond. So, in all these years, only a few persons have provided the requested documentation.[3] Hence, the quotations in this article are the result of interviewing people, and asking pointed questions, as well as including the information from the few essays we received.

In facing the challenges of MS, we have found a remarkable sex difference in how people deal with information provided to them. For persons who suffer with MS, their work and learning inevitably centre around their *isolation*, their high need for *control*, and their *abandonment of their bodies*. We believe we treat people of both sexes in the same manner in our programs. When they are given breathing exercises, and invited to engage in dialogue with friends, women do much better at following advice. Women seem to have more perseverance, and willingness to face themselves. Women will dedicate themselves to breathing, relating, and working through the process; men seem to sink back and give up. As a result, women are generally more solid in their healing than men. The men commonly protest that it is so difficult to follow a routine regimen of breathing; while the men are resisting, women just get down to work and apply themselves to the exercises. Perhaps this is the expression of greater endurance and perseverance on women's part; on the negative side, perhaps they are simply better at complying with instructions. One professional woman who has had the diagnosis of MS said the following:

> *A woman is closer to her body than a man; hence a woman will be able to find her way into her body better than a man. Women have had experiences with childbirth and menstruation, and are more familiar with the general experience of their bodies; they know their bodies a little, and are more ready to live in them. A man has never known his body except as a tool or as a function, and has a difficult time finding his way home.*

One man learned to walk without his cane when he had the stimulation of being in a program; when he returned home, he did not continue his exercise and went back to a wheel chair. Another woman from the same city sold her wheelchair to acquire the funds to attend a residential program; when her healing became her purpose, she quickly came into health, and remained so after she returned home.

Blame

People with MS are often invested in *blame*, either blaming themselves for getting the illness, or blaming some external factor (parents or some infectious agent). This blame serves to cement the illness process, and indeed is a factor in it; blame operates against symptom improvement. One woman devoted much of her energies at the beginning of her program to complaining about how handicapped people were not being adequately considered; she politicized the situation, instead of working on her own capabilities. When she was wrapped up in this, she did not have time or energy left to investigate her own relationship to the disease process. As long as the victim/blame stance persists, the MS process also persists. People often confuse personal responsibility with self-blame. When people begin to try to be accountable, they often shift from a victim stance into blaming themselves for what has happened. To facilitate healing, they must learn to distinguish between *victim* and *responsibility* and blame. One MS client said,

> I knew I was responsible for being sick, but I thought that it was just stupidity. I had allowed my defences to drop, and I got sick from an external agent. It was my bad luck to get MS rather than the flu. There was nothing I could do when the external agent had attacked.

Isolation

As long as people are stuck in fault-finding, they are failing to see beyond their own version of the world. Hence, they are kept from genuine dialogue. They perpetuate their isolation where they are trapped, and they seem unable to find the healing that would come with personal responsibility and interpersonal dialogue. These comments illustrate:

> I withdraw into myself when things get tough.

> I learned early to confide only in myself.

> Not needing help got distorted into helplessness. The last people that I would confide in were my parents. The logical extension was withdrawal.

Willfulness

MS involves a disorder of the will. Such people are usually very *willful*; they force themselves through life, and often the only way they can relax is to acquire an illness condition that makes them rest. Often, they are driven to fulfil obligations to others, and are involved in the self-hatred cycle of the path to glory towards the Ideal Self. When they try to become responsible for their illness, they often try to will themselves into wellness, which further fixates the MS process. There is a difference between willfulness and will. This statement is pertinent:

I did not want to use my will power, since it produced more pain. I didn't really believe that anything could change.

High Achievers

People with MS are often high achievers, with all the difficulties associated with a life attitude of striving, self-denial and self-discontent. They are driven:

I had to be great.

With this high achievement, I always felt inadequate. I could not choose what to do, since the risk of choosing poorly and not keeping great was too great.

I don't know when to stop.

Since so many people with MS are over-achievers, we wonder if MS provides a way to rest that the person could not otherwise accept? Literally, they have to be struck down in order to accept rest and help from others.

"Misunderstood"

The personal history often involves strong achievement ethics, accompanied by the loneliness of believing that they are misunderstood. One young man, whose parents were part of academia, said:

I had to be self-reliant. In my relationships with my parents, I felt like I was in a university lecture; I never felt understood, and to them, my pain and sadness were not important...I was told to 'buckle down' and be a little stronger.

We came to know this young man's parents, and discovered that their view was quite different from his. In our experience of his mother, we believed that she did care about his pain and sadness. This opened our minds to the possibility that the individual with MS possibly had a different view of the parents (and himself, and others). So, again, perhaps the MS was from a particular vision, in which the man believed that he was unloved, and was expected to achieve. The problem was not with the parenting, but with the individual's *experience* of the parenting.

Mental Correlates

There is a distinctive *mental lassitude* that accompanies the muscular weakness. Previously productive people become very undirected, with only occasionally episodes of vitality:

> I lived in a semivegetative state with odd bursts of excitement.

> I was full of self defeating behaviour, never completing anything. When I didn't complete anything then I couldn't be judged, and I had an excuse. Underlying this is a fear of failure, or of being condemned.

> My decision making has been poor. I have a paralysis of action. There is a split between thought and action. Thought is not translated into action. My whole life feels paralysed.

In at least one of the cases we have seen, there was evidence of an underlying mental disorganization. In this particular young woman, she kept her body tight, and she stiffly went through her days as a manager. She was in control of herself, and in control of the business she managed. However, inside, she was a frightened child who was afraid of going crazy. When she finally gave in and shared her panic and anxiety, she drew closer to her life partner, and the symptoms of MS subsided. She had to share her fear of going crazy; she had experienced a craziness in other members of her family, and she was keeping herself in stern control to keep herself from flying away, or disintegrating into madness.

Self-Hatred

The characteristic self-hatred process interferes with the self-awareness that could lead to healing:

I've been afraid to look at myself—because when I did, I turned it against myself.

Whatever I found [about myself] I used for self-blame.

People with MS become frustrated in never being perfect, even though they will attempt very large tasks. Thus, even though they often accomplish a great deal, they don't reap the fruits of their labours, often succumbing instead to self-hatred for falling short of their grandiose expectations of themselves.

Work hard enough, with enough will power, and you can do anything—that's what I thought. The result was that I was never great at anything. People would always do better than I. I compared myself to the encyclopedic 19th century writers, and always came up wanting.

Procrastination

Mixed in with a strong achievement ethic is a common tendency to procrastinate. One woman who became fascinated with her illness process, and indeed learned to have the symptoms of muscular weakness turn around inside of minutes with dedicated breathing, was subject to procrastination. She applied to graduate school, and intended to write up her experiences with MS as a doctoral dissertation. For years she obsessed about the thesis, and could not get down to writing it, even though she had the information at hand that she was ready to synthesize. She never did finish the dissertation for her Ph.D. This same woman was fascinated to discuss her MS process when we began the conversations; and she brought forth many valuable insights when we did converse with her. Yet, she never did summarize her experiences into a written form. Thus, she did not directly provide any material for this article.

Often, people with MS are exceptionally intelligent. They sometimes tend towards idealistic dreaming, rather than dedicating themselves to practical pursuits. Thus, they will fantasize and procrastinate, and not engage themselves fully in their lives. They often come to understand their illness process very well, without doing anything about it. They know what they should do; but, they would rather think about it than do it. Their capability to rationalize is very marked. They are like a powerful automobile with the transmission disengaged—they can't seem to get into gear! This same process seems to show in their muscular weakness: they are very capable physically, but often do not engage their strength.

> My character is basically flawed. I am intelligent, but the flaw prevents me from using my intelligence in the real world. I succumb to gross absurd self-idealizations as a substitute for actions.

Is this a failure to translate idea into action? Procrastination and idealistic dreaming seem to replace physical engagement and incarnation. Instead, they abandon their bodies, to take up residence in the dream states of their minds.

Disembodiment

MS is a disease of *disembodiment*. These people are often afraid of their passions, and reluctant to surrender to the energies that flow through them. Repressed and self-denying, their bodies tighten as they exert increasing control over their feelings and expression. Literally, they are leaving their bodies, and living in their minds. Often, they are uncomfortable with their sexuality.

In MS, the body itself is denied. Often, the body is a tool, rather than a source of pleasure. Sensations of all kinds are ignored, and sexual inhibitions are often hidden in their symptoms. *Their healing involves incarnation.* In this process, these people often will show *fears of intimacy*, and *discomfort with sexuality* in specific, and sensations in general. One young woman did not want to shake, because she thought this was "gross." In the Chinese medicine theory of the Five Elements, MS is a disease of the earth, with failure to incarnate fully, failure to be present and in the flesh. This is seen in Chinese medicine to be accompanied by a failure of *yi* (purpose or intention). As facets of this earth imbalance, there are disturbances in boundaries and in relationships.

Their bodies are not their own. They experience themselves as the victims of a disease process that takes over. Indeed, the disease sometimes appears to be a devil that inhabits the body. One woman in her forties struggled to take charge of her process, and was learning to breathe to relax her tight muscles. She had previously been unable to shop, since her body would seize into painful contractures after she had visited a couple of stores in a shopping centre. After her dedication to breathing, she learned to accept the tightness that would come when she breathed; it was as if some internal devil was fighting her attempt to relax. She would breathe through the tightness, and her muscles would relax again. Her triumph came when she walked several miles around the lake at the family cottage; for years prior to this time, she could scarcely enjoy even a brief walk in nature, since her body would seize up. Coming to attend a program was an act of self determination and self-definition. Her disease process was attempting to prevent her from improving, by making her tight and tired. A typical comment:

I was out of my body.

Control

MS people are afraid to be out of control. Hence, they keep their symptoms secret, and don't talk about the fears they have when they experience muscular weakness, or a decline in vision. They struggle to *maintain an image* to others as being in control, and needing no one. Hence, they are often in positions of responsibility, and look very capable. Their fears and suffering are kept private. Consequently, they do not have the comfort that could come in sharing their feelings and experience with a friend or co-worker. They are isolated, and tend to want to take care of everything themselves.

MS is an issue of *domination and submission.* Strongly controlled and controlling people, MS people hold their bodies in a rigid fashion, and literally will themselves (and others) through life. They submit reluctantly to authority, and often resist in passive ways when they must submit. In relationship to themselves, they can be cruel in their dominance of their own physical and mental being. Usually, MS people *use their bodies*, rather than inhabiting them. We have noticed that such a rigid body armouring is usually held in place by severely limited breathing. They do not feel their bodies; they use them as tools. In a fundamental way, they are not in their bodies, and need to learn to reinhabit their physical being. When these people learn to breathe more deeply, their symptoms (which they often hate) will exacerbate. They will shake more, and they might experience panic or anxiety. They tend to want to tighten up, resist the symptoms, and in this way fight the expression of feeling and energy that comes from more breathing. When they contract and resist, they are in a mode of *submission* to their symptoms, which have taken over to dominate their lives. If they persist in breathing, and *surrender* to the release that comes, their muscular strength often will return, and they will find more energy for physical activity. They frequently find this frightening, as they inhabit the bodies that they had previously abandoned. Their temptation is to *submit* to the symptoms of tightness and disincarnation, rather than *surrender* to their feelings.

Often, they report that they are *afraid* of the shaking that comes with breathing practice, because it represents a loss of control to them; we encourage them to let go, to surrender to the body's vegetative responses, and relax. They are often *embarrassed* to shake in public; when they learn to share this shaking instead of hiding it, they are already well into the process of surrender.

Denial of Passion

The passions are denied too. The woman described above discovered that her tightness was not random. She would contract when she was not expressing her feelings. In particular, she had shut down her sexuality, and she discovered in an educational program that she would tighten up around attractive young men. When she learned to express her attractions to these young men (without any intention to act on these attractions), she began to feel more free with these feelings, and her symptoms subsided. A similar easement came as she learned to express her anger in a more open and direct fashion. She had previously used a "nice" mask to cover her feelings (she herself often didn't know when she was displeased); when she learned to identify her negative feelings, and express them, her symptoms declined remarkably. So, MS can be seen as a failure of expression, and a failure to accept and live with one's passions. One begins to heal when the sensations and pleasures of the body are accepted:

I'm now doing things I haven't done since I was seventeen years old.

Caretaking

A frequent theme is that of being a *caretaker*. In relationships, people with MS smooth the waters, and take care of others. In several instances, people with MS have seen it as their duty as children to take care of one or both of their parents. For example:

> *I was a caretaker for my mother.*

Having lived as a caretaker, perhaps the only way they can relax is to become ill themselves, and then have someone take care of them. Perhaps the mental framework of seeing relationships as caretaking endeavours is a feature of the MS process. These people fail to connect; instead, relationships are largely seen in terms of taking care of others, or being taken care of themselves. In one case, a grown man discovered that his mother wanted to move from his home town; when he was unhappy about this, she did not move, because she was afraid he would get worse. She didn't tell him directly, she only talked to her friends about this. This illustrates the failure of dialogue, wherein the mother objectified the son as unable to face these issues directly. She was afraid he would get sicker if she moved away; under the social proprieties, she believed his health was under her control. She was martyred to his illness, and the rest of his family and friends got caught up in the victim attitude and accompanying objectification. Thus the mother limited herself, and in this way, kept her son ill (and herself too—she had the "mother of MS" syndrome).

Pleasing

These people are often overly nice in their demeanour. Their desire to be liked and accepted gives them an accommodating air, and a superreasonable placating quality. They are so afraid to be rejected that they try desperately to please others. They often have been "good children," pleasing their parents; they grow up to be adults who fit in. Thus, they deny their own passions, and are afraid to express anger or negative feelings. They keep themselves (and others) under control by limiting the expression of negative feelings.

They tend to be political rather than personal. They would rather talk about how things should be, and what is wrong with society, or other people; they do this often in a very cool cerebral fashion. Inside they are often very angry (at their spouses or family, or at the disease itself); but they convert this anger into political discussions, rather than express the anger directly.

Failure of Vision

MS can be seen as a "failure of vision." They often refuse to see that they can take more responsibility for their illness process. For example, we generally recommend that people who are suffering from chronic or severe illnesses should breathe in a concentrated fashion as much as possible—at least fifteen minutes four times per day. Also, we recommend to people with MS that they get some regular exercise to encourage their muscles to move in a synchronized fashion. Often, we suggest that people go the gymnasium to build up muscular tone, or embark upon walking or calisthenics.

Rather than put these suggestions into practice, these people seek answers and advice from an authority or a guru; they seem to prefer someone else's reframing rather than take the courage to find the meaning of the disease state in themselves. In this *limited field dependent vision*, people are filled with self-hate, and strive to live up to someone else's suggestions (parents, healers, gurus etc.) instead of meeting the challenge of facing life for themselves, to make up their own minds about things. Often, these very intelligent, capable people have a long history of subjugating themselves to teachers and authorities. We have seen numerous people who would rather look for another guru who can tell them how to become spiritually enlightened, rather than face up to the messy day to day task of coming into their bodies through breathing and personal responsibility.

Healing Through Revision

What would facilitate a healing is a "revision"—literally, coming to see with original eyes what comes from inside. Possibly these persons once had such a self-directed vision, and lost it; or perhaps they never developed the ability to "see" for themselves. Thus, they are sick because of faulty vision.

A revision would involve an updating (revision=revising) of their self-concept and their attitudes about others. Probably, parents, authority figures and self have all been objectified; they can appear very different with updated perspectives. This revision takes courage, and when people fail in courage, they succumb instead to self-hate. A note from one courageous person:

> I am my disease "This has been a total revolution in thinking from where I was at. I am now open to change things. I could still have MS. My patterns in life were the disease. All I had to do was change my life, and I would not be sick.

Often, desperation brings the person to the brink of self-discovery:

> The paralysis was increasing, and I was having increasing difficulty translating my thoughts into actions. My right side was paralysed for two weeks. I believed that it was just a matter of time, and I was scared. I couldn't walk, and I had to radically change my life.

As in many illness processes, a nuclear problem involves *fixated attitudinal positions*. Healing often progresses when individuals recognize their participation in the illness process. One man said,

> The assumptions that I was holding were dead ends. I could not heal because my body was fixed, and was basically a container. I used the 'cash register approach' to life—I collected experiences and rang them up. I thought if I could collect enough experiences I could change.

When they come to a new attitude, wherein they can learn about the illness, and take responsibility for it, the healing can progress:

> On the advice of my friends, I realized that I could do something. I now realize that I wasn't a victim.

The notion of energy is very useful in working with MS people. Previously, a client had believed that he was running out of energy, and that his physical body which generated and stored the energy was failing. Then he began to see in terms of the Chinese acupuncture theory, where energy is universally abundant, and is merely blocked or fixated in illness states. As he began to become interested in unfixating the energy (through breathing, and open dialogues with significant others), he began to feel more energetic:

> *I have a new perspective. I believe in the energy body; the energy body and I are constantly in flux, in transformation.*

Acupuncture, and other energy approaches are very helpful:

> *I am actually being transformed after needles. You still recognize me because enough of the old pattern persisted.*

To work with the illness process, the practitioner is more of a friend. Helpers can establish relationships in which clients can learn without the harshness of their oppressive superego. They will often express a feeling of gratitude that someone reached out, and appreciated them, even when they were not accepting themselves:

> *You accepted me as a friend.*

Awareness Into Action

With awareness, people with MS can learn not to give in to the tendency to disengage. Instead, they can engage with life, and move ahead with healthier, more active perspectives. Much improvement comes with the ability to laugh:

> *I don't have to succumb to this flaw. Now, for the first time in my life, I'm happy. I can take responsibility for myself. Now, I can laugh at myself, and not take my idealizations and superego so seriously.*

As they become more aware of the memes that run through their illness process, they can learn to understand and take more responsibility for themselves. Generally, they will acknowledge that they knew that their illness would wax and wane in relation to their attitudes and life experiences:

> *Deep down, I knew all along what was going on.*

A New Attitude

When people come to see their illness process as themselves, they are no longer doing battle with themselves and the disease. They are then engaged in a learning process, wherein they come to accept and appreciate the meaning of their illness process. Some comments:

I'm more curious than afraid now.

My plan now is to listen to my superego, and then go about my own business.

Getting MS has been a blessing in disguise. I have been learning to appreciate my symptoms.

We believe that healing from MS involves a change in relationship with self, others and the world:

When I interact with anyone, I become different. Relationships heal. The healing process is in interaction.

Individuals who improve come to see their disease process as a learning opportunity, rather than an illness that they have acquired. They become interested in their personality configuration, and come to see more and more how their attitudes and actions determine the course of their illness:

Understanding the patterns led to these awarenesses.

They become less intent upon the final outcome of being disease free, and become more interested in learning about the process itself:

The symptoms I still have will slowly recede.

Individuals can gradually come to think of themselves in a new way, where they are no longer a disease, but rather a person involved in a life process:

It's been a phenomenal experience realizing I don't have to be sick.

I no longer have MS. My neurologist, however, has a different assumption system; he thinks I still have it, in remission.

Summary and Recommendations

Some common recommendations came from all the clients who have responded. We ourselves endorse the following in learning to deal effectively with the issues relating to Multiple Sclerosis:

- Learn about the victim stance, accept it, and take responsibility for it.
- Even if one is afraid, take the courage to take action, rather than sitting back from life.
- Breathe! Symptoms ultimately will regress with routine breathing. Clients do feel increased strength and vitality after breathing; but also they feel more anxious and exposed.
- People with MS have abandoned their bodies, and have thus avoided experiencing their feelings (thus limiting their sexual expression, and their creativity). Learn to come home into the body.
- Interacting meaningfully with others in open honest communication, owning objectifications, and not succumbing to them—this is the path to healing through dialogue.
- Learn to accept instability, insecurity and shaking.
- Express anger, and other uncomfortable feelings more directly. In this way, the feelings will not be stuck in the body, and the tightness will gradually recede.

A Radical Thought

The prognosis in MS is extremely variable; even the most severe cases can have sudden deterioration followed by striking improvement. So, when someone improves, it is difficult to assess what is the normal course of the ebb and flow of the disease, and what is the result of some beneficial activity or treatment. Our radical hypothesis is this—perhaps the disease itself does not wax and wane, but instead maybe it is the changes in the person that express themselves as improvements or deteriorations.

We have seen numerous people make some very strong and enduring changes in their lives, with a marked lessening of their symptoms. With some, the improvement has been so dramatic that they seem to be free of disease. Conventional medical thinking suggests that the lesions are still there, but are somehow quiescent ("MS is a disease that is characterized by exacerbations and remissions"[4]). We wonder if the lesions of the central nervous system can somehow vanish. In other words, is the disease necessarily always there? We have seen an upgoing plantar response (evidence of central nervous system dysfunction) change to a downgoing normal response after one episode of body work. Perhaps the lesions also vanish when these people breathe and inhabit themselves. If this were so, we would be challenged to re-think many of our assumptions about other serious illnesses, such as cancer and heart disease.

Notes

1. R. Blackwell, R. and H. MacPherson, "Multiple Sclerosis: Staging and Patient Management." *Journal of Chinese Medicine*, No. 42, May 1993.

2. Ibid.

3. Jody Wright, "A Personal Experience With Multiple Sclerosis," *Shen*, Issue 15, Spring 1995, pp. 2,3.

4. R. Blackwell, R. and H. MacPherson, "Multiple Sclerosis: Staging and Patient Management." *Journal of Chinese Medicine*, No. 42, May 1993.

Part Six:
ISSUES

You will still sleep many hours
here on the beach,
and one clear morning you will find
your boat tied to another shore.

—Antonio Machado [1]

1. Antonio Machado, *Times Alone: Selected Poems of Antonio Machado*, trans.
    by Robert Bly (Middletown, Connecticut: Wesleyan University Press,
    1983), p. 29.

Creation-Centred Spirituality

Imaginary Biography

First childhood, no limits, no renunciations,
no goals. Such unthinking joy.
Then abruptly terror, schoolrooms, boundaries, captivity,
and a plunge into temptation and a deep loss.

Defiance. The one crushed will be the crusher now,
and he avenges his defeats on others.
Loved, feared, he rescues, wrestles, wins,
and overpowers others, slowly, act by act.

And then all alone in space, in lightness, in cold.
But deep in the shape he has made to stand erect
he takes a breath, as if reaching for the First, Primitive . . .

Then God explodes from his hiding place.
                                  —Rainer Maria Rilke [1]

The Holistic View

Most people will wrestle with issues of spirituality and meaning, regardless
of their particular problems and their motive for embarking on a voyage of
self-discovery, personal growth, or self-healing. The fields of education,
religion, psychology, sociology, and politics also must ultimately address
the issue of spirituality. From a holistic point of view, the spiritual
dimension reflects the state of being of the other levels of each person's
existence; when there are fixations at any level, these will be manifested
spiritually too. Although a person's awareness and focus may be on one of
these levels, any movement or change will find expression on all of the
levels. Thus, shifts in body, emotions, or mental attitudes will have spiritual

implications; and vice versa, alterations on the spiritual plane will be manifest mentally, physically and emotionally.

Religion and Spirituality

The term "spirituality" refers to the level of being that addresses the issues of *meaning*. Too often, spirituality is confused with religion, which is a codification of spirituality. Religion is a sort of map of meaning that is used by institutions and governing authorities to provide a group of people with a morality—rules of behaviour and thought aimed at a common goal.

> *Religion is tending to degenerate into a decent formula wherewith to embellish a comfortable life.* —Alfred North Whitehead [2]

Redemption-Based Spirituality

Many people suffered from church experiences in childhood, and so they resist any exploration in the direction of spirituality; they confuse religiosity with spirituality. Their resistance is often based in their belief that spirituality will be accompanied with morality, control, limitation of their behaviour, guilt, recrimination, self-denial, and ultimately self-denigration. Such a belief is based on experiences arising out of the commonly held belief and teachings of the neo-Platonist *redemption-based spirituality*.[3] In this view, humans are imperfect in sin, and need to be redeemed through the intercession of an external agent.

This conservative view, which dominates most traditional western religions, assumes a higher power (God) existing outside the self. Hence power, control, and morality are issues to be discovered beyond oneself, dictated by some wiser, stronger, and more invulnerable being. The authority for correct behaviour exists with that being ("God") or the agents of that being ("church"). Most people, in their struggle toward autonomy and personal growth, must reclaim the strength and personal integrity that they lost in their upbringing and social training. The authorities that they usually have rejected include parents, education, and religion, when those have exerted a dominating influence. In this rejection, they can become locked in a power struggle, which tends to obstruct their growth, rather than aid it.

Creation-Centred Spirituality

There is another possible view of spirituality, in which the authority remains within the individual. This is *creation-centred spirituality*, in which each person is seen as a part of, and reflective of, the totality of existence ("God"). In the view of the philosophy of structuralism, each person is already whole, although the wholeness is usually not clearly expressed; hence, structuralism is compatible with creation-centred spirituality (see above, "The Helping Relationship"). There is nothing to be rid of, or added to, or punished for; there is only more self-awareness and self-responsibility to be experienced. There is no need to struggle toward perfection; each person is already whole. Instead of striving, people can devote themselves to know and to accept themselves in the process of self-compassion (see above, "The Idea Self: Striving For Perfection"). In that process, they can be more revealed to themselves and to others, manifesting what already exists within. This is a practice of *revelation* and unfolding wholeness, rather than a striving toward a perfection dictated by greater authorities. People then can be involved in creating the expression of themselves, and are released from the obligations to become what others want them to be. We could put it this way:

> In redemption-based spirituality, we ask the question and God provides the answer. In creation-centred spirituality, God asks the question and we are the answer.

Comparing The Two Views

These issues related to external authority have had a significant impact on the lives of most people, whether they had direct early experiences with a religion or only grew up in a society dominated by religious ideas. For the individual, denying or reacting against religions will not help; such actions only serve to fixate the person's energy all the more, creating more walls and resistances that produce more blocks. Many people drop out of formal religions, often seeking some other expression of their spirituality. In North America, where alternative life-styles have become acceptable, people are sometimes drawn toward eastern religions, which seem to offer the promise of liberation and ultimate answers. Ironically, too often the very people who are attempting to escape from the tyranny of authoritarian rule will submit to the authority of a guru or another form of religion (such as the teachings of some New Age leader) in the hope of finding enlightenment or absolute truths.

In creation-centred spirituality, the authority for meaning remains centred in each individual. Alternative meanings or even opposing points of view can be considered, sorted, and digested; no one position should ever be swallowed whole or taken on as "the truth." Each person (being God) is considered to be whole, capable of discovering personal meaning or individual truth from within. Sometimes advocates of this position unwittingly adopt an isolationist perspective, forgetting that this point of view recognizes the God within every person, which is the same God for everyone, thus connecting us all. Our task is not to become God, or to fashion ourselves to please God, but rather to *discover* God (the elements of meaning of the self) within. As an expression of a structuralist philosophy, creation-centred spirituality would have us discover the patterns of existence (God) in any of our levels of being—in our bodies, our feelings, our minds, and our relationships.

To love another person is to see the face of God. [4]

Sin

Redemption-centred spirituality assumes that we are born imperfect or incomplete (in sin) and that we need to make reparations and submit to a higher power to become perfect; this is the moral interpretation of sin (we are "imperfect" or "bad"). In creation-centred spirituality each person is believed to be whole, connected to all others and the universe, as part of a total energy flow; however, because of a limited state of consciousness, the experience of being connected is lost; sin (meaning "separation") is the state of being *unaware* of that connection. In redemption-based spirituality, human life is rooted in "original sin"; in creation-centred spirituality, human existence emanates from "original blessing."[5]

The goal of creation-centred spirituality is to rediscover that connection, reaffirming the wholeness of existence through self-awareness and raising the level of consciousness; authority remains within the person, not in outside people or structures or institutions.[6] Creation-centred spirituality is self-centred—but is not selfish, self-indulgent, or self-promoting. Creation-centred spirituality assumes that God can be found in all of life's experiences, including those that appear to be negative, dark, and frightening.

Transcend or Transform

Redemption-centred spirituality, found in both eastern and western religions, offers redemption or enlightenment through renunciation, atonement, self-denial, or disengagement from the material, physical world; salvation offers relief from guilt, pain, and suffering. Spiritual practices in redemption-centred spirituality are often *transcendental* in nature, through self-denial, self-punishment, or disengagement from oneself.

On the other hand, creation-centred spirituality emphasizes living more fully in the present, acknowledging all aspects (both dark and light) of the person, becoming more self-aware, with a higher level of consciousness. Learning through relating is one of the *transformational* approaches; discovering creative expression of all aspects of the person is one of the goals. Spirituality can be experienced at all levels of being, at all times. God can be expressed by each man and woman being fully alive, as free of fixations as possible, willing to allow the energy flow into all niches of experience, without bias or prejudice.[7] Creation-centred spirituality acknowledges a oneness, with responsibility (response-ability) but not license. In eastern practices, this is the "every-minute Zen" notion of being fully present and fully aware. Because God is assumed to be ever-present in all things, the discovery of God requires mindfulness and awareness, rather than striving toward perfection.

> *God's being is my being*
>   *and God's primordial being*
> *is my primordial being.*
>
> *Wherever I am,*
>   *there is God.*
> *The eye with which I see God*
>   *is the same eye with which*
> *God sees me.*
>   —Meister Eckhart[8]

Notes

1. Rainer Maria Rilke, "Imaginary Biography" in *Selected Poems of Rainer Maria Rilke*, translated by Robert Bly (New York: Harper and Row, 1981), p. 171.

2. Alfred North Whitehead, quoted in M.Fox, *Original Blessing* (Santa Fe: Bear and Company, 1983) p. 10.

3. M. Fox, *Meditations with Meister Eckhart* (Santa Fe: Bear and Company, 1983), p. 5.

4. From the musical *Les Misérables*, by Alain Boublil and Claude-Michel Shönberg, lyrics by Herbert Kretzmer (Original Broadway Cast Recording, Geffen Records, 1986).

5. M. Fox, *Original Blessing* (Santa Fe, NM: Bear & Co., 1983).

6. J. McKeen and B.R. Wong, *The Relationship Garden* (Gabriola Island, B.C.: PD Publishing, 1996), pp. 203-204.

7. Ibid., pp. 172-73.

8. M. Fox, *Meditations with Meister Eckhart* (Santa Fe: Bear and Company, 1983), pp. 20-21.

Myths (Not) To Live By

"When I use a word," Humpty Dumpty said, in a rather scornful tone, "it means just what I choose it to mean—neither more nor less."
"The question is," said Alice, "whether you can *make words mean so many different things."*
"The question is," said Humpty Dumpty, "which is to be master —that's all."

—Lewis Carroll [1]

Our "New Age" helping professions are beset by a raft of unquestioned and frequently untested beliefs that are used by many practitioners in their attempts to serve their clients. Consequently, many such recipients are finding themselves trapped by a whole new set of untenable assumptions that enslave rather than liberate. The following is a partial sampling of some of the myths that are in danger of being reified into "truths." They are offered as propositions which hopefully will stimulate discussion and investigation, rather than themselves becoming "truths" or "falsehoods."

People are entitled to a happy life free of stress, poverty, accidents and danger.

This myth has been the basis of the current prevalence of victimhood that has contributed to many people no longer taking responsibility for themselves. Instead, numerous individuals take for granted that they have a right to be clothed, fed and generally cared for, without having to contribute anything in return. They live lives of dependency and resentment, always seeking retribution for their needs being unmet or their "rights" being transgressed. Such a situation finds expression in the politics of the welfare state and in the faultfinding in the courts of law (euphemistically referred to as the discovery of "responsibility"). Within these individuals, the cost of buying into such an attitude is high—the limitation of personal growth. Helplessness and revenge become their ways of life; these are expressed in illness symptoms and unsatisfactory relationships. By supporting such attitudes, the helping professions often contribute to the problem rather than help with solutions.

Poverty breeds social ills.

The adoption of this attitude by governments and social helpers in general is what underlies much of the welfare state. Supporters of this belief rarely stop to consider how much happiness that financial success has had on various countries. Are people living in "poor" countries more unhappy than those enjoying economic success? Attempts at the redistribution of wealth have produced little positive results. Bulldozing slums and replacing them with new buildings frequently fails: in time, the displaced inhabitants manage to create slums out of their new quarters. Surely it is time to consider that both poverty and social ills are products of a *mental attitude* which can only be altered with proper education rather than the dispensing of funds.

Change is possible.

Because of this assumption, many helpers find themselves frustrated at trying to make silk purses out of sows' ears. Common sense and experience show that people are limited by their basic nature and biological assets or handicaps. The important issue is not *change* (which is a questionable possibility), but rather people's *relationship* to situations. Becoming aware of this provides individuals with an opportunity to *transform* the expression of their behaviour, to take more *responsibility* for themselves, to make freer choices in their future, more realistically based upon the circumstances of the present. Much therapy is based upon the assumption that change is possible; perhaps the impossibility of change could partly explain the lack of success of psychotherapy that has been reported by a number of studies.[23]

Childhood traumatic experiences will produce adult emotional problems.

Currently, this is a very fashionable notion, especially in the area of childhood sexual abuse. Although many practitioners staunchly believe this—to the point of explaining most, if not all problems to be results of early childhood trauma—there has been little scientific data that can substantiate such claims. However, because of the widespread publicity given to such beliefs, many current emotional problems are being *blamed* on such experiences. Little investigation has been done on a probably greater number of instances of early "abuse" in which the "victims" have used those experiences to effect positive life choices. It would be interesting to discover how and why such people have been able to do so. From our own work we have arrived at the conclusion that the past should be able to *inform* the present, but not be used to *excuse* it. When people adopt this attitude, they can take more *responsibility* in their lives, and diminish their inclination towards *blame* and *revenge* which tend to arrest personal development.

We are "responsible" for our own illnesses.

Indeed, we agree with the original intent of this statement—that each person *participates* and makes necessary life *choices* in the process of developing illnesses. However, many in the field of holistic health have interpreted this to mean that people are to *blame* for their own illnesses; they have assumed a *moral* position which is readily transmitted to vulnerable clients. As a consequence, as if they did not already have enough problems, many ill people are now having to secondarily wrestle with a *guilt* that is not primary to the process of the development of their illness.

You are what you eat.

This is an especially compelling dictum to health addicts who are compulsive and paranoid about everything that they ingest. They appear to ignore the amazing faculties of sorting, choosing, absorbing and storing that is characteristic of the human body. Rather than spending so much energy at investigating every calorie, mineral and molecule that passes their lips, perhaps more could be gained by considering why the body would choose to select the elements it does. If it chooses to store fat in order to defend the self from intimacy, would it not be more worthwhile for that person to work on relationship issues rather than on the discovery of the ever-new diets? And wouldn't it be interesting to decide on what you eat without a morality of right or wrong? Probably it is the *moral* component of your diet that is most destructive to your health, whether you are vegetarian or carnivorous. Taking the "you are what you eat" argument to absurdity, vegetarians must slowly be changing into plants!

Related to this subject is the current belief in low-fat diets to assure good health and longer life. Although that idea seems simplistically appealing, there does not seem to be much hard evidence to support it. One study seems to suggest that strict adherence to such a diet over a lifetime might prolong a man's life by days, and a woman's life by weeks.

Compromise is necessary for a successful relationship.

Many counsellors believe that in order for a couple to adjust to one another, each partner must give up something in order to reach a compromise. Although on the surface this seems harmless enough, closer examination reveals that what is being advocated is the *reduction* of each of the involved parties to the lowest common denominator. Thus, the cost of having a relationship would be for both to become less of themselves, to diminish the potential of what each person could possibly be. In our experience, most couples that stay together through compromise end up either living together with growing resentment, or they sink into despair and apathy; in many cases, they ultimately separate with negativism and vengeance.

When partners are responsible for themselves, there is no need for compromise. Instead, they can become curious about differences, and share their varied points of view. Ultimately, they can arrive, not at compromises, but *agreements* about what course to take, without either partner having to relinquish values or opinions.[4]

Peace is possible.

Throughout history, it has become apparent that world peace is beyond our grasp. As with most interpersonal relationships, one negotiated compromise after another is temporarily achieved, and then is lost; the only variable is the amount of time between broken agreements and renewed negotiations. During the periods of respite that seem calm on the surface, submerged and repressed resentments breed and grow, ultimately bursting forth in renewed hostilities.

Instead of wasting time and energy in negotiating new terms for peace, an alternate choice would be to focus on *educating* the involved parties to appreciate diversity rather than viewing differences with hostility and suspicion. To do so would require a general acceptance of the principle of *self-responsibility* and a *raising of consciousness*, both individual and collective. The expansion of consciousness would make room for more *appreciation* (as opposed to tolerance) of one another. The past would then be useful to *inform* the present rather than controlling it. Instead of reverting to old patterns of behaviour, the focus would be on developing new patterns, a new sense of *harmony* with one another.[5]

Rebellion is necessary for independence.

In many ways this is so; however, is it desirable? In growing from a state of dependence, rebellion ties the individual to the very tenets that are being negated. Adolescents who rebel against the rule to come home early are shaping their lives *in reaction to* authority, hence remaining negatively dependent upon that same authority. In rebellion, the important factors governing behaviour remain located *outside of the self*.

On the other hand, a person could become involved in achieving *autonomy* rather than independence. An autonomous person's centre remains *within* the self. Decisions are made on a realistic basis rather than in reaction to somebody else. Ironically, many people fighting for their independence really would prefer autonomy, and are disappointed when they achieve an independent state.

Personal power is important for individual growth.

Many current social movements seek more personal power as an antidote to grievances of oppression in the past. Too often, this is converted into expectations for more consideration, special status, or more privileges. When these are not met, the cry of "victim" demands redress of grievances. Too often, society collaborates to punish transgressors and reward "victims" who can now feel "powerful" in their revenge. But in the end, what actually has been gained? What are the rewards of revenge?

We distinguish between "power" (having control over external events and others) and "strength" (which involves confidently accepting and expressing oneself); the former is *other*-related while the latter is *self*-referred. To have power and dominance over others is actually a position of weakness because of the dependence on the submission of others. On the other hand, when people have an internal sense of strength, they are more full and authentic. Power diminishes the self; strength stimulates growth.

High self-esteem is important for personal success.

The self-esteem movement is gaining much ground in the fields of education and psychology. There are now governmental ministries of self-esteem, and educational systems have placed self-esteem among the top goals of education. Already, casualties of this movement are beginning to appear. Students and teachers who have failed to elevate self-esteem are experiencing self-hatred and depression. Unwarranted praise to bolster flagging self-esteem encourages self-deception; if this distorted mirroring continues, children remain undeveloped in their faculties for self-evaluation and self-motivation, and become increasingly out of touch with their authentic nature.

It is better that people learn more *self-acceptance* and *self-compassion*—to be more ready to acknowledge and love themselves in their struggles to survive and belong. To have the initiative to try, to accept themselves if they fail, and to rely upon themselves as the judges of what is deemed success—these are the hallmarks of individuating people. We know many people with a low sense of self-esteem who are creating happy lives for themselves, because they have learned the secret of self-acceptance.

Shame is responsible for unhappiness.

There is much confusion regarding shame and guilt, which are frequently interchanged in usage and dictionary definition.[6] Guilt, not shame, underlies many of the problems people have in life.

When people are in guilt, they are punishing themselves for a breach of conduct that violates a law or a moral tenet (either real or imagined); they are less of themselves in the objectification and self-hatred that accompany guilt. Guilt is associated with the problems of striving for perfection (see above, "The Ideal Self: Striving For Perfection."). In guilt, people are cold, tight, distant, objectified and objectifying; they thus are not standing forth in their authentic nature. Guilt involves a closure of the self; hence, the myriad problems that come with withdrawal can ensue.

On the other hand, shame is an experience of warmth that involves self-recognition; it is a personal response to being revealed, wherein the reference is to the self. In shame, people are undefended and vulnerable, and hence capable of intimacy and growth; with the revelation that accompanies shame, people can be more aware of themselves. So, indeed, shame involves a sense of fullness about the self, and can accompany a deep happiness.

Bad things only happen to bad people.

This statement is a symptom of immature minds that primarily operate from the moral rather than from expanded awareness and heightened consciousness. Underlying this notion is the propensity for people to ascribe guilt before wrongdoing is actually proven. Related to this is the frequently misinterpreted karmic idea that each person is atoning for wrongs committed in the past. The simplistic moral corollary is that doing good ensures a good life.

The New Age concept of personal responsibility is often misused to mean that each person is to *blame* for all action and results (hence "bad" occurrences are the punishment for bad people). This moralistic twist is often misapplied to illness conditions. That you are *responsible* for your illness or accident (i.e., you have participated in the lifestyle that contributes to everything in your life) does not mean that you are *to blame* for the illness. So, people cannot be assessed as "bad" based upon what has occurred with them.

People are basically good.

Once human behaviour is divided into "good" and "bad" through moral beliefs, social convention attempts to eliminate the bad. The "bad," the dark, and the negative forces within are generally repressed and denied;

then people see no need to address them. Instead, society holds up an unrealistic "ideal" type of person whom all citizens are expected to use as a model for their own behaviour. Usually people adopt this denial, refusing to address themselves to the inherent "evil" capabilities that lie within them; this leads to the expression of the repressed energy in indirect (and frequently socially acceptable) ways—such as wars, petty crimes, ruthless interpersonal relationships, "dirty" politics, and exploitative kinds of businesses that ignore personal and ecological considerations. The main issue is that people are probably capable of the whole spectrum of moral behaviour; it is important for them to know and acknowledge this, so that they can choose not to use their energies destructively.

Get out of your head; trust only your body!

This was the war cry of many who lived in the rebellious era of the 1960s and 1970s; this statement made thinking politically incorrect. The mind was held suspect while the body, its functions, meanings, and feelings were held in high regard. Responsibility and cause-effect considerations were discarded, as adherents to such a philosophy wanted to live "in the moment," impulsively catering to emerging desires. Information, history, theory, books, philosophy, and literature (all products of the mind) were relegated to the dustbin, thus fostering an epidemic of anti-intellectualism, anti-planning and anti-commitment. This situation prepared the way for the next, more profound denial, "You are not your body, or your mind."

You are not your body or your mind!

This is the maxim of the spiritually ambitious who would desire to grow *beyond* themselves through transpersonal methods, such as those proposed by gurus of eastern religions and philosophies. All the uses of the will are seen to contribute towards illusion and earthly desire, preventing the person from experiencing the "oneness" of universal consciousness. As in the eastern cultures that foster such transcendental ideas, adherents find living and supporting themselves in regular society to be too difficult; hence they tend to gather in "spiritual" and "intentional" communities that support their spiritual quest. In their rejection of society's traditional standards, their search for "oneness" results in a degree of social isolation.

People (especially children) need to be loved.

This myth is likely impossible to dispel. It is based on the assumption that "love" is a commodity like light or heat—that people are born deficient, needing to be filled with love, first from parents and then from other people. Indeed, children need to be stimulated—but *they do not need to be loved!* Most people live as though they will only be happy when they obtain a dependable source of love; most carry with them a sense of being entitled to love, resenting parents and partners who do not live up to that expectation. Yet, they are actually only going to feel fulfilled when they discover their own ability to love, realizing that there is no such thing as "love"; there is only the activity of "loving," a feeling that is only growth-inducing when it emanates *from* them, not when it comes *to* them. Depending on love from without seems to provide security; but this attitude results in issues of control, and does not foster the development of autonomy.

Our feelings can be hurt by others.

Although much of people's behaviour is governed by this myth—fearing that what is said may hurt another's feelings, or believing that what others do or say will hurt their feelings—actually, the entire mechanism of pain exists solely *within* the interior of the individual, under the complete control only of that person. Whatever is said or done by anyone else, it is the individual's own interpretation of the deed or word that stimulates the brain to initiate whether to laugh or to hurt. The trigger exists primarily within the recipient's cerebral cortex, and secondarily in lower brain centres. So, more accurately, people hurt their own feelings over what others say or do—it is impossible for it to be otherwise!

Trust your feelings.

Feelings provide the texture and quality of experience. Since they are directly dependent upon our perceptions and judgments, they themselves provide an unreliable source upon which decisions should be based. People would be better served by developing more accurate perceptions and checking out the accuracy of their judgments. Since feelings are generated so arbitrarily and are so context-based, they are readily contaminated by prejudice and past experiences, when individuals were too immature to be able to arrive at competent conclusions. Thus, making decisions in the present based upon such feelings is filled with the possibility of many errors. Some tend to interpret this admonition as meaning "trust your intuition," using what is sometimes postulated as the "sixth sense." In some rare people, this sense is highly developed, so that it is worthy of trust; but, for most people, this is not the case.

All cults are bad.

Webster defines a cult as "a system of worship of a deity" or a "great devotion to some person, idea or thing."[7] By this definition, all religions would be seen as cults; so would any hockey or movie star's fan club. We refine the definition to mean any organization which demands strict allegiance to persons, or to a set body of rules and basic assumptions that are proposed to be "truths." In usual practice, the term "cult" tends to be used by members of one organization (such as a church or a political system) when referring to other organizations that have dissenting views. Individuals are encouraged to abandon their own critical ideas, and sometimes even their own history. Such an organization then expects its members to slavishly adhere to the its "truths"; it may even be prepared to propose violent actions to eliminate the "truths" of others. Over such stuff are wars fought and laws enforced.

All socially unacceptable organizations tend to be labelled as "cults." Actually, in any society there are those in control (*socially acceptable* cults, that see themselves as being "moral" and "ethical," that generally don't call themselves "cults"), and those that are *marginalised* (which are referred to as "cults" by those in power, and are seen to be "immoral" and "unethical"). From the perspective of individual autonomy, it is the *cult activity* (i.e., the abandonment of individual thought) that creates a problem for its members. The cult ideas themselves (whether socially acceptable or unacceptable) might be worthy of consideration, and could even be beneficial if *freely* adopted by the individual will, without coercion. In our view, what is "bad" is not the ideas, but rather, the restriction placed upon an organization's members from thinking for themselves.

If you really understood, you'd agree.

This is one of the commonest myths that is used in interpersonal relationships. It is based upon an arrogant concept that one's own perceptions and judgments are so "true" that if other people *really* understood, there is absolutely no chance that they could arrive at another (especially an opposing) interpretation. Frequently, it is possible to fully understand another person's point of view without having to agree. At those times, even though the person who understands makes no claims to being "right," the other person will argue, apparently believing that if others understood, they could not do other than to agree. We believe that it is possible to understand, to disagree, and to still remain close to another person.

Good communication ensures a long-lasting relationship.

To assess this statement, so much depends on the definition of "good communication." Some research into the current high divorce rate suggests that good communication is not a definite indicator of which couples will remain together; what seems more important than their style of communication is a high level of *intent* to remain together.

Well documented studies published by John Gottman showed that even couples with difficult marriage styles such as argumentative or avoidant ones (i.e., what many would call "poor communicators") can enjoy longevity if they learn, and agree upon some ways to remain respectful, empathetic, understanding, accepting, present and engaged. We believe that these are the characteristics of an enduring intimate relationship of high quality. For some couples, their communications might be messy or flawed; their longevity in relationship is more determined by these underlying values.

Other couples who seem to have good communication, but lack these underlying values, do not maintain an ongoing relationship. Communication is not enough; indeed, the attitude and intention are highly significant. According to Gottman, the main threats to an intimate relationship are the "Four Horsemen of The Apocalypse": criticism, contempt, defensiveness, and stonewalling.[8]

Jealousy will destroy a relationship.

Jealousy is a feeling of anxiety related to the possible loss of a valued person to some other. It is an expression of unresolved insecurities from past childhood experiences.[9] When jealousy arises in intimate relationships, it can be seen in a positive light:

- It is an expression of how important and meaningful the other has become to the jealous person.
- It reveals the areas of fixation and immaturity within the jealous person; often these have previously been hidden or denied.
- It can signal a readiness for the jealous person to share with the partner those areas of vulnerability.
- When these feelings are shared *without the element of control*, intimacy grows stronger and both parties have the opportunity to grow, both individually and together.

Jealousy becomes destructive when people blame their insecurity and pain upon another, and when they use their hurt to control others. An example of a basic blame message is, "I am hurting because you are showing attention to her." *The usual controlling option* would be, "My pain is being caused by you—so stop seeing her and pay more attention to me!"

The sharing pain option is different: "I want you to know about my pain without your having to change anything about yourself. I am exploring the origins of my insecurity, and will continue to keep you informed. In the meantime, I want to hear about your attraction and desire for her. Also, I want to check your intentions in this matter."

By choosing the latter option, both partners are capable of becoming more responsible, with a golden opportunity for personal growth. Using jealousy for control will invite hostility and distance between them.

Intimacy equals sexual excitement.

The human being is capable of experiencing a great variety of sexual feelings in different areas for myriad reasons. What is usually called "sexual excitement" is related to an objectifying symbolic system that carries an underlying story of pursuit and capture. The expression of that basic story varies from culture to culture, ranging from romance to economics, seductions to family arrangements. The romantic version would have us believe that, as intimacy develops, the sexual excitement will grow. In practice, this is not the case. Certainly, at the beginning of romance, when the people are relatively unknown to one another, there is usually high level of sexual excitement. However, over the years, as these lovers have come to know much about one another (familiarity), or have really come to *know* one another (intimacy), their sexual excitement usually wanes (see above, "A Perspective on Sexuality").

That the sexual excitement decreases with time and familiarity is the source of much anxiety, disappointment and frustration in many couples. Often, they interpret the diminishing sexual appetite as a sign of some problem in their relationship. Indeed, in many instances it can indicate a high level of shared intimacy. It may mean that because they know one another so well, they are having difficulty in objectifying one another. This is a common problem.[10] It signals a need for partners to be creative and curious about one another, to deepen intimacy while rekindling sexual excitement as they choose.[11]

Money can't buy happiness.

Actually, happiness is a state of being within people, for which they are fully responsible. Because of this, individuals can choose to be happy over anything, including money. Unfortunately, most people don't have the opportunity of creating happiness over money; so all they can do is fantasize about it. Those with money can easily squander it on things and activities of little consequence, resulting in little enjoyment. Some people create happiness for themselves wherever they go, in whatever they do; the money only increases the style and variety of things with which they will do that.

Parents should stay together for the sake of the kids.

Children probably flourish best in a loving environment (whatever that may be). Too often , people judge that to be a particular form (usually a two parent family, with a mother and a father). Nowadays in North

America, more than half of the children are either raised in a single parent family, or with one parent who is not blood related. Does this spell trouble for our future generations?

We think not. In our experience, couples that stay together "for the sake of the kids" create an unstable, unloving family environment. Even though the basic needs for accommodation and food may be met, the general atmosphere can be confusing. Although the children might never say, they can experience the lack of caring between the parents, the possibility of hostility and conflict (both open and covert), the differences over how the children are to be handled (or not handled, as in many instances), and the lack of real communication between all members of the family. Furthermore, children have a tendency to blame themselves for their parents' differences. When parents stay together under these circumstances, children have a daily opportunity to feel bad about themselves.

When parents separate with consideration and respect for one another, there will be minimal trauma. Parents who are separated or divorced can both creatively provide their own consistent presence to the children, in their own fashion.

Notes

1. Lewis Carroll, *The Annotated Alice* (New York: Penguin Books, 1965), p. 269.

2. J. Efran, M. Lukens and R.Lukens, *Language, Structure and Change: Frameworks of Meaning in Psychotherapy* (New York: W.W.Norton and Company, 1990), pp. 12-13.

3. James Hillman and Michael Ventura, *We've Had A Hundred Years of Psychotherapy—And The World's Getting Worse* (San Francisco, Harper Collins, 1992).

4. J. McKeen and B.R. Wong, *The Relationship Garden* (Gabriola Island, B.C.: PD Publishing, 1996), pp. 126-28.

5. J. McKeen and B.R. Wong, "Peace Is Not Possible!" in *Association For Humanistic Psychology Perspective*, March/April 1995, pp. 23, 25.

6. J. McKeen and B.R. Wong, *The Relationship Garden* (Gabriola Island, B.C.: PD Publishing, 1996), pp. 30-31.

7. *Webster's Collegiate Dictionary* (Springfield: G. and C. Merriam Co, 1947), p. 246.

8. J. Gottman, *Why Marriages Succeed Or Fail*, New York: Simon & Schuster), 1994

9. J. McKeen and B.R. Wong, *The Relationship Garden* (Gabriola Island, B.C.: PD Publishing, 1996), p. 39.

10. Ibid., p. 169.

11. Ibid., p. 76.

The Walking Wounded: A Way of Life

Working with people over many years, we have heard and encountered many horrifying stories of childhood trauma, including the blind outbursts of alcoholic parents, the pain of neglect, and the ravages of early child sexual abuse; we have also worked closely with a number of individuals whose unfolding memories reveal episodes of repetitive ritualistic assaults. The degree of objectification of young lives invites outrage, horror and pain on the part of the attending professional. We ourselves have been shocked to discover the extent of this objectification that has occurred for so many people. Many times, these people have tried to forget, to bury their previous pains with patterns of coping and withdrawal; they are often plagued by seemingly inexplicable fears, and myriad psychophysiological symptoms. It is in this state of current distress and disability that they seek the help of professional counsellors and other helpers.

Caring Is Not Enough

Professionals can help to uncover early memories, and to provide safe nutritive environments where people can update themselves, and learn to trust and to care in open and sharing atmospheres in the present. Counsellors can help people to revisit old wounds, so that they can express their pain and outrage in the present, in order to unlock the restrictions in themselves, mentally, physically, emotionally and spiritually. These people do need a caring, supportive environment in which they can face their lives, put their history into perspective, and practise using underdeveloped wills. *But caring is not enough!*

The problem has now been recognized; agencies have been established to help, and programs to provide rehabilitation. Social services are now involved with prevention, by working with young people who are in need. Professionals can often recognize the signs of child abuse, and can sometimes take action to ease a child's pain. Generally, these solutions are legal and political. Laws are passed, which society endeavours to enforce. There are concerted efforts to ferret out perpetrators, to rectify so-called wrongdoing. However, there is another insidious aspect, which helpers, agencies and clients are not facing squarely.

The Concept of "Survivor"

It has become fashionable to talk of the "wounded child." As counsellors help people to reclaim earlier memories, and to express previously repressed pains, these clients then are prone to explain all of their current circumstances as being caused by their earlier abuses. Others unconsciously feel pity for them, and want to try to rectify past wrongs with current caregiving. Some become their champions and want to be their saviours. Unfortunately, in the attempt to provide help and services, caregivers are now involved in fixating people as victims.

Now, it has become a way of life to be a "survivor," and an "adult child of...(fill in the blank)." Guilt-ridden agencies and institutions provide much support for this stance, and many well-intentioned counsellors are conspiring to keep clients fixated as helpless nonparticipants in earlier life activities. Early abuse is becoming an icon to be worshipped, a talisman to wear proudly, as a testimonial to endurance and fortitude. Unfortunately, for some people, it is also used as a justification for complaining, and to wallow in past pains rather than face life in the present. Although we believe one can find self-respect in expressing indignation and outrage, the self is diminished by blame and faultfinding. As long as people use their past traumas and abuse to justify their current life, they are ignoring the importance of their own will. They can use this as an excuse not to develop themselves, and not to learn and grow in their current relationships. Often their counsellors are conspiring with them, to keep them fixated as victims.

The concepts of the "wounded child," the "child within," and other similar notions imply that there is indeed a young person within an older body, who is injured. This has been useful in giving language to feelings and memories that have been difficult to access. However, as with most concepts that begin as fresh innovations, these ideas are now becoming trite and over-used. Often, adults who have been abused become like spoiled children in their bid for attention. Strangely, these people who have often had so little, become entitled and demanding. They want to be attended, fixed, heard, and pitied. Their attitude becomes "give me what I want to make up for what I missed," or "I have been wronged, or damaged, and I need caretaking," or "I am incomplete, and need help." Thus, these people fail to individuate. In a way, they fail to take ownership of their past. Instead, their past was something that "happened" to them.

The Task of the Professional

The task of the professional is to provide a safe atmosphere in which these individuals can uncover their past hurts and pain, and investigate them in the light of their current lives. Generally, these people have not learned to relate in consistent boundaried ways. They did not have the circumstances to learn to say "no," or to use their will to determine what they wanted. They often have shrunk back from life, tightened up in fear and denial, and are living restricted lives. These individuals can learn to take ownership of their feelings from the past, and move on into fuller lives.

Working with victims involves sequential facilitation. At the beginning, the person needs support and help to uncover repressed material and feelings. This early "dependency phase" makes up for early childhood experiences that were missed. Then when the person has some personal strength, and has experienced dependability in interacting with another, (s)he can develop more mature relationships in the present. Often, the counsellor is the first healthy relationship that this person has dared to have. Once a strong bonding is made with the counsellor, the next step in the project is for the person to extend newly found interactive skills into relationships with peers.

Stages in Working Through Past Trauma

There are four stages in working through past trauma.

- Stage 1. *Awareness*: The client is helped to recognize past experience, to uncover earlier memories and to acknowledge them.

- Stage 2. *Affect Expression*: The client is helped to express the pent-up pain and anger, to go through these emotions, rather than bury them (as they probably have done to this point). This should not be only verbally; instead, an energetic body approach is encouraged, to unlock the energy that is stuck in the body. At first, this expression will likely be heavily laden with blame. As the work progresses, the client will be more involved in self-affirmative expression of feeling without so much blame. In this way, the person begins to shift from blame to responsibility for his or her own feelings.

- Stage 3. *Sharing*: Clients share their feelings and experience with others—with individuals, or in safe group settings. By relating their experiences to others, they can reduce the charge of secrecy, and begin to see their lives in a broader context. By others' empathetic witnessing, people can learn to see that they are not alone in the present. The person can have time-limited comfort, and then be encouraged to engage in life. This is a fine line. Impoverished people certainly need to experience compassion, caring and empathy; however, they must move through and beyond the dependency upon the attentions of others to discover their own curiosity for life, and their own empathy for others.

- Stage 4. *Discovery*: The person begins to discover life without the victim stance, and to develop responsible relationships.

The Challenge

Health professionals themselves often lack the personal development and tools to help people work through such issues. They are commonly afraid of their own pain, and try to relieve pain in others, rather than experience their own in response to others. Often, they might be willing to help, but don't know what to do. Although counsellors are generally well-intentioned, they are prone to conspire to keep these people dependent and fixated on their pasts. It is tempting to contribute to a prolonged dependency because of a need to be important to someone else. Rather than encourage gradual development in the present, counsellors are tempted to keep these people weak and dependent *to serve their own inadequacies*. Often, helpers are arrested at the same level as their clients, and gain false power by taking care of them, rather than facing their own fears of inadequacy. Many times, counsellors have themselves experienced similar traumas to their clients, and are prone to fuel the clients' distress with their own. Instead of participating in mutual pity, professionals should be encouraging their clients to live in the present, and put the past into its place—as a memory.

One Woman's Story

A 37-year old woman, who had endured early abuse and sexual violence, described her uncovering of memories in counselling as follows:

> Remembering all these experiences really shook up my world. It explained many of the struggles I've had in my life, especially regarding my sexuality. It also changed the way I saw myself. I began to see myself as a victim of sexual abuse—small, powerless, helpless, bound. I didn't like the word "victim" so I thought of myself as "wounded" instead. And since I had been wounded, I needed to be healed.

Her counselling proceeded:

> I spent the next three years seeking to be healed of the effects of being sexually abused. I faithfully saw a counsellor, attended workshops and a support group, prayed, made retreats, journalled, drew and read books. I found all these things helpful and I could see progress, but I never seemed to attain that elusive goal of being healed. Since I was not yet healed I felt unable to make decisions about my life. I put my life on hold waiting to be healed.

She waited for healing from outside of herself:

> I realize now that in seeing myself as a victim I believed that my healing was out of my control. Since I'd been abused by someone else I needed to be healed by someone else. At first I thought that my counsellor would be the one to heal me. When I realized that this wouldn't happen, I decided that it was God who would somehow heal me. I tried hard to do my part and carried on faithfully with my process while waiting for God to do His part. Yet this never seemed to happen and I began to despair that I would ever be healed. I had become stuck on a merry-go-round of feeling victimized and powerless, waiting for something or someone to magically heal me, and feeling even more victimized and powerless when that didn't happen. I became frustrated, exhausted and stuck, unable to get on with my life.

She then attended a residential personal development seminar:

> *I came to [the group] looking for someone or something to heal me. My turning point came one day when [the leaders] explained how we live in the future instead of the present when we live in hope. I realized with surprise that I was living in hope for the day I would be healed and could get on with my life. I decided I could let go of the idea of being healed, and live my life as it is today. I shared this with [one of the leaders], and he said, "Yes, and you don't even have to think of yourself as injured!" I suddenly understood! I'd never thought of myself as injured before all this—why did I think of myself as injured now? I'm the same person I was before I started remembering all this stuff! At that moment I stopped believing I was an injured victim waiting to be healed. I began to see myself once again as an intelligent, caring and competent woman. I know that I have experienced sexual and physical abuse, but I no longer see myself as powerless or helpless. Rather, I believe that I have developed a lot of inner strength as a result of my experiences. I feel freer and once again able to make decisions about my life. And now I can make these decisions much more fully than I ever could before.*

She was amazed to discover:

> *I'm not injured or flawed ... I'm whole.*

She had thought her life was doomed because of her early experiences, rather than to see that she was now an adult who could make different choices with more authority than when she was young. She said,

> *I have been afraid of men, but now as an adult, I can make choices not to simply avoid men.*

Common Misconceptions

Too often, counsellors leap to the conclusion that any current trouble is the expression of past abuse. Indeed, some people endured much violation; however, there does not seem to be a clear correlation between degree of abuse and degree of current difficulty. The health care field is now poised to turn the therapeutic endeavour into a parody where all people coming to a counsellor think they have been abused; in this environment, the counsellor is certain that everything in the present is explained by past traumas. Without denying the seriousness of early abuse, professionals must not make the mistake of trying to witch-hunt every vestige of the past. Not all current problems can be explained by early abuse.

Not everyone who has a memory was abused. We know of a young man who is explaining his delayed adolescent rebellion with his parents by his assertion that he was sexually abused by his parents as a child. There is no substantiating evidence, except for a vague memory, that we believe was constructed after a well-intentioned therapist suggested it to him. The old dictum, "Follow your clients, don't lead them," is crucial. Helpers should not put more ideas of abuse into people's minds.

Fixation on "Abuse": A Second Story

For counsellors, there is a danger that they will become so fixated on "abuse" that they will miss hearing what a client is trying to tell them. Another woman had sought help from a counsellor for a depression following the untimely death of a close friend. These are her words:

> *At age 51, this was my first psychotherapeutic experience. I had no idea what to expect, no frame of reference with which to evaluate the quality of the therapy other than an acquaintance referral plus my blind faith in the counsellor's friendliness, to which I immediately was attracted. Friends seldom mentioned therapy except as an adjunct to their failing marriages or their kids' brushes with drugs or delinquency. With a healthy marriage of 30 years and four "good" kids, I had remained a counselling virgin who had managed life to that point with no knowledge of the risks or benefits of therapy.*

She began to experience improvement.

> *Weekly sessions at $80 per hour commenced with my commitment to attend three sessions. My depression improved immediately, just from the counsellor's warmth and empathy. Then I agreed to stay on in therapy to address other life improvements. Since insurance was not reimbursing this therapy, there were no external checks or time limits. Five years and more than $20,000 later, we were still locked in a therapeutic alliance.*

In the course of her therapy, she disclosed an early experience to her therapist:

What seemed to cement my need for long term therapy was my disclosure toward the end of our fifth session that I had been incested by my father from age 2½ to 11½. Sucking in her breath, my counsellor had grabbed my knee as if to capture a "live one" before it got away. I was surprised by her zeal to explore this issue that I had relegated to the dustbin of past history, not knowing that this was a hot issue in the world of psychotherapy.

She describes her ongoing efforts to discover her anger over the past incidents:

Attempting to access my anger over nine years of incest was sine qua non on my counsellor's agenda from then on. Any positive feelings I shared about my father's enjoyment of my body, the nurture I had experienced in his warmth and cuddling, fell on deaf ears or were contradicted. My father was labelled a criminal who had "abused, molested and betrayed" his daughter. I remember those words exactly, because I carried them on a flash card in my purse for several months. I found these indictments hard to swallow because they invalidated my feelings, distorted my reality. Instead of anger at my father, I became furious at my counsellor.

My confusion was compounded when I attended several agency-facilitated survivor groups over the next few years. In each case, the main agenda was to access rage over the all-inclusive, heinous crime of child sexual abuse. In many cases, I judged that a survivor's anger was justified. I shared buckets of tears with them over beatings, burnings, bondage and other hurtfully inflicted perversions; but I felt like a white elephant when expected to kick and scream on my own behalf against my incestor. He had acted tender and loving with me. I had for the most part enjoyed being cherished, being aroused sexually, being penetrated by his penis, being enveloped by his warmth. My healing could not be predicated on accessing an anger I did not feel.

The counselling continued:

Private weekly counselling continued with the same therapist, to whom I was now inextricably bonded, all during the group work, of which she was not a part. In an attempt to please her, I kept trying to feel anger toward the incest so my counsellor could "wash me clean" and we could get on with other issues, now stacking up like cord wood. Compulsive eating, yo-yo dieting with a loss and regaining of over 100 pounds, low self-esteem, neurotic behavior patterns, emptying nest, uterine cancer followed by a radical hysterectomy, instant menopause, resumption of smoking and drinking, sudden onset of asthma and arthritis, fibromyalgia, strabismus, spiritual crisis, career change—nothing could get my counsellor's attention like the incest/anger issue. We locked ourselves in stalemates for months at a time, always with her implication that once the anger was released, other issues would fall into place. Where, oh where was my anger?

She remained dependent upon her counsellor.

After our fourth year together, my counsellor periodically broached the subject of termination. Each time, I would panic. How could we abandon each other when I still had not found my anger? What about all those other unprocessed issues? Was I to flunk counselling as I had almost flunked college statistics, because I was missing a point? Childhood memories were triggered about feeling abandoned by my absentee mother, and the numerous housekeepers who filled in for her. I felt like I would die without my counsellor's support. I wanted to be her friend forever, or be locked in therapy with her for the rest of my life. We terminated three months ago. Her door closed forever on future contacts except for once a year tune-ups. I still often feel bereft, and silently grieve the loss of that significant relationship.

After leaving counselling, she attended a residential personal development seminar. In a session, the simple question "Is it possible that you enjoyed your sexual relationship with your father, and that you don't have anger about it?" brought a shocked look, and a sudden outpouring of relief from the woman. She concludes her report with the following passage:

As of this writing, I am attending a two month program of personal development at an educational retreat centre. A new way to look at the issue of child sexual abuse has been suggested for me to consider, one that seems to be more in line with my own sense of reality. "Who told you that you had to get angry when you're not?" asked one of the directors. Am I being heard at last? Are my feelings being validated? Am I now free to invest energy in new directions of personal growth?

The Lesson

Both offenders and victims need to learn to stop objectifying each other, and see that both of them have poor boundaries, and lack ability to feel themselves. Both need to move beyond the objectification of the "bad" perpetrator, and the "wounded" victim. Both are human beings, who are lost and underdeveloped. Generally, the perpetrators of violence or abuse become objectified as the "bad one," the "offender," the "guilty one." This objectification does nothing to help either the perpetrator or the victim. Perpetrators have objectified their victims; then the victims remain stuck in objectifying the offenders. In one of our programs, we had a very intense and dramatic encounter between a young woman and an older man; she was a previous subject of childhood violence, and he was the person who had actually committed the offenses against her. As she faced him with her rage and pain, exploding with pent-up frustration and suppression, she asked him "How could you have done this?" The perpetrator, suddenly faced with the real life feelings of the person rather than his objectified victim, broke down crying with remorse and impotence. He wept to see her pain, and was suddenly shocked loose from the impersonal world of objects into a human dialogue. If the young woman had remained stuck in just punishing him, she would have remained fixated in litigious revenge. As she cleared her feelings, she began to develop a genuine curiosity about him. He was stimulated to look into himself, and cried openly about his own childhood trauma. Suddenly, both people were looking beyond their own entitled fixations on power and revenge, and were seeing the humanness of each other. This young woman has gone on to develop a meaningful relationship; the perpetrator continued to seek help to uncover the sources of his own poor boundaries. Everyone in the abuse situation, victim and perpetrator alike, is contending with poor boundaries, and inadequate personality development.

Counsellors Who Have Experienced Abuse

Counsellors who have had early trauma can be an inspiration, if they have worked through the situation. Often, the client can benefit from relating to someone whose life is working well, who can say, "I made it out ... so can you." We have worked with a young woman who was a victim of a satanic cult, raised from infancy in horrid rituals to be a high priestess. At this point in her life, she has no regrets for her past, even though she has come through several life-threatening illnesses that were associated with buried memories.[1] She is now a counsellor, and she says,

I can resonate with people who have experienced pain like me, and have compassion for them. My training as a counsellor has come from my living

through the pain of my earlier life. Now, in a strange way, I'm glad I have this experience, although I wouldn't wish it on anyone else.

As she continues in her personal development process, she writes:

I am also very aware now that I have maintained a "victim's" position throughout a great deal of my life. I have had trouble acknowledging that I often feel victimized, but my language and my stance in difficult situations has brought this information to my awareness. I had always thought of myself as someone who was tough, but now I see that even though I toughed my way through a lot of things I often did not acknowledge the fear or the hurt and it has built up over time. I think through using the communication model and noticing the number of times I say "she did that" or "you make me," I have finally realized that on a deep level I take a position of being the victim to my life. That is changing. I laugh now at how I slip so easily into blame. My partner is also a constant reminder, always commenting when I say something using language that implies I have no control or responsibility.

She has much insight to share:

Since being ill I have had to look at almost all the areas in my life that I avoided—my sexuality, my relationship to my family, my style of communication, my sadness, my incredible neediness and desire to remain helpless. At times I have been repulsed, scared, ready to quit. I believe the journey has taken a tremendous amount of courage and the outcome has not been glory or sympathy but simply life. I think I wanted to get even on some deep level, to draw attention to myself, to not have to become interested in anyone else, and to be able to avoid caring. Instead I have learned about loving, I still sometimes want more than that. But I know that comes from a place of fear. Life is not about glory or honour or right and wrong; those paths have led me to death. Life seems to be more unpredictable and has little to do with fairness.

Conclusion

Counsellors or friends cannot make up for someone else's past; nor can they undo it. They can hurt and rage with them, and help them to discover appropriate forms of expression in their current lives. The line of questioning should not be "How were you abused?" but rather, "What did you experience?" The former question keeps the person stuck in moral strictures; the latter brings forth the individual's own experience, which often involves ambiguities of pleasure and coexisting pain. If some of the acts were pleasurable, the person might have repressed guilt feelings, which can be expressed in a variety of ways.

When individuals discover that they have been abused, this revelation does not provide the answers for the rest of their lives. Even when people have horrible things to work through, there comes a time when they must let them go, and move on. This is not to excuse the inhuman violences of the past, nor to deny the importance of the political and legal efforts in this area. However, professionals must go beyond political and legal solutions, into personal sharing with the people who are in danger of becoming lost or fixated in the concept of themselves as wounded children. James Hillman describes the importance of listening deeply to people, instead of quickly labelling them, in the following passage:

> *Whenever treatment directly neglects the experience as such and hastens to reduce or overcome it, something is being done against the soul.* [2]

The goal is for people to *understand* themselves, but it not to *rationalize* current shortcomings. Thus, no one should *excuse* people's behaviour in the present because of past memories. The task for everyone is to learn to use the *will* to have maturing interpersonal relationships, and to develop a growing sense of *responsibility* for the self. As counsellors, colleagues or friends, empathetic understanding offers much more than does pity and caretaking. The traumas of past experiences need to be *honoured, but not venerated.* Dealing with the pain and suffering from the past can be a way of discovering life; *but, this should not become a way of life!*

Notes

1. B.R. Wong and J. McKeen, "A Case of Multiple Life Threatening Illnesses Related to Early Ritual Abuse," *Journal of Child and Youth Care*, Special Issue, 1990, pp. 1-26.

2. James Hillman, *Suicide and the Soul* (Dallas: Spring Publications, 1976), p. 23.

Memories of Abuse—
A Call For A Balanced Perspective

Memories are to the mind what feelings are to the heart. In their own way they both provide texture to our lives. —Bennet Wong

Frequently, people seek help from counsellors to integrate painful past experiences. More and more reports are emerging of people who have been trying to come to peace with memories of past sexual and ritualistic abuse. As the alarms were sounded, both in the therapeutic literature, and in the press, we became increasingly alarmed ourselves. However, the nature of our alarm has been shifting. At first, we were shocked and outraged, as many others have been, at what was reported to have occurred. Then we were shocked at the extent that such incidents have been reported to have occurred. But now, we are concerned at how the whole issue is becoming a *cause célèbre*, and is being skewed. We ourselves began to write about the issue of memories, expressing concern that early abuse memories are becoming substitutes for living[1]; the substance of this endeavour appears in this book (see above, "The Walking Wounded: A Way of Life."). This issue has developed and mutated over the past twenty years since we have been speaking and writing about it.[2] This chapter is an attempt to clarify some important issues.

Fixation Upon Memories

Human beings have a remarkable proclivity to become fixated, to become repetitious and addicted in attitudes and activities. People seem to abhor newness, and want to set things into a familiar pattern. The majority tend to become fixated to find something dependable, as a way of alleviating ontological anxiety (See above, "Anxiety: Friend or Foe?").

Now, it is fashionable to come to "know oneself," to look into one's past, and find explanations for current circumstances from recollections of early childhood experiences. In our opinion, Investigating oneself and one's past life is acceptable, for a period of time, and for perspective. However, there is a very great danger that a person can become addicted to this procedure, and become more interested in indulging in the memories; the person becomes self-stimulated by more and more memory unfolding—a sort of experiential masturbation. The memories supersede lived reality. A few visits to one's traumatic past should be enough; any more verges on indulgence and sentimentalism. One can become fixated upon self-investigation, becoming a "memory junkie." This is the same as with the process of any addiction; the addiction becomes more important than contact. To the alcoholic, the drink supersedes the contact and relationship with the world and people around. The current fashion of focussing on remembering provides a dangerous situation, wherein the individual can indeed become addicted to the memory seeking, and lose perspective with day to day life. One young woman wrote the following:

When I first started experiencing memories of ritual abuse, I was overwhelmed; the images I saw terrified me. Somehow, though, they excited me. I believe I began willing myself to have more and more memories because as frightening as they were, there was an enormous charge in the suffering. In fact, the more terrifying the memory, the more I could indulge in self-pity, and since self-pity is extremely gratifying, I became obsessed with remembering. It became like an addiction, and eventually the abuse was all I thought about. Soon, the addiction took the place of contact.

The investigation of past memories can become indulgent, and the person does not mature until this indulgence is overcome. The same young woman wrote:

I would often come to dinner, buried in my pain, and arrogantly expected everyone else to jump right in with me. "If they really loved me," I told myself, "they would hurt because I'm in pain." What I didn't see, however, was that they loved me enough to show me how self-indulgent and selfish I was being by holding on to my pain. They showed me it's important to experience the memories, and to have your feelings about them, but it's equally important to let them go and to get on with your life. I had been defining myself as a victim, and [my counsellors] helped me to realize I could choose not to be. It's that choice that's made all the difference, and has allowed me the freedom to establish relationships, go back to school—to live my life.

This loss of perspective, and tendency to become fixated also happens in chronic illness process, wherein ill persons become more involved in their disease processes than with other people around them. We know a young woman who at 22 years of age already qualified as a chronic illness case, with a life-long disability allowance. She had been investigated for all manner of autoimmune disorders, with no certain diagnosis found. And yet, when she learned to take responsibility for herself and her own experiences, rather than dwell in past memories, she lost her symptoms. Today, she is healthy, and shows no evidence of the former chronic conditions. Indeed, we have witnessed the miracle of another young woman having cured four different cancers (four distinct locations and cell types); today, she is cancer free.[3] Another young woman who used to suffer from multiple sclerosis no longer has anything but precursor symptoms. We have known numerous people who have struggled with extreme allergies and chronic fatigue; they have also found their way out of the oppression of the victim position. The common factor among these people is this: when they decide not to *succumb* to the illness process, but rather to become *involved* with it, they find new resources of life, energy and health, and their symptoms often improve.

In addictions, the person directs more and more attention towards the addiction, and correspondingly, less energy is left to enter into genuine dialogue with self and other and the world. In self-investigation, one can derive bodily sensations and pleasures and pains from the reliving (or re-creation, or creation) of memories. This can become indulgent and addictive. Probably there is a biochemical loop established, (likely involving endorphins, serotonin, and other related chemicals), that serves to facilitate the fixation. Such obsessive investigation is akin to becoming lost in a maze. There is often a sickly sweet driven quality to the pursuit, that even can have elements of pleasure. This is much like reading a Stephen King novel—you feel kind of ill, but you can't put the book down.

When therapists and counsellors become involved in the revisiting of such memories (or, indeed, sometimes participate in helping to create them de novo), they also may derive an erotic experience from witnessing the horror and wonder of the remembered experience. The investigation can become very indulgent, with the therapists experiencing pleasures and pains in association with their clients. Carl Whitaker once said, "One-on-one psychotherapy is emotional incest."[4] Perhaps he recognized the self-stimulating and voyeuristic behaviours that can occur in self-investigation. The therapists might be living their lives through their clients, rather than having the courage to have lives of their own. In crude terms, counsellors are in danger of "getting off" on their clients, rather than being in genuine dialogue with them.

The Uncertainty of Memory

Often, one obtains much valuable perspective by reconsidering and reliving one's life memories. Having done so, one can often put history into order, to close past chapters, to forgive and move on. But, everyone must keep in mind—they are just that, memories. And the process of memory is a very flawed activity at best. One cannot be certain from one moment to the next what *actually* occurred. People can only know that they remember this or that. No one can say for sure that it actually happened.

In the professional literature, public press and media, the question has been raised about the validity of repressed memories.[5] On the one hand, investigators caution against the tendency to believe all memories to be true, thus abandoning discriminating intelligence. On the other hand, now that "false memory syndrome" has been named, there is danger of a backlash, where no one's memory is to be believed. There is a fine line here. Surely there is a middle road that allows for the importance of the memories without becoming fixated upon them.

Freud's Evolution of Thought

Early in his work with clients, Freud believed that the cause of hysteria was from early sexual experiences that produced the later neurosis; this came to be known as "The Seduction Theory." He gradually shifted in this understanding. Marie Jahoda writes the following:

> Freud came to realise that what his patients had reported to him were memories not of actual events but of phantasies and early wishes; he also realised that there did not exist an ultimate cause of hysteria . . . Substantively it led him to realise that memory does not distinguish between reality and phantasy.[6]

He became acquainted with people who reported childhood sexual experiences with adults, who apparently did not manifest hysterical behaviour. Thus, he thought that early sexual experience did not necessarily result in neurosis.

Then he began to be impressed with the number of reports about child sexual experiences, and was at the same time recognizing that for the child, reality and fantasy are often indistinguishable. Hence, he gradually moved away from the notion that the sexual experiences had always actually taken place, and replaced this notion with the idea that the child often had fantasied them having happened, as an expression of wish fulfilment. As the child's body was eroticised, the child fantasied sexual experiences with the parent who was the love object. Often the notion of actual sexual events was retrospective; memory played a part in having the experiences be seen as sexual. The memory introduced an adult's retrospective viewpoint on early experiences.

Freud was also impressed that so many of the reports had to do with oral and anal sex. Thinking these both to be perversions (and hence unlikely to occur in such frequency), he began to think that it was not so much that all the fathers of his clients had been actively seeking such sexual experiences with their children; rather, he considered that there were psychological events in play (possibly an atmosphere of seduction), wherein the child fantasized (subconsciously) such activity. Proceeding in this fashion, he ultimately revised his notion that the memories arose from actual events, and instead, saw them as usually being fantasies emanating from the localization of libido in the anus and genital regions.[7] Many gender feminists have never forgiven him.

By 1905, when Freud was writing "Three Essays on Sexuality," he was already revising earlier positions:

> In the foreground we find the effects of seduction, which treats a child as a sexual object prematurely and teaches him, in highly emotional circumstances, how to obtain satisfaction from his genital zones, a satisfaction which he is then usually obliged to repeat again and again by masturbation. An influence of this kind may originate either from adults or from other children. I cannot admit that in my paper on 'The Aetiology of Hysteria' (1896) I exaggerated the frequency or importance of that influence; though I did not then know that persons who

remain normal may have had the same experiences in their childhood, and though I consequently overrated the importance of seduction in comparison with the factors of sexual constitution and development. Obviously seduction is not required in order to arouse a child's sexual life; that can also come about spontaneously from internal causes.[8]

Later in 1905, he elaborated his changing perspective on the Seduction Theory:

I thus over-estimated the frequency of such events . . . moreover, I was at that period unable to distinguish with certainty between falsifications made by hysterics in their memories of childhood and traces of real events. Since then I have learned to explain a number of phantasies of seduction as attempts at fending off memories of the subjects <u>own</u> sexual activity (infantile masturbation). . . . They [symptoms] were now no longer to be regarded as direct derivatives of the repressed memories of childhood experiences; but between the symptoms and the childish impressions there were inserted the patients <u>phantasies</u> (or imaginary memories), mostly produced during the years of puberty, which on the one side were built up out of and over the childhood memories and on the other side were transformed directly into symptoms.[9]

He went on in the same writing to recognize individual differences. It was not the trauma or absence of trauma that determined the person's ultimate condition:

Thus it was no longer a question of what sexual experiences a particular individual had had in his childhood, but rather of his reaction to those experiences—of whether he had reacted to them by 'repression' or not.[10]

In "Notes Upon a Case of Obsessional Neurosis" (known in popular terms as "The Rat Man" published in 1909) he noted that childhood memories are retrospective, and coloured by more current attitudes and perspectives:

If we do not wish to go astray in our judgement of their historical reality, we must above all bear in mind that people's 'childhood memories' are only consolidated at a later period, usually at the age of puberty; and that this involves a complicated process of remodelling, analogous in every way to the way in which a nation constructs its legends about its early history. It at once becomes evident that in his phantasies about his infancy the individual as he grows up <u>endeavours to efface the recollection of his auto-erotic activities;</u> and *this he does by exalting their memory-traces to the level of object-love, just as a real historian will view the past in the light of the present. This explains why these phantasies abound in seductions and assaults, where the facts will have been confined to auto-erotic activities and the caresses or punishments that stimulated them. Furthermore, it becomes clear that in constructing his phantasies about his childhood the individual sexualizes his memories; that is, he brings commonplace experiences into relation with his sexual activity, and extends his sexual interest to them—though in doing this he is probably following upon the traces of a really existing connection.[11]*

He goes on in the Rat Man case to say that it is difficult to know for sure whether the memories are based in fact, or are from fantasy:

It is seldom that we are in the fortunate position of being able, as in the present instance, to establish the facts upon which these tales of the individual's prehistoric past are based, by recourse to the unimpeachable testimony of a grown-up person.[12]

In 1910, writing about Leonardo Da Vinci, he elaborated his views about childhood memories and fantasy:

Quite unlike conscious memories from the time of maturity, they [childhood memories] are not fixed at the moment of being experienced and afterwards repeated, but are only elicited at a later age when childhood is already past; in the process they are altered and falsified, and are put into the service of later trends, so that generally speaking they cannot be sharply distinguished from phantasies.[13]

By 1918, Freud believed that the notion of having sex with a parent was a common mental form, "a phylogenetic heritage."

These scenes of observing parental intercourse, of being seduced in childhood, and of being threatened with castration are unquestionably an inherited endowment, a phylogenetic heritage, but they may just as easily be acquired by personal experience . . . All that we find in the prehistory of neuroses is that a child catches hold of this phylogenetic experience where his own experience fails him. He fills in the gaps in individual truth with prehistoric truth; he replaces occurrences in his own life by occurrences in the life of his ancestors.[14]

He thought that the explanation for a report of sexual experience could be from actual experience (ontogenetic possibilities) or from thought forms that were from the mental structure of the human (phylogenetic possibilities):

> *I fully agree with Jung in recognizing the existence of this phylogenetic heritage; but I regard it as a methodological error to seize on a phylogenetic explanation before the ontogenetic possibilities have been exhausted.*[15]

In "A Child is Being Beaten," which he wrote in 1919, Freud noted the frequency of a fantasy wherein a child is being beaten. As he investigated this, he began to see that this was very common, and probably had "an auto-erotic satisfaction." He thought at first that these fantasies were the domain only of children who had experienced corporal punishment at home; however, he decided that they often happened in individuals who were very seldom beaten in their childhood.[16]

This was the watershed that Freud encountered at the turn of the century. As Freud saw more and more of his patients reporting childhood sexual experiences, he gradually realized he could not be certain whether or not the reported incidents had actually occurred.[17] And today, it is still impossible to be certain.

In recent years, critics of Freud have denounced him for contributing to a conspiracy to keep the secret of incest and child abuse hidden. And yet, it is noteworthy that almost a century ago, this great pioneer was considering and noting his questions about the same issues which society is now facing. Are memories real, or is fantasy a component? Interested people should now be continuing to ask the same questions that Freud was posing so many years ago.

Memories Induced by Therapists

Next, there is the consideration of therapist-induced memories. Not only can professionals not be certain that what a client remembers is based in fact or not, it is possible to induce remembrances or attitudes that are not grounded in fact at all. Dr. Herbert Spiegel, a hypnotherapist from Columbia University in New York City, conducted experiments into implanting of memories decades ago. To a client under hypnosis, he spoke a simple sentence, saying that members of the media were involved in communist activities. When the client came out of the hypnotic state, he became distressed, and increasingly agitated, and revealed that he felt a pressure to alert authorities that there was a widespread plot in the media to spread communism. And then he began to name names. Although the original suggestion did not involve names, this person was filling in and embroidering the original statement, with increasingly elaborate detail; he even reported fictitious names as part of his account. It was evident that the person was unconsciously fabricating the story, and was believing it to be true.[18] How often does this occur in people's day to day life? It seems that individuals can easily pick up on some suggestion, and then embellish or alter it, without conscious awareness.

Elizabeth Loftus, an experimental psychologist at the University of Washington, is recognized as an authority on memory.[19] In her extensive experimentation, she noted that the very act of asking a question such as "Was there a barn in the scene that you remember?" would, in time, result in the remembering of a barn in the scene at a later recollection, *even though the barn was not remembered until the question had been put.* These memories induced by interviewer input have been dubbed "Trojan horses":

> Through hundreds of experiments performed on some 20,000 subjects, Loftus found that memories could change simply through the questions asked about them. She found that through the fallibility of retrospection she could turn stop signs into yield signs, or make barns appear in a landscape, merely by slipping them into the subjects' consciousness disguised as questions. Unannounced as Trojan horses, these suggestions subtly transformed the memory.[20]

Counsellors think they know what actually happened, and they think they know what the client actually means when he or she is reporting. And yet, the interpretation of what clients remember or report is subject to the errors of the counsellors' own filters, which are coloured by their own biosocial conditioning.

Certainly, most people have had the experience of hearing someone say a word, and then attaching their own significance to the word, and going off on a whole train of ideas related to that word, without checking the person's intended meaning. If someone were to ask whether they knew what the other person meant, they would say with assurance that they did. It is common for people to be sure they know what another person means, without checking. They associate to their own meanings and predetermined interpretations, and then think that what they interpret is fact. And when people come from different cultures, there are different meanings attached to simple elements. For example, white is the colour for purity in North American culture, and thus is prized for a bride's dress; in Asia, white is associated with death, and traditionally would not have been the colour of choice for a wedding. For clear communication, all must realize that they cannot possibly know for certain what another person means, and they must continually check with what the other person intends, in order to achieve optimal (but not perfect) understanding.

The Witch Hunt

Each culture decrees what is "real." And having established what is real, then the process goes on to determine what realities are "good" and what are "bad." Having arrived at these categorizations, then the powers in the society set about on political activity to assure that the good is maintained, and the bad is punished, or stamped out. And yet, philosophically, reality is a shaky phenomenon at best. One can never be sure what is "real." Bertrand Russell wrote, " . . . we can never prove the existence of things other than ourselves and our experiences."[21] Even if people could be perfect listeners, and could know exactly what a person means in reporting (without the filter of their own cultural conditioning, prejudices, inadequacies of language, mental limitations, etc.), they would still not be able to know what is real and what is imagined, or embellished by the other.

Jim Fadiman calls for a balanced, sane approach to memories in relationship to the subject of abuse and memory. He wrote the following passage concerning issues in remembering past violence and abuse:

> Do all the perversions so zealously elaborated truly exist in reality? Certainly the images exist, and trouble us all, like the dragons which occur in the imagery of almost every civilization but nowhere in flesh and blood, scale and bone. It is still unclear how much of what has been reported as real is real. So far the answers from research and litigation show that some is real, but most is not.[22]

In most cases, when working with clients who report abuse or historical sufferings, counsellors should not devote so much attention to how much truth there is to the memory. Certainly, there is a legal obligation to report to the appropriate authorities when there is current potential danger to a child. But in many cases, the memories pertain to events from many years ago. The important point is that whatever their clients remember, they can work with the feelings that arise from having such a memory, without having to determine whether or not the memory is real. No one can ever know for certain whether the remembered experience actually occurred.

Counsellors can accept their clients' experiences as just that—these are their experiences, and they have feelings and thoughts associated with them. It does not matter whether the experiences are factual, or "real." Furthermore, helpers should avoid the diversion of determining what is good or bad (the moralizing overlay on experience). Hence, caregivers should steer clear of the politics of trying to punish wrongs, or tell people what should be so. Counsellors, teachers, and other people-helping professionals can be fair witnesses to people's experiences, without judging the reality, or the morality of them. In counselling, people are involved in a process of confession in the original sense of the word. Professionals can be present with their clients, to live through their experiences, in dialogue with them. And they can assist them in becoming free of past experiences and memories. When people succumb to moralizing, or political activity, they lose their opportunity for freedom, and become mired in the morass of limitations. When professionals do this, then their clients become lost with them. When caregivers perpetuate a limited, fixed viewpoint, the open sky of possibilities will disappear. The task for counsellors is to remain as a fair witness, with feelings and compassion, without judging what is real, or moral, or politically correct. And if helpers find their clients deviating down these roads (of morality, political correctness or righteousness), they can call them back to a more nutritive ground, where they can fully experience themselves, and their own feelings and thoughts. If people go down the route of moralizing and political correctness, they are in peril of being lost.

This loss of self in interaction is shockingly displayed in the play *Oleanna* written by David Mamet. In the drama, a young female university student comes to her middle-aged male professor's office to discuss her difficulties in learning. In the drama that ensues, the audience is horrified to witness that neither party listens to the other; each is caught in a rigid world view. In the professor's attitude, education supersedes the feelings of the young student; to the student, her increasing association with politically correct thought helps her to see her professor's paternalistic intentions as assaultive rather than helpful. Finally, the play takes its dramatic conclusion into the hell where both are lost in their own realities.[23]

We denounce the hideous tendency these days to affirm that "If you think you were abused, you were." Therapists are ready to assign child abuse as the cause and problem in many current life situations, and to relentlessly harass their clients until they will acknowledge the "truth" of what the counsellor is saying.[24] In Fadiman's words, it becomes ". . . difficult to separate the denied reality from the socially approved of and endlessly reinforced fantasy."[25] In short, some therapists claim to "know" what is true, and then set out to convince their clients. This can become a form of indoctrination; and this process itself is abusive.

Professionals should not be collaborating in the fervour to play the game of "ain't it awful." The episode of the "Little Rascals Day Care Centre" in the eastern United States is a chilling example of what can happen when experience, therapy, the police, and the legal system become embroiled. A single report from a very young child turned into one of the biggest trials involving sexual abuse in the history of the U.S. legal system. In a small town in North Carolina, an incident was alleged to have occurred where one of the caregivers in a day care centre had disciplined a young child. As this story was reported by the child to a parent, somewhere in the process the suspicion about possible sexual abuse arose. One set of parents talked to another set of parents who had children in the day care, and gradually through the small town, children were being questioned by well-intentioned, concerned parents. After some time, a number of the children came into counselling. Then the accusations of sexual abuse of the children in the day care centre began to come out. After a period, a high number of the children reported in increasingly graphic words the details of sexual abuse by a number of the staff members of the day care centre. The small town became polarized, as some citizens refused to believe such allegations, while others became militant about investigating them, and having charges laid. We find it noteworthy that amongst the children who reported abuse, all were involved with therapists or counsellors in the same town. None of the children who were sent to counsellors out of the town reported any abuse. It appears possible that something occurred in the dynamic with the police and the counsellors that brought forth memories of abuse from the small children. It is possible that the "memory" of abuse that the young children had was somehow infectious, or could be enhanced, rather than merely uncovered. To compound this, when the matter came to trial, some of the jurors actually believed that the accused staff were innocent, and yet gave in to the pressure to vote to convict them, "to get it over with." One of the jurors reported, "I didn't see no hard evidence"; nevertheless, under the pressure of one very aggressive and moralistic juror, the entire jury convicted the defendants, and sent them to prison for long terms.[26]

Commonly, therapists go on a crusade to punish alleged wrongdoers, believing that this somehow helps a person who is not coping in present life. Jim Fadiman writes:

> It is disturbing that psychotherapy seems to be accepting that a deliberate attack on the fantasied attacker will lead to a cure. Have we learned so little from the each-one-murder-one situation in the tattered scraps of Yugoslavia that we need to incorporate tactics of revenge into the process of psychotherapy?[27]

When Memories Differ in Families

Some years ago, we reported the case of a young woman who remembers violent and extreme traumas that involve satanism and ritualistic abuse.[28] We also know her sister, who grew up in the same family, and does not remember any such activity. We ourselves don't say that either sister is wrong. We only can say that one sister has these memories, and the other sister does not. What actually occurred, we can never know. The sisters are becoming closer, as they realize that they do not need to have the same memories in order to care about each other. The sister who remembers the abuse wrote the following:

> Because my story involves an incredible amount of violence in my childhood, it had only seemed possible to believe that my sister would either present some of the same story, show obvious signs of repression or I would be lying about my version of the story. This had been my belief and my experience prior to being in

this environment over time. But I have learned that there is another possibility . . . that we do each have our own experience. And although there are few if any similarities, we can each be here and learn and grow and heal. I experience such freedom—because it means that I can do whatever I need to do to transform and heal without having to be concerned that the cost would be pain, punishment or vengeance towards others who may or may not be involved in the violence as I have remembered it.

The woman with the memories went through a period of trying to convince others that her family was "bad" and that her memories were "true." She now is moving away from the perspective of blame and weakened victimhood into a stance of responsibility, and is discovering some acceptance for her family. She writes to her counsellors:

I have thought that I wanted people to hate my parents like I did—but in actual fact that would be very difficult. Because I am now seeing that at times I have cut myself off from remembering anything but the pain, and in the pain I wanted revenge. But now over time I have come to open to much more and the hate is not primary. So revenge is no longer the issue. I am very thankful now that you never wanted that either. And that you were always able to encourage me to see the person behind the object. That has been of tremendous value to me. And one of the primary beliefs that I want to bring into my own counselling setting.

I find great comfort in knowing that even if I never find peace with my family there is a place or process in which each of our experiences would be accepted. And in that knowing . . . I too am beginning to accept us all.

Advice to Counsellors from Previous Clients

A young woman who reported memories of severe childhood sexual and ritualistic abuse has now become a therapist herself. She describes her current stance:

I want to respect and have empathy for myself as a person who has memories of incredible violence and a great deal of anger about the events that occurred in my life, but I don't want to move into a position that supports and creates "victims." I have found that this is at times challenging.

She goes on to write the following advice:

I believe that what would be of value to others training and working with people who are viewed as "victims," or in a helpless position, is the value of maintaining the ability to accept and not become judgmental of the people that are involved in the violence or abuse. For myself I hope that I have learned this. Not that I will not judge or become angry—but that I will have the ability to work through these feelings in such a way that allows me to come into the relationship with my client, open not only to their experience but to the experience of the other. Thus I will not make them a victim, but will remain clear about my empathy and support of their own experience within our relationship, but open to the possibility of other experiences. And that if that were not the case I would have the courage to reveal that I may no longer be helpful to the healing process of my client. Because when I begin to believe only their experience we both become limited and closed. It is difficult enough to live with my own sense of guilt about the things I have said my parents did. But if I not only have to accept and move inside my heart, but also then must try to open the heart of someone who my story may have impacted—then the work becomes a great deal harder.

Conclusion

There is a possibility of erring on either side of this controversial issue. Counsellors can dismiss all memories as not being based in fact, and thus disallow the individual's experience. Or they can go on a righteous rampage to punish perpetrators of remembered past traumas. Let us not make either error. Caregivers can live along with their clients and friends who remember the most hideous things, empathize and work with them, without having to get caught up in whether or not the memories are true.

Memories

Memories are subject to
distortions
in the forest of mirrors
we call time

Twisting spirals
whorl in space
reverberating
through the rhythms of
the mutable geometry
of past recollections
—Jock McKeen[29]

Notes

1. B. Wong and J. McKeen,. "The Walking Wounded: A Way of Life," *Journal of Child and Youth Care*, vol 7., no. 3, 1992, pp 78-89.

2. J. McKeen and B.Wong,. "Memories of Abuse: A Call For A Balanced Perspective," *Journal of Child and Youth Care*, vol 10., no. 3, 1995, pp 67-81.

3. B. Wong and J. McKeen, "A Case of Multiple Life Threatening Illnesses Related to Early Ritual Abuse," *Journal of Child and Youth Care*, Special Issue, 1990, pp. 1-26.

4. Carl Whitaker, Personal Communication.

5. Leon Jaroff, "Lies of the Mind," in *Time*, November 28, 1993, pp. 52-57.

6. Marie Jahoda. *Freud and the Dilemmas of Psychology* (New York: Basic Books, 1977), pp. 28, 29.

7. Ernest Jones, *The Life and Work of Sigmund Freud* (New York: Basic Books, 1961), p. 213.

8. Sigmund Freud, *The Standard Edition of the Complete Psychological Works of Sigmund Freud* (London: The Hogarth Press, 1955), vol. VII, pp. 190, 191.

9. Freud, Vol. VII, p. 274.

10. Freud, Vol. VII, pp. 276, 277.

11. Freud, Vol. X, pp. 206, 207.

12. Freud, Vol. X, p. 207.

13. Freud, Vol. XI, p. 83.

14. Freud, Vol. XVII, p. 97.

15. Freud, Vol. XVII, p. 97.

16. Freud, Vol. XVII, pp. 179-181.

17. Freud, Vol. XI, p. 83.

18. M. Métivier and S. Kleinfeld, producers. "Mistaken Identities." shown on *The Fifth Estate*, CBC Television, Autumn, 1993.

19. Elizabeth F. Loftus, "Creating False Memories," *Scientific American*, September 1997, pp. 71-75.

20. Kathryn Robinson, "Memories of Abuse," *Seattle Weekly*, August 11, 1993, p. 22.

21. Bertrand Russell, *The Problems of Philosophy* (New York: Oxford University Press, 1959), p.22.

22. J. Fadiman, "Overcoming Abuse," *Perspective*, July/August 1993, p. 24.

23. David Mamet, *Oleanna* (New York: Dramatists Play Services, 1992).

24. B. Wong and J. McKeen, "The Walking Wounded: A Way of Life." *Journal of Child and Youth Care*, vol.7, no. 3, 1992, pp. 79-89.

25. Jim Fadiman, "Overcoming Abuse," *Perspective*, July/August 1993, p. 25.

26. Ofra Bikel, "Innocence Lost: The Verdict," a television documentary presented by the Documentary Consortium, July 20, 1993.

27. Jim Fadiman, "Overcoming Abuse," *Perspective*, July/August 1993, pp. 24, 25.

28. B. Wong, and J. McKeen, "A Case of Multiple Life Threatening Illnesses Related to Early Ritual Abuse." *Journal of Child and Youth Care*, Special Issue, 1990, pp. 1-26.

29. Jock McKeen, previously unpublished poem, 1998.

Epilogue

If you have been able to persevere to the end of this book, you will have a general idea of some of our basic assumptions about life, relationships and the exigencies of human nature. By now, you will have probably discovered that in developing these ideas, we have borrowed extensively from a wide variety of sources. Furthermore, these ideas have been tried and tempered through our interactions with the thousands of people who have graced us with their presence. To all of those—participants, thinkers, scientists, theologians, authors, professionals, seekers, artists—we express our deepest gratitude.

We agree with the eastern philosophers and some existentialists who posit that the human being is suspended somewhere between the earth and heaven, facing the need to survive while yearning for a felt sense of meaning, some reason to survive. Since survival needs seem to be best served through corporation and organization, each individual frequently finds the demands of the self at odds with the demands of society and culture. Individual development reflects that dynamic tension. Most often, the self is sacrificed for conformity and security; however, the inner yearning for fuller expression of that self cannot be completely extinguished. Throughout history, many different kinds of political systems have come up against that irrepressible desire for freedom of expression of the self.

When the self cannot be fully expressed, the cost is enormous, although often subtle and disguised. These disguises may take on a wide range of symptom formations at all levels of being—emotional, spiritual, mental, physical and environmental. At root is a common thread of isolation and anxiety resulting from a separation not only from others, but more fundamentally, a separation from the self! It is our observation that much of human endeavour is aimed towards healing those separations; it is also our experience that most people lack many of the basic tools to effect such a healing. Instead of exercising personal responsibility, many people tend to ascribe power and authority to others. We believe that the project of establishing a meaningful dialogue in a relationship of intimacy can be a most fruitful way to overcome isolation and rediscover our relationship to ourselves, to each other, and to the cosmos.

We hope that this book has provided you with some of the understanding and tools for you to use to heal your own personal rifts, and has contributed to the development of some faith in yourself.

You are not alone!

We wish to close with one of our favourite poems:

Oceans

I have a feeling that my boat
has struck, down there in the depths,
against a great thing.
And nothing happens!
Nothing . . . Silence . . . Waves . . .

Nothing happens?
Or has everything happened,
and are we standing now, quietly, in the new life?
—Juan Ramón Jiménez [1]

Notes

1. Juan Ramón Jiménez, in Robert Bly trans., *News of the Universe* (San Francisco: Sierra Club Books, 1980), p. 105.

Index

Other Titles By The Authors

Books

The Haven By-the-Sea and PD Seminars Experience (1992)
As It Is In Heaven (1993)
In And Out Of Our Own Way (1995)
The Relationship Garden (1996)

Audio Recordings

As It Is In Heaven (Audio Cassette, 1993)
In And Out of Our Own Way (2 Compact Disks, 1998)

Videotape Recording

The Relationship Garden: Boundaries, Chaos and Intimacy (1996)

To order, or for more information:

PD Publishing
RR#1, Site 9, 240 Davis Road
Gabriola Island, B.C., Canada V0R 1X0
Tel: (250) 247-9211   Fax: (250) 247-8454
Email: havreg@island.net
Website: http://www.island.net/~jockben